WITHDRAWN

Open Borders?
Closed Societies?

Recent Titles in
Contributions in Political Science
Series Editor: Bernard K. Johnpoll

More Than a Game: Sports and Politics
Martin Barry Vinokur

Pursuing a Just and Durable Peace: John Foster Dulles and International Organization
Anthony Clark Arend

Getting the Donkey Out of the Ditch: The Democratic Party in Search of Itself
Caroline Arden

Elite Cadres and Party Coalitions: Representing the Public in Party Politics
Denise L. Baer and David A. Bositis

The Pure Concept of Diplomacy
José Calvet de Magalhães

From Camelot to the Teflon President: Economics and Presidential Popularity Since 1960
David J. Lanoue

Puerto Rico's Statehood Movement
Edgardo Meléndez

Foreign Relations: Analysis of Its Anatomy
Elmer Plischke

Conflict over the World's Resources: Background, Trends, Case Studies, and
Considerations for the Future
Robert Mandel

Lyndon Baines Johnson and the Uses of Power
Bernard J. Firestone and Robert C. Vogt, editors

Trotskyism and the Dilemma of Socialism
Christopher Z. Hobson and Ronald D. Tabor

Policy Studies: Integration and Evaluation
Stuart S. Nagel

OPEN BORDERS? CLOSED SOCIETIES?

The Ethical and Political Issues

EDITED BY
MARK GIBNEY

CONTRIBUTIONS IN POLITICAL SCIENCE, NUMBER 226

GREENWOOD PRESS
NEW YORK • WESTPORT, CONNECTICUT • LONDON

Library of Congress Cataloguing-in-Publication Data

Open borders? Closed societies? : the ethical and political issues /
  edited by Mark Gibney.
        p.   cm.—(Contributions in political science, ISSN 0147–1066
  ; no. 226)
     Bibliography: p.
     Includes index.
     Contents: Citizenship and freedom of movement : an open admission
  policy? / Frederick G. Whelan—Nationalism and the exclusion of
  immigrants : lessons from Australian immigration policy / Joseph H.
  Carens—The force of moral arguments for a just immigration policy
  in a Hobbesian universe : the contemporary American example / John
  A. Scanlan and O.T. Kent— [etc.]
     ISBN 0–313–25578–4 (lib. bdg. : alk. paper)
       1. United States—Emigration and immigration—Government policy.
  2. Refugees—Government policy—United States.   3. Emigration and
  immigration—Government policy—Moral and ethical aspects.
  4. Refugees—Government policy—Moral and ethical aspects.
  I. Gibney, Mark.   II. Series.
  JV6493.064 1988
  325.73—dc19   88–15484

British Library Cataloguing in Publication Data is available.

Copyright © 1988 by Mark Gibney

Library of Congress Catalog Card Number: 88–15484
ISBN: 0–313–25578–4 ·
ISSN: 0147–1066

First published in 1988

Greenwood Press, Inc.
88 Post Road West, Westport, Connecticut 06881

Printed in the United States of America

The paper used in this book complies with the
Permanent Paper Standard issued by the National
Information Standards Organization (Z39.48–1984).

10   9   8   7   6   5   4   3   2   1

Contents

Tables

Introduction

Immigration issues have received a great deal of attention the past few years as the United States, like many other industrialized nations, has attempted to cope with what has been perceived as an "immigration problem." Most of the efforts in this country have involved the attempt to deal with the flow of illegal aliens crossing our national borders. Passage of the Simpson-Rodino bill late in 1986 culminated many years of struggle to reform U.S. immigration law. One of the two major provisions of the new law prohibits private employers from hiring those who have not been lawfully admitted to the United States. The other noteworthy feature of Simpson-Rodino is an amnesty provision for those who are in this country illegally, but whose long-term residence was thought to warrant legalization as members of the American community. (Agricultural workers with even a rather fleeting residence in the United States are deemed to have a sufficient tie.)

The United States, then, is embarking on what may or may not be a bold new experiment in the area of immigration policy. The driving force behind Simpson-Rodino was the sentiment—seemingly universally shared by policymakers—that this country had lost control of its borders. What seemed essential was to "do something," although there was apparently much less agreement on what policy prescriptives were needed, as evident from the many unsuccessful attempts to pass various versions of immigration reform. What emerged, finally, was the Simpson-Rodino bill; its effects we are only now beginning to see.

Although Simpson-Rodino was heralded at the time of its passage as a landmark piece of legislation, it warrants this description not so much for the changes it makes in U.S. immigration law, which are relatively minor, but more on the basis of coalescing so many diverse opinions and approaches to immigration reform. This not to say that Simpson-Rodino will not bring about enormous changes in U.S. immigration practice. The jury is still out on this question. What seems evident from this legislation, however, is that unlike other attempts at immigration reform, Simpson-Rodino concerns itself less with attempting to produce or perpetuate a certain vision of American society through immigration channels. For example, the now discredited national origins quota legislation from the 1920s attempted to maintain what really did not exist—an American society that was derived from the "superior" races of northern and western Europe. The McCarran-Walter Act of 1952 likewise pursued this elusive goal. Immigration reform in 1965 abandoned the national origins quota system because it had a different vision of the American community. This new vision truly did accept the idea of the American "melting pot," an image that had previously existed, in name only.

It is not apparent what vision of the American community Simpson-Rodino hopes to create. To a large extent its only goal is to maintain the essence of the American community as we now know it, however one might define that. Unlike some of its predecessors in reform, Simpson-Rodino focuses on one aspect of U.S. alien admission policy—keep out illegal aliens—and it does not concern itself (or really even attempt to concern itself) with the larger question of the direction that U.S. alien admission policy should take. In short, Simpson-Rodino is "political" in the sense that it is a political response to a rather narrow political problem.

The essays in this volume attempt to step back from the political fray and place alien admission issues into some broader context. As the book's title suggests, these essays address both the political and the ethical (and the meeting of the two), but there is a decided focus on the latter. The former has already had center stage, not only in the recent policy debates, but in intellectual circles and writing as well.

The aim of this book, then, is to examine the basis for an ethical or moral alien admission policy for Western societies. This stated aim itself should cause some controversy. The admission of aliens has historically been viewed as inherent in the very nature of sovereignty. Along with this assumption has been another: that nations admit aliens only when it serves the national interest, and exclude aliens when that, too, serves the national interest.

Much of U.S. immigration history—the exclusion of the Chinese and then the Japanese; the national origins quota system; the designed exclusion of Jews both during and after World War II; but also becoming the home for millions of the huddled masses—can largely be explained on what was politically feasible, but also what was purportedly in our national interest. This is not to say that moral concerns never played a role in U.S. alien admission policy, but one would have to search deeply to find such goals, and even more deeply to see those particular goals actively pursued.

Simpson-Rodino is premised upon two assumptions: that sovereignty gives a nation absolute control over its borders, and that aliens are only admitted when it serves our "national interest." Having said that, however, it must also be noted that to a certain degree Simpson-Rodino recognized some limitations on these assumptions. For one thing, Simpson-Rodino ran squarely into the problem of attempting to differentiate between "member" and "stranger" in a society where those distinctions are no longer clear. Immigration reform in this country also recognized that control of our national borders might come at a price to the civil liberties of all. Finally, although Simpson-Rodino came about as the result of the violence and poverty of our borders, these "push" factors driving immigration were essentially ignored in designing the policy prescription, raising the question of whether effective and meaningful immigration reform is possible without these considerations.

Although Simpson-Rodino recognized that some of the basic assumptions of alien admission policy were changing and had changed in many respects, this bill was a concerted effort to reestablish these old assumptions. What the essays in this book do instead is to challenge these assumptions. In addition, all these essays focus on immigration and refugee issues as being a part of a larger concern: the relationship of citizens in this country to individuals living elsewhere. Among the questions raised are the following: Can closed borders be morally justified? To what extent should a nation be able to maintain its "communal autonomy" through its immigration policies? Should moral concerns play a role in a country's alien admission policy, and if so, which moral concerns? Should constitutional guarantees be afforded to those seeking entrance to the United States? Finally, to what extent has the United States met the moral goals it enunciated in the 1980 Refugee Act?

Part I focuses on immigration questions as such, while Part II devotes itself to issues involving the admission of refugees. This collection begins with Frederick G. Whelan's contribution, "Citizenship and Freedom of Movement: An Open Admission Policy?" This essay, like others in this volume, addresses what had been assumed for so long—that nations should have absolute control over their borders. Whelan notes, and examines, some of the seemingly contradictory strains in our liberal, democratic society, and applies this discussion to the area of alien admissions. Whelan maintains that on one level the notion of a nation being able to close its borders goes against the most basic tenet of liberalism: the equal moral worth of all individuals. This vision of liberalism drives toward open borders, where individuals

would have unfettered liberty and true equal opportunity. Whelan maintains, however, that there is another strain in liberalism that drives us away
from open borders (and perhaps to borders that are sealed) and that is the
need, or desire, to maintain and cultivate the liberal society that we have
or hope to achieve.

Joseph H. Carens resists the temptation to address the question of whether
open borders are morally justified, but his undertaking is related. Carens
examines the degree to which a society ought to be able to maintain a certain
way of life through its immigration and refugee practices. His example of
the White Australia policy, which until 1971 restricted immigration to individuals of Anglo-Saxon descent, is a provocative one. In a sense Carens is
saying that it is too easy to dismiss legislation like the White Australia policy
(or the national origins quota system) because beneath the racist surface is
a very real, and, in some cases justifiable, goal: maintaining communal autonomy. This issue will not leave us. We see it in France with the fear and
reality of Turkish and Middle Eastern ghettoes. We have seen the same
issue in Britain, where even immigrants from Commonwealth countries have
experienced problems and hostility in becoming members of that society.
Finally, the United States certainly is not immune to such concerns. The
border between the United States and Mexico is, at times, quite blurred.
Some of our largest cities—Miami and Los Angeles, to name two—have
ethnic populations that outnumber the native population, if one could ap-
propriately use that term.

The last essay in Part I, by John Scanlan and O. T. Kent, is "The Force
of Moral Arguments for a Just Immigration Policy in a Hobbesian Universe:
The Contemporary American Example." Scanlan and Kent recognize, and
work under the assumption, that we live in a Hobbesian world where nations
pursue their own versions of their "national interest." An integral feature of
the Hobbesian universe is the well-accepted principle that nations have
absolute control over their borders. Scanlan and Kent trace this view in
American immigration policy and practice from the earliest immigration
restrictions to the present day.

The quintessential argument by Scanlan and Kent is that moral concerns
and discourse can and should play an important role even in this Hobbesian
universe. Thus, the pursuit of national goals is not necessarily anathema to
the pursuit of moral goals, and Scanlan and Kent point to such practices in
the immigration area, particularly the humanitarian response of admitting
refugees. Yet, although moral considerations rightfully come into play, not
all justifications are equally valid. The authors make a significant contribution
to the debate about which refugees the United States should be admitting
by arguing that certain features of current U.S. practice cannot be justified
on moral grounds, particularly the notion of admitting refugees in the pursuit
of ideological goals. Here Scanlan and Kent take sharp issue with Michael
Walzer's position that out of the universe of refugees in the world, a country

like the United States can pick and choose which refugees it will admit because of a purported ideological connection or an ethnic affinity. Scanlan and Kent maintain that these rationales differ little from now-discredited immigration criteria based on race or ethnicity.

Part II examines a more specific aspect of immigration concerns, that of refugee admissions. We begin with the general and then pursue the specific. The argument developed by Peter and Renata Singer in their essay "The Ethics of Refugee Policy," is that developed nations are not doing nearly enough to provide a safe haven for the world's teeming refugee population. The Singers argue that developed nations continue to maintain the position that assistance to refugees is simply charity, not based on any moral or legal obligations. Accordingly, while developed nations claim to recognize and honor the equal moral worth of all individuals, the Singers argue that they pay only lip service to this principle. Instead, the interests of members of a society are given absolute priority over the interests of refuge seekers.

The Singers attempt to bridge the ethical and the political by examining Australia's refugee policy. The 12,000 or so refugees that Australia is admitting in 1988 are far too few, they maintain. From an ethical perspective, the vast majority of Australians are thus allowed to enjoy luxuries while literally millions of refugees live on the edge of existence. Moreover, from a political perspective, the Singers argue that additional refugees will not have a deleterious effect on the nation, and, if anything, the empirical evidence points in the opposite direction. How many refugees should Australia admit? Without providing a ready response, the Singers maintain that opponents of increased refugee admissions should not be allowed to perpetuate fears by positing absurd conclusions and numbers. At some point the negative consequences of large-scale refugee flows will become certainties, but developed nations have not come to this point yet.

Andrew Shacknove's contribution continues this theme of duties to refugees, but within the context of the American constitutional system. Shacknove's concern is with the moral and legal responsibilities that host nations have to those who are refugees, with a particular focus on U.S. law and practice. Shacknove notes two strains in American constitutional law with regard to the rights of foreigners in this country. One is to maintain that the Constitution and constitutional guarantees do not apply to foreigners, as evidenced in such cases as *Knauff v. Shaughnessy*. The other strain, indicated in cases like *Yick Wo v. Hopkins*, recognizes that foreigners are not without constitutional protection.

Of particular concern to Shacknove is whether constitutional protections ought to be afforded to those seeking refugee status in the United States, and he answers this question in the affirmative. He premises his position on two related grounds. One is to honor the principle of the equal moral worth of all people. The other is to recognize the interest at stake to the individuals who claim a well-founded fear of persecution in their homeland.

Shacknove concludes that the principle of equal moral worth generally does not obligate the United States to treat citizens and foreigners alike. However, where a refugee's life is at stake, different considerations come into play, which dictate constitutional protection.

In their contribution, "Human Rights and U.S. Refugee Policy," Mark Gibney and Michael Stohl present one of the first empirical studies of U.S. refugee/asylum policy. They examine the relationship between different levels of "political terror" in other countries and the U.S. refugee/asylum response. In particular, Gibney and Stohl have attempted to determine whether the United States is more likely to admit as refugees, or grant asylum to, individuals from countries where the most serious human rights violations occur. In their work, Gibney and Stohl introduce the notion of different levels of persecution, with their argument being that there is generally a stronger duty to aid those who suffer from the most serious forms of persecution.

The empirical evidence strongly suggests that neither in refugee admissions nor in the granting of asylum is U.S. policy particularly geared to the level of human rights violations in other countries. This is most striking in terms of U.S. refugee admissions where very few individuals from countries with the worst human rights violations are admitted to the United States. Instead, the empirical evidence indicates that U.S. refugee admissions favors countries with moderate levels of human rights violations.

In conclusion, the essays in this book are provocative in the sense that they raise questions that have been conveniently ignored not only historically, but also in most of the recent policy debates. The aim is to examine both the political and the moral, with the ultimate aim of providing a moral basis for the alien admission policies that nations will be pursuing.

PART I

IMMIGRATION

1

Citizenship and Freedom of Movement

AN OPEN ADMISSION POLICY?

Frederick G. Whelan

IMMIGRATION AND SOVEREIGNTY

Questions regarding immigration (including the special issues of refugee admissions and guest worker programs) are increasingly prominent in the public policy debates of advanced countries, particulary such important traditional and current immigrant-receiving countries as the United States. These questions, moreover, are widely expected to take on increasing urgency over the coming decades if the disparities in wealth between "North" and "South" and the population pressure in some of the main sending countries (and in all of the potential sending countries of the Third World) continue to mount. This is a case in which certain very real problems and choice-compelling situations of the contemporary political world challenge political philosophers to reconsider some fundamental concepts and practices of political life: the sovereign state, citizenship, and the proper scope of individual freedom as expressed in the possible freedom to move across state borders and to choose one's place of residence. In particular, we are challenged to inquire into what (if any) justifications can be offered for the power universally claimed by states to exclude foreigners from their territory—especially from *permanent* admission—or to control and restrict alien admissions in any way they choose.

The purpose of this essay is to survey and evaluate several arguments that might be offered in defense of some version of this exclusive power, both in general and in the circumstances of the world as it is today. This exercise represents a reaction against a previously enunciated challenge both to the institutional status quo of actual state practice and to the conventional opinion that has, until recently, sustained it. This challenge, some facets of which I explore in the following section, has arisen within contemporary liberal thought in countries where it matters most—countries like the United States and Australia which (it is often assumed) would be chosen as destinations by many more migrants than they are now were it not for immigration restrictions that are in effect even in those relatively open states: it appears to express conscientious self-doubts on the part of citizens of affluent and comparatively thinly populated countries with respect to the additional privilege that the sovereign power over alien admissions confers upon them. In any event, arguments have been advanced that call radically into question the legitimacy of state borders as barriers to the free movement of people, or the moral justifiability of the authority of the sovereign state (or of the citizens collectively, if we are thinking of a democratic state) to enforce an exclusive, restrictive, or selective policy regarding the admission of foreigners. (The matter of admission into a state, of course, has two dimensions that normally receive two distinct legal expressions: geographical admission into the country, or immigration, and civic admission into the association of citizens, or naturalization; but except for the important question of guest workers, these usually go together and may be considered as two steps in a single process.) These arguments do not normally go so far as to deny the propriety of there being independent, self-governing political units, having borders and making distinctions between citizens and aliens. Both of these features of the political world as we know it, however, would be greatly diminished in significance if people, foreign in origin, were effectively free to cross borders and acquire membership in a new state virtually at will, subject only to administrative formalities. It is this vision of states that are open in this sense—open to voluntary inflows of foreigners—or of states that are required to maintain "open admissions" policies, that I wish to subject to a critical review.

It is important to note that the views I consider below do not constitute an argument against immigration, or for a relatively restrictive admission policy—although they might do so if supplemented by certain empirical findings concerning the consequences of immigration in particular cases. Their point is rather to support the moral *permissibility* of exclusion in principle: conversely, they constitute objections to the view that states (or in some versions, wealthy states) are morally required to be open to the entry of foreigners (perhaps especially needy foreigners), and thus to the view that people have a moral right to immigrate into a state other than that of which they are nationals. Of course, under the prevailing conception of sovereignty, a state might adopt a generously open, even a relatively non-selective, admissions policy. Such a course might be motivated by a special twinge of moral sensibility, like the feelings that lead a state to decide to admit refugees, perhaps a group for whom its citizens feel special affinity or responsibility. More often, it might arise from an opinion that immigration is in the national interest, as it is with "normal," economically motivated immigrants, especially if they are suitably selected for skills (or if those with clearly undesirable traits are denied admission). On these grounds, and under current conventions, a state such as the United States might find that it could and should admit more foreigners than it now does—a number which, incidentally, is quite large in absolute terms both by world standards and by historical U.S. standards, though not in proportion to population.[1]

Immigration may clearly be in the national interest as specified in some particular way. Immigration may bring the benefits of a growing population, or it may contribute to a population having certain desirable demographic features, or to economic development, or to cultural diversity. In this case, enlightened policymakers would see that the country is correspondingly open; actual immigration would depend on the supply of would-be immigrants meeting the selection criteria imposed by law. However, it seems unlikely in the 1980s, on any plausible account of the national interest of the United States or any other likely receiving country, that nationally set immigration policy would be completely open the way that of the United States was before the 1880s. However generous in a quantitative sense the policy might be, one would expect it to be qualitatively restricted, and the imposition of selective criteria is as much an expression of a state's sovereign powers in this matter as are numerical restrictions or closure itself. If the state is democratic, so that policymakers are responsive to the will of the people, one expects the policy to be open in proportion to the belief that immigration is beneficial to the present citizen body as a whole, since the public or national interest is the accepted standard for democratic policy, especially policy regarding foreign affairs or foreigners. Pluralist democracy as practiced in the United States, of course, deviates from the model that imagines a unified "popular will" pursuing a "public interest," since well-organized and clearly intentioned groups can often get their way even in the face of an opposed majority view, if the issue is not especially salient or the majority view not very intense. This dynamic of American politics has probably been responsible for keeping our immigration policy more open than it would otherwise have been (under a more populist kind of democracy): employers and other groups have successfully resisted a more diffuse nativist and restrictionist sentiment both during the key 1890–1920 period and perhaps again in recent years (as witness the fortunes of the Simpson-Mazzoli bill). Also contributing to this outcome has been the fact that in the United

States (in contrast, perhaps, to Australia) tradition and thus legislative inertia have been on the side of the proponents of openness, thus placing the burden of effort on the restrictionist majority, if such in fact exists.

A country may thus be open in practice to immigrants, either because this is thought to be in the national interest, or as a result of historical inertia; either as an expression of a democratic will, or as a result of a qualified or distorted democratic political process. In any case, the policy represents, as international law now stands, an expression of state sovereignty. It may be framed and altered by a purely internal political process, in which foreigners (including the would-be immigrants) not only have no voice, but in which their interests need not be considered at all and often in practice *are* not considered, at least not on anything like an equal basis with those of the present citizens. Here, given prevailing moral theories and attitudes, a problem of justification seems to arise. May states or their citizens unilaterally determine their admissions policies, disregarding or discounting the interests and therefore rejecting the petitions of applicants for admission, especially if the latter appear to have pressing reasons for desiring to enter? May citizens, by virtue of their sovereign powers, enact a closed society, or, in what would seem to be a morally similar use of the same powers, set limits and criteria that are designed to ensure that immigration serves the interests of themselves (and their descendents), the interests of those admitted being served in this fashion only indirectly? Finally, since control over the entry and naturalization of foreigners has been acknowledged, in positive international law, as a fundamental right or power of the sovereign state as long as such states have existed, these questions imply an even deeper one regarding the justification of sovereignty itself in one of its more clear-cut manifestations.

LIBERAL MORALITY AND THE WORLD OF STATES

The questions about immigration policy in the preceding section are derived from recently influential currents of liberal moral and political philosophy, although they are only beginning to be voiced explicitly. The modes of thinking that concern me here may be called abstract in at least two senses. First, they arrive at practical conclusions, including conclusions about fairly specific matters of public policy, on the basis of reasoning from moral premises, or in pursuance of sophisticated methods of moral reasoning that typically do not take account of or attribute moral weight to the concrete particularities of different communities, historical traditions, and ways of life. Second, the moral premises to which contemporary liberalism (like classical liberalism) resort make reference to individual human beings, with their rights and their generalized basic interests, abstracted from the identity that actual people have by virtue of being members or citizens of particular communities or participants in actual networks of relations with certain other people.

I start with this observation not with the intent of casting suspicion upon such modes of thought: abstraction may be a source of acuity in moral reasoning as in other theoretical fields, and in ethics it is, furthermore, often thought to be required as an aspect of the impartiality required in moral judgment. But it seems clear from the outset that a moral theory that sets out to attend to the claims of all human beings as such, on an equal basis, is going to have some difficulty in justifying borders that set off groups of people from each other and act as barriers to the free movement of individuals. This might be true even if the groups in question were in fact "separate but equal," but it is even more the case when, as in the real world, the groups are significantly unequal by various measures and when (as with the effect of labor mobility on wages in liberal economic theory) cross-border movement might be expected to have an equalizing effect. Likewise, it appears that views upholding the integrity of distinct communities, and their right to seek to maintain their character and their flourishing condition, are going to be on the defensive as upholding a kind of group preference (and thus, sometimes, group advantage or privilege) that seems illicit. A few brief exercises may serve to illustrate the way in which abstract liberalism poses a challenge to contemporary opinion and practice with respect to immigration.

Although John Rawls' theory of justice is developed so as to apply to a particular society (with its membership taken as fixed),[2] several of his critics, including some who are friendly to his enterprise, have made a cogent case for its global application. Since, under the veil of ignorance, the parties in the original position would not know which society they belong to, but since they would presumably know that at any point in history the various existing countries are unequally endowed with resources and unequal in development (including political development, or the development of liberties), it seems reasonable to suppose that they would seek to alleviate some of the disadvantages that would attend the accident of birth in a less favored society. This thought has been developed mainly with respect to Rawls' third principle (the difference principle) and accordingly applied as an argument for ongoing international redistribution of wealth from rich to poor societies.[3] An extension of Rawls' theory to the international realm with respect to freedom of movement (including the freedom to immigrate), however, appears to offer several possibilities:

1. Freedom of movement might count among the basic liberties. Rawls (like other liberals) gives first priority to protection of these liberties. In keeping with the classical tradition that he follows in this part of his theory, Rawls at one point lists "freedom of movement" (presumably internal movement and choice of residence) as among the basic liberties of citizens;[4] but if it has this status, would the global perspective of the original position not dictate the addition of international free movement (of persons, not citizens) to the list as well? The same reasons that make internal freedom of movement

important as an expression of individual liberty would seem to apply internationally, especially from the point of view of someone who does not know
in what country he is going to find himself. Although the existence of reasonably stable, bounded political and administrative units, and individuals
having a legal domicile, may be desirable institutions, there is no special
reason why free movement across international borders need be more inconsistent with these institutions than are municipal, county, and U.S. state
borders with the practice of internally free movement as it exists in the
United States. The lexical priority of liberty to material welfare in Rawls'
theory would mean that freedom of movement into a country, if it *is* regarded
as a basic liberty, could not be restricted out of consideration for maintaining
the income level of the current residents of that country—or, for that matter,
of any group of people. Freedom of movement could be restricted only in
order to secure some other similarly important liberty or to strengthen the
overall system of basic liberties. The problem posed by transience for democracy (or, in the case of international migration, the need for some degree
of political assimilation) suggests the need for a compromise between freedom of movement and the right to vote, perhaps in the form of a durational
residency requirement (as exists for U.S. naturalization), and temporary
restraints could be imposed on persons involved in compulsory judicial proceedings. But aside from these cases, it is not obvious how the exercise of
a right to migrate in or out of countries would threaten the civil liberties of
others.

   2. Rawls' second principle of justice, which also takes precedence over
considerations of welfare, is that of fair equal opportunity—that is, an equal
right of access, on the basis of one's demonstrated qualifications, to any
desirable social position. Equal opportunity and freedom of movement have
of course gone closely together in the liberal world. The main reason that
people move (physically) is to seek or take advantage of opportunities for
improvement of their condition or career prospects (or those of their children); social mobility is a counterpart to geographical mobility. The aspiration
of people to migrate from a poorer to a richer country in the modern world
normally represents this same process—one that liberals have traditionally
viewed (in the aggregate) as socially beneficial as well as indicating a praiseworthy trait of individual character. Aspirations for mobility today simply
make themselves felt on a larger scale, as a result of more far-flung information networks and cheaper transportation. Classical liberal economists
assumed that international labor mobility (as with the mobility of other factors
of production, and of goods in trade) was desirable, subject to the cost and
the psychological constraints of human migration; and higher professional
positions (in science, the arts, academia) in liberal societies today are often
thrown open to international competition. Why would the parties to the
original position not insist that all positions (jobs) in every society be open

to any qualified person, regardless of international borders or the nationality of the applicant?

3. Finally, there is the difference principle, which states that basic goods (other than liberties) may be distributed unequally as the result of some institutional arrangement only if those who are worst off under this arrangement are nevertheless better off than they would be under any feasible alternative. This principle is designed to apply to economically scarce goods like income and wealth and to intrinsically scarce (positional) goods like authority, whereas free movement (like other liberties) need not be scarce at all. It is scarce only as the result of artifical restraints such as borders and visa requirements. Still, the difference principle can perhaps be held to apply to the matter of immigration in several ways. First, national immigration regimes are institutions that clearly affect the distribution of income in such a way as to perpetuate or bring about inequalities—both of the would-be immigrants, whose income (on the average) would presumably rise if they were admitted, and of the present citizens, on whom the effect of immigration of different kinds and degrees is more controversial: it would presumably affect different groups differently, but the income of at least some would no doubt decline under conditions of open admissions, thus effecting something of an overall equalization between the natives and the newcomers. If the would-be immigrants are the worst-off group in this scenario, then application of the difference principle would dictate their admission to the extent of the economic-absorptive limits of the receiving country, taking into account the robustness of its economy over the long term. Second, we could simply think of immigrant visas as economic goods (rather than as permits for exercising a liberty), as equivalent to jobs with prospective earnings, their value varying according to the number issued and the state of the economy (the labor market) in the receiving country. Then again, if the would-be immigrants constitute the worst-off group, the issuance and distribution of visas could be regulated with an eye toward enhancing the propsects of as many of these people as much as possible. Finally, it has been argued that the difference principle applied globally would prescribe redistribution in the form of transfer payments (foreign aid) from rich to poor nations; assuming that some such argument is valid, one could make the case that the migration of people from poor to rich countries accomplishes at least part of the same end (and thus satisfies to some extent the requirements of justice) in reverse. This possibility is discussed further below.

From this sketchy exploration it appears that all three of Rawls' principles of liberal justice (all of them widely persuasive, on their face) could be construed to favor an "open admissions" policy, especially into more affluent countries, either as a basic right of individuals (and thus virtually unrestricted) or as an instrument of economic distributive justice (and thus on a scale that would probably greatly exceed current levels of immigration in the United States or anywhere, assuming sufficient demand). This apparently radical result is not surprising in view of two major features of Rawls' (and kindred) theories: their tendency to egalitarianism, not only with respect to human rights and opportunities but also with respect to economic well-being, subject only to their concern for the continued productive capacity of economic systems; and their rejection of common claims made on the basis of what they regard as morally arbitrary factors, including the favorable or unfavorable circumstances of a person's birth. Rawls applies the latter argument to an individual's natural talents and inherited wealth, but it seems inescapable that a person's nationality (acquired as it nearly always is by birth), and by extension the restrictions on life chances that are due to exclusive national borders, are just as arbitrary from the perspective of the original position, or of strict moral impartiality.

A second influential strand in recent liberal moral thought that seems relevant to immigration questions has arisen from reflection on the disparities in wealth between the affluent Western nations and the poorer Third World states—between the high standard of living enjoyed by citizens of the former in contrast to the extreme poverty (even actual starvation) among many people in the latter. An intuitively compelling principle of "mutual aid" or limited altruism suggests that one ought to relieve the great distress of another person if one can do so at comparatively small cost or risk to oneself.[5] Peter Singer in his "famine relief" argument, and others, have developed this principle into an argument for a moral duty on the part of the wealthier countries to provide aid to the world's poor at a higher-than-current level, asserting that neither distance nor national borders nor differences of culture ought to restrict the scope of the moral requirement.[6] Furthermore, a more rigorous utilitarian view holds that those who are in a position to relieve distress and contribute to the happiness of others ought to do so up to the limit of their capacity, or, in the present case, that rich countries (or their inhabitants) ought to transfer their wealth to the very poor to the point where they would be sacrificing something of "comparable moral worth," or where the marginal utility to them of what they would be forgoing equals the utility of the transferred resources to the needier recipients.[7]

Pleas along these lines—especially perhaps in the former, less drastic form—evoke a response from the consciences of residents of liberal, Western societies; more analytically, both the mutual aid principle and utilitarianism (with its austere demand for systematic altruism) offer plausible philosophical alternatives to rights-based versions of liberalism. Like Rawls' and other liberal doctrines, they are founded on what may be summed up as an equal consideration of the basic interests of individual human beings.[8] Accordingly, they give equal weight (when it comes to determining the moral obligations of individuals or governments) to the equivalent rights or needs of any persons, whoever and wherever they may be, irrespective of political boundaries or nationality. An ethical doctrine and the moral sentiments that support it thus appear to be significantly at variance with the political organization of the world and the political sentiments that nearly everywhere dictate a preference or a greater level of concern for one's fellow citizens or neighbors than for foreigners, however great and acknowledged the hardship of the latter.

Arguments for foreign aid drawn from duties of benevolence or from utilitarianism, like those drawn from more elaborate distributive criteria such as the difference principle, have a bearing on the present topic insofar as immigration—that is, the immigration of people from poor to rich countries that might be predicted if a general practice of feedom of movement were adopted, or simply if rich countries embraced an "open admissions" policy—could serve as a (partial) equivalent to the transfer of resources. This reasoning seems intuitively plausible: it is a simple matter of bringing needy people to the resources they need rather than sending the resources to them. A poor person who immigrates and either finds a livelihood or is supported by welfare programs in an affluent country has basic needs satisfied, and the emigrant's departure relieves pressure on the scarce resources of the native country. It may be granted that proponents of international redistribution are mainly worried about "absolute poverty" or starvation, which is found on a large scale in places that are remote from and that lack traditions of migration to the West.[9] Most recent immigrants to the United States, for example, even the illegal ones, have come from semi-developed rather than from direly impoverished nations (Mexico and Korea, not Ethiopia or Mozambique; Haiti may be an exception). But migration patterns as well as volume might well change under conditions of "open admissions," and in any event immigration need only be regarded as a partial equivalent of foreign aid in order for openness to acquire a sense of moral obligation, assuming that the ethical arguments for foreign aid are valid.[10]

Foreign aid can be defended as preferable to migration in that it can be directed to people who are unable or unwilling to uproot themselves and move to a distant country, and it can take the form of development projects that might contribute to long-term improvements in living standards.[11] On the other hand, there are a number of considerations weighing in favor of migration over aid, from the point of view of the poor themselves:

1. The moral argument for aiding poor countries has reference to the distress of the poor *people* in those countries, but proposals for international redistribution run up against familiar problems of state-to-state (or government-to-government) aid: the aid may be wasted by inefficient administration, or spent on ill-conceived projects, or diverted by corruption into the hands of the ruling elite and its allies. At the same time, efforts by the donor government to ensure that the aid reaches those for whom it is intended, or the attachment of "strings" to it, may constitute infringements of sover-

eignty.[12] Aid programs that are administered privately at the receiving end exist by the sufferance of the local government. Opportunities for migration, by contrast, benefit directly those individuals who avail themselves of them, that is, people who have reason to believe that they will be better off by moving and frequently people who are clearly poor (if not the poorest) by Western standards. Assuming that transportation is paid by the immigrant, there are no overhead costs other than those that attend immigrant reception (and possible welfare services) in the receiving country. Foreign aid, moreover, is sent to people who are distant and anonymous, whereas would-be immigrants are specific individuals standing on the doorstep. The facts that the potential beneficiaries of immigration are identifiable persons and that the benefits to them are more certain than they may be with foreign aid, constitute strong psychological if not moral foundations for this alternative,

2. Among the very needy we may have an obligation to assist are refugees, defined as people who are out of their country of (nominal) nationality and/ or who are victims of persecution by their own government. Since their governments obviously cannot serve as conduits of aid to these groups (often the neediest of all), and since refugee camps are both temporary and unpromising sites for any but the most immediate kinds of assistance, opportunities for immigration (somewhere) and settlement would appear to be the only substantial means of relieving this form of distress.

3. Arguments in favor of international transfer payments (in common with many theories of social justice) often address the question of a just distribution of economic goods as though this were independent of questions regarding the production of these goods; Singer, for example, simply asserts that since plenty of food exists (at present) in the world, "the problem is essentially one of distribution rather than production."[13] This is simplistic: a different distributive regime would certainly have an impact on production, with respect both to what and to how much was produced, and a plausible theory of justice should be concerned with this relationship. Much immigration from poor to rich countries, however, can be interpreted as flows of labor from areas of low to areas of high demand for it (from lower to higher wage markets); the immigrant is aided by acquiring not a piece of wealth produced elsewhere but a job in a productive economy. To the extent that migration flows are responsive to labor market signals (as it is thought they often are, even in the case of illegal immigration into the United States), this method of redistributing resources would be (indirectly) coordinated with production.[14] From this standpoint one might also be able to make a case for the investment of private capital rather than governmental aid in poor countries as an alternative to the flow of labor in the other direction.[15]

4. The moral argument for aid is frequently addressed to individuals in the affluent countries, rather than or in addition to calling for governmental action: shouldn't each of us, without further ado, send half of our income to relief programs abroad, rather than spend it on comparative luxuries if doing so will save a certain number of people from stravation?[16] However, if just

a few of us did this and most did not, we would be incurring a very great sacrifice of our own well-being relative to those around us *and* making a negligible contribution toward relieving world poverty. We would encounter both the "cut-off for heroism" and the "cut-off for triviality" that Fiskin argues limit our moral obligations.[17] Poverty in Third World countries is not like the hardship of a neighbor or an acquaintance, where spontaneous benevolence can help; it is a large-scale problem, and its alleviation requires collective action in the interests both of fairness and efficacy. Therefore, it is often regarded as the proper business of government, notwithstanding the difficulties pointed out in (1) above. Open immigration, however, as a public policy, would (like taxation for foreign aid) be a collective response to the problem. If it resulted in costs in the form of a reduced standard of living in the receiving country, these would be widely (if not equally) distributed, while at the same time the aggregate effect on relief would be substantial and visible.

5. Finally, adoption of the principle of freedom of immigration would represent an enlargement of the sphere of individual liberty as well as being an equalizing welfare measure and as such it is more consistent than compulsory redistribution with the principal concern of liberalism as traditionally expressed. The possibility of free movement internationally would open new options for everyone (especially for the poor) just as the removal of barriers to internal mobility created new opportunities for the lower classes of European states several centuries ago. Those who took advantage of these opportunities would do so voluntarily, taking account of their personal position, skills, job prospects, aspirations for their children and the like. The enterprise that could be released by such an expansion of choice might seem promising, especially when set against the danger of continuing dependency that could be fostered by transfers of wealth. Freedom of movement has another related advantage as well. An alleged obligation to give material aid, and a right to receive such aid, are positive, but freedom of movement, if it is thought of as a right (with a corresponding obligation in others not to impede movement), is negative. Theories invoking negative rights and obligations are weaker, less controversial, and more in keeping with traditional liberalism than are theories of positive rights. A call for "open admissions" is simply a call for the removal of an obstacle that citizens have previously erected in order to prevent other people (foreigners) from doing what they wish to do (enter), thereby making them worse off than they would otherwise be. Advocating "open admissions" is simply a call for noninterference of a certain kind with the liberty of others in a very clear sense of the term.

I conclude, then, that arguments that advocate redistribution of wealth from rich to poor countries could also be invoked to support open borders and free immigration from poor to rich regions of the world: such movement of people (in some respects perhaps even preferable to transfers of resources) would have similar effects in promoting greater equality, a more just distribution of goods and opportunities, or the relief of extreme economic hardship. More generally it appears from the foregoing survey that both of the main types of contemporary liberal political philosophy, if suitably developed, could be harnessed to this proposal: Rawls' relatively complex theory supports freedom of movement in several different ways (in terms of rights, opportunity, and its likely distributional consequences), whereas utilitarian theory does so more simply in terms of the effects of such a practice on overall welfare, taking account of the interests of all who would be affected by it (foreigners and citizens alike), given standard assumptions regarding the declining marginal utility of extra units of wealth or income. The apparent inability of either of these versions of liberal philosophy to justify the restriction of opportunities or welfare preferences to the members of politically bounded units stems from their fundamental commitment to accord equal weight to the interests of all human beings, in abstraction from the actual features of political life.

This conclusion, however, is paradoxical in the strict sense of the word: it is contrary to common opinion, and startling in its radicalness. Nearly everyone rejects it, preferring instead to stand on the established principles of state sovereignty and of protection of the interests of members of one's own nation in preference to (though not necessarily in total disregard of) those of members of foreign communities. Citizens of well-off countries are not likely to embrace in practice the conclusion of strong versions of the theory—that they should give aid or admit poor immigrants to the point where living conditions in all countries are equalized—nor do citizens of poor countries demand that they do so. Foreign aid is given, and immigrants are admitted, and many argue that the levels of both should be increased, but it is widely granted that these are properly matters of sovereign political choice, not obligations in a strict sense, that is, actions to which the beneficiaries have a right. As matters of sovereign discretion, they are issues that are fittingly assessed by the citizens or officials of a given country in terms of its national interest and security, and arguments in favor of both foreign aid and immigration therefore are usually couched in these terms.

In saying that adherence to the principle of sovereignty remains the common opinion, I have in mind both the prevailing attitudes among citizens of Western countries and the views officially affirmed by the rulers of all contemporary states—Western, Communist (most vociferously of all), and Third World. To this one might respond that the doctrine of state sovereignty is embraced by the affluent because it legitimizes protectionist policies (such as exclusion of foreigners) that perpetuate their advantages, and by the spokesmen for states because the principle of independent statehood reflects the interest of governing elites everywhere. It is conceivable that different, though inarticulate, views are held by the masses of people in impoverished regions who would presumably be the principal beneficiaries of free migration, or of large-scale transfers of wealth, or indeed of some alternative kind of world order altogether.[18] Now as in the past, statism may express simply the existence of states and hence the interest of statesmen in preserving the states system; on this view it is not surprising that the United Nations, as an association of states, has been prominent in asserting the principle of sovereignty. Nevertheless, it is risky to attribute beliefs, or even a predisposition to certain beliefs, to people merely on the ground of their supposed interest in the state of affairs that might follow from the beliefs being generally acted on. Therefore, in the absence of any significant breach, except among philosophers, in the statist consensus, it seems safer to conclude that the philosophical conclusions are in fact paradoxical. This is of course not in itself a reason for rejecting the conclusions, but I believe that it is a reason for scrutinizing them more closely, considering the possible validity of alternative premises and inquiring into the possible grounds of the opposed sentiments of the adherents of traditional opinions.

Finally, it is perhaps worth noting that, so far as can be discerned, the liberal arguments outlined here (though not proposals for foreign aid) lack a constituency in the poor countries of whose interests they seem to be solicitous as well as in the West. Third World governments have been quick to embrace the traditional doctrine of state sovereignty (or the similar U.N. principle of the "right of peoples to self-determination"), which on any account includes the power of restrictive border control with respect to aliens.[19] If the principle of freedom of movement or open admissions were taken to be a basic human right, it would (apart from possible special conflicts of rights) apply with equal force to poor as well as to rich countries. Although the philosophical discussion of immigration in Western countries takes place against a background of presumed pressure of needy Third World nationals to enter the more advanced countries, one should recognize that similar prospects are faced (and resisted) here and there in the Third World as well: India copes with disturbances arising from the influx of Bangladeshis into Assam, Malaysia and Thailand try to draw the line against Indochinese refugees, the Sinhalese of Sri Lanka face secessionist terrorism as the result of historic migrations of Tamils, Nigeria has expelled large numbers of illegal aliens. The world is not neatly divided into rich and poor nations; rather, any country that is relatively better off than neighboring areas may be attractive to would-be immigrants and is accordingly likely to invoke the principle of sovereignty in order to protect the position of its current citizens. Another factor may be forebodings resulting from a lingering association of national aggression with claims for free migration across established borders, as most notably in the cases of German and Japanese demands for *Lebensraum* for their growing populations in the 1920s and 1930s.

Third World states, moreover, have been particularly concerned to assert the additional principle of national sovereignty over the natural resources located within national territories as the common property of the people or nation.[20] This principle applies, of course, to rich as well as to poor states, and if "resources" may be extended to include the national wealth created collectively by the labor of a people (and their ancestors) in addition to raw materials, then this principle amounts to a claim of national property rights that would appear to rule out any demand for international redistribution as a matter of justice. If a given people (the citizens of a state as presently constituted) is entitled by right to have and enjoy its resources, finally, then there can be no claim by foreigners to share in them through immigration either—although of course a people remains free to invite outsiders to come in, as a matter of interest or out of generosity. It is thus striking that, whatever might be the real interests or wishes of their people, the governments of some of those states that one might suppose would benefit most from transfers of resources or an international free migration regime have been notably insistent on asserting doctrines of international law that confirm the traditional rights of sovereign nations.

RESTRICTIVE ENTRY TO PROTECT LIBERAL INSTITUTIONS: THREE VIEWS

In this and the following section I turn to a survey of possible arguments to support the common opinion against open borders or free immigration understood as something that is morally required (as opposed to a policy that a state might choose to have), in other words, possible ways of defending the acknowledged power of a sovereign state or a political community to restrict the entry of foreigners. This project is motivated by a desire to air as fully as possible all sides of an interesting question of political theory, especially considering its practical bearing, and also, as suggested, out of a certain distrust of (or a failure so far to achieve "reflective equilibrium" concerning) a paradoxical result of abstract philosophizing. In this section I consider an argument that can be made from within "pure" liberalism, drawing from illustrative purposes on three representative American writers from different periods of our history. The final section will take up arguments that draw on considerations supplementary to liberalism.

Let us assume the validity of liberal moral and political principles in their main outlines (leaving aside details and variations). Assume that the realization of liberal institutions would be a good thing, not only for us (who currently support them), but for everyone, including those many people around the world who are not currently liberals and who indeed in many cases know nothing whatever of liberalism (and who thus have no desire to promote it). Assume also that liberal institutions are in the interest of future generations and that we therefore should be concerned to preserve and develop them for their sake as well as for our own: this too is a liberal perspective because it encompasses all humanity without distinctions. Finally, let us accept the view (based on arguments like those in the preceding section) that liberalism in its fully realized form would require the reduction if not the abolition of the sovereign powers of states, at least the sovereign powers, and especially those connected with borders and the citizen-alien distinction, that lend themselves to maintaining advantages and inequalities among different populations. (States of some sort, with sovereign powers of legislation and compulsory jurisdiction in their territories, would probably continue to exist.)

The question then arises: What strategy should a liberal adopt for promoting the liberal program in a world in which, at present, liberal institutions are far from being fully realized? In the existing world a conviction of the value of liberal principles is distinctly a minority viewpoint, and only a minority of states are even nominally committed to liberal practices and in even partial compliance with their requirements. Liberal institutions are not only scarce, but hard-won and fragile, and where they exist, they are vulnerable both to domestic challenges and to threats emanating from the hostile or indifferent external environment, as the historical record indicates. In these circumstances it seems reasonable to say that a liberal's first concern should be to nourish and defend liberal beliefs and institutions, even imperfect ones, where they presently exist, as a base from which their influence may someday expand when more favorable circumstances permit. And a liberal may properly compromise liberal principles in practice, in the non-ideal world, when this appears to be necessary *in order* to preserve or strengthen them where they have a foothold, while at the same time seeking ways of promoting their expansion and eventual full realization. In this spirit a liberal might, as things stand in the world today, not only uphold the traditional (and admittedly nonliberal) sovereign power over borders and admission to citizenship, but might also support restrictive policies on these matters, insofar as there were good reasons to believe that uncontrolled cross-border movement of people—in particular, the influx of nonliberal people into liberal states—would pose a threat to the survival or perhaps simply to the flourishing and strengthening of liberal commitments and institutions where they exist. The persuasiveness of this argument is suggested by the fact that it has been advanced, in different forms, by liberals of different types in different periods of U.S. history, as may be illustrated by the arguments of Thomas Jefferson, Richmond Mayo-Smith, and Bruce Ackerman.

Thomas Jefferson represents important currents of early American thinking on these matters. The liberalism to which he subscribed emphasized the natural rights of individuals, among them the right not to be subject to political authority without one's own freely given consent. For Jefferson this entailed a denial of the English common law doctrine of "perpetual allegiance" stemming from birth in the "dominions" of some government and a defense of a natural right of emigration or expatriation (a right Americans had exercised) as a means of ensuring that "choice not chance" might determine civic membership.[21] Although Jefferson presumably believed that people were free to enter and settle in "vacant" territories or wilderness (or more precisely, into lands not yet organized into civil societies), he did not, however, advocate a corresponding right of individuals to immigrate into and be granted membership in established states. On the contrary, he not only accepted the sovereign right of a state like Virginia (or after 1788 the United States) to set rules for admission, but at one stage in his career he also expressed support for restrictiveness along the lines just suggested.[22]

After first commenting on the apparent desirability of populating the new American societies as rapidly as possible, including the encouragement of immigration, Jefferson immediately expresses some misgivings. Every government has its own "specific principles." American principles, that is, republican (or liberal) principles derived from "natural right and natural reason," are "peculiar," even unique in a world otherwise pervaded by monarchies and despotism.

To ["our" principles] nothing can be more opposed than the maxims of absolute monarchies. Yet, from such, we are to expect the greatest number of emigrants. They will bring with them the principles of the governments they leave, imbibed in their early youth; . . . These principles, with their language, they will transmit to their children. In proportion to their numbers, they will share with us the legislation. They will infuse into it their spirit, warp and bias its direction, and render it a heterogeneous, incoherent, distracted mass.[23]

This passage, written during the Revolutionary War, may reflect a fear that American republicanism was still in an experimental and precarious stage, still threatened by "monarchical" power from abroad. More important, however, is the fear that American principles of government could be undermined from within if membership were extended to excessive numbers of those (such as emigrants from German principalities) who were unfamiliar with these principles, not having "imbibed" or internalized their spirit. Although the dependence of regimes on widespread inculcation of their principles was a general tenet of (Montesquieuian) political science, the danger of instability is especially pressing in republics for two reasons.[24] Republican government, being founded on citizen participation and assertiveness with respect to individual rights, is more demanding than other systems, and it thus requires a more intensive civic education for its members. Furthermore, republican government, by extending the suffrage to all inhabitants, is directly vulnerable to the distortion of its ideals, through the process of government itself, if sufficient numbers of voters are deficient in the requisite attitudes. It follows that republican government must take care to nurture its own foundations in the moral and political qualities of its citizens through oversight of the upbringing of the children of citizens, through care for the civic assimilation of newcomers, and, perhaps, through restrictions on the number of those from nonrepublican backgrounds who are admitted.

It may be added that Jefferson did not in fact press this worry to a particularly restrictionist conclusion. He affirms that he has no doubts about the value of the immigration of "useful artificers" (as opposed to more servile peasants?), who are good potential citizens. Moreover, he has no objection to those who "come of themselves," a voluntary, individual decision to emigrate perhaps constituting in itself sufficient evidence of the desired spirit; he opposes only "extraordinary encouragements" or subsidies for mass emigration.[25] Finally, whatever fears he had seem to have withered away later, since during his presidency the earlier Federalist naturalization law was replaced by one with a comparatively brief residency requirement, one designed to encourage the absorption of immigrants into the American body politic.

Richmond Mayo-Smith was a professor of sociology at Columbia who published a major study of immigration in 1890, in the context of the growing movement for restriction of the "new" (non–Western European) immigration that was becoming visible and worrisome to many old-stock Americans. It is an even-handed and relatively liberal work when read against the background of nativist and restrictionist sentiment, and it expresses certain distinctive currents in late nineteenth-century liberal thought.

Mayo-Smith begins the argument with which I am concerned by affirming what had emerged as the consensus of positivist writers on international law: notwithstanding the merits of permissive (laissez-faire) *policies,* sovereign states have the legal *right* to control migration both in and out of their territories. The Jeffersonian idea that "expatriation" is a natural right of the individual belongs to an earlier, now generally repudiated, phase of thinking on the subject. Nevertheless, from the moral point of view states may have a "cosmopolitan duty to admit other persons to their soil if they desire to come."

A nation, it is said, has a right to the soil only on condition of making the best use of it, and if it have more land than it really need, it is in duty bound to share it with others. It is on this basis that the colonization of America by the nations of Europe is theoretically justified. The Indians were the original occupiers . . . but the white men were more highly civilized, and could make better use of the land. What once barely kept a few thousand savages from starvation, now sustains millions of men in an advanced stage of culture. So it is said that the present inhabitants of the United States have no right to appropriate a country fitted to support several times their number. . . . We have no right to keep these struggling millions out from our fertile fields and broad prairies.[26]

This argument, Mayo-Smith says, is perfectly sound, based as it is on this underlying principle—that "it *is* the right of the higher civilization to make the lower give way before it. . . . for it is in this way that the world progresses." This is, I think, a basically liberal argument (though of a kind that is no longer in fashion), since Mayo-Smith assumes that the mark of "higher" civilizations is their greater realization of liberal institutions; the triumph of

higher over lower societies means in effect the spread of liberalism around
the world, a process that in 1890 perhaps seemed to be in full sway and
could be equated with the "progress" of humanity in general. Mayo-Smith
here simply echoes well-known arguments of John Stuart Mill, for whom
conduciveness to "progress" and the spread of civilization—meaning liberal
civilization—was often invoked as a criterion for assessing practices and
indeed for limiting the application of principles (such as those of liberty and
nationality) that in the right circumstances were desirable.

Although the imperative to spread civilization justifies a right of migration
in some circumstances (especially a right of civilized people to settle in vacant
or less civilized regions), it has other implications as well. So long as the
final triumph of civilization is not assured and while "barbarism" poses a
threat to its achievements where they exist, the more civilized must take
precautions to protect what they have—not so much in their own interest
(in this case their interest coincides with a more general interest of humanity)
as in that of the world as a whole, which in the long run stands to benefit
from civilized institutions wherever they may be based: "A conquest by
barbarians does not raise even the average civilization of the world. . . . One
nation on a high plane of civilization is better than half the world in a state
of semi-civilization." From these general points follows a particular worry
about uncontrolled migration: "There is this danger in indiscriminate immigration; it may be composed of elements which tend to pull down rather
than build up."[27] This argument would seem to be susceptible to a strong
or a weak interpretation: that the immigration of people of a lower cultural
level (or of less well developed liberal sensibilities) into more civilized countries ought to be restricted if it reduces the maximal flourishing and development of liberal institutions there; or, more weakly, that it ought not to
be permitted on such a scale that it threatens the very survival of liberal
civilization in a country that has attained it. In either form we would face
the prospect of a threat that has long haunted the Western liberal imagination—a "barbarian invasion" that, however peaceful, would represent a
setback, with possibly irreparable losses, for civilization and human progress
in general.

For a third, contemporary variant of this same basic argument, I turn to
Bruce Ackerman's theory of justice, which includes an explicit treatment of
nationality and immigration. This theory is in crucial respects, as its author
proclaims, a liberal theory—in its individualism, its conception of the neutrality of public authority vis-à-vis private values and pursuits, and its foundation in a universalist commitment to rationality. When pressed, these
themes appear incompatible with the collective pursuit of any substantive
form of political community. The most distinctive feature of Ackerman's
theory is its insistence on an absolute equality of starting points for individuals
as they set out in life, each to pursue his or her own conception of the good,
or life plan, as the individual sees fit. Although it shares with traditional

liberalism a commitment to equality of opportunity, it vastly extends this notion to mean an actual equality of material opportunities or abilities to pursue and realize one's conception of the good, to the point of calling for the abolition or neutralization of any inequalities in life chances that individuals may face as the result of the circumstances of their birth. This means that the natural "genetic lottery" must be corrected (pending the invention of a "techonology" to correct its defects at their root) by compensation payments from the more to the less fortunately endowed. Similarly, it means that the results of what might be called the "nationality lottery," by which some people are unaccountably born into less advantaged countries, must be evened out, both by international redistribution of resources and by the opportunity of free movement by individuals from, for example, the "poor East" to the "rich West."[28] For the citizens of a particular (rich) country to attempt to exclude aliens who seek to immigrate would be to attempt to exercise a "power" over them that Ackerman believes cannot be defended in a "neutral dialogue," since (he supposes) it would entail making the untenable claim that having been born on one side of a border makes one a "better" person than one born outside, and hence entitled to advantages. Nor could one properly appeal to one's descent from ancestors who were the first to occupy the territory: temporal priority of citizenship does not yield a right to deny this status to others who apply later, since "people who arrive first" are not "better" than those who come later.[29] Geographical boundaries and the civic identities and privileges associated with them are morally arbitrary and thus indefensible when they cause inequalities or interfere with the pursuit of individual life plans. Freedom of movement across borders, on the other hand, furthers both the remedial goal (in an imperfect world) of equalization of resources and the ultimate end of equal opportunity for self-realization.

This conclusion is, however, qualified in one significant way. While liberalism itself (with its commitment to equality, neutral dialogue, and so forth) is a scarce and fragile resource in an imperfect world, liberal societies can never be obliged to do what might imperil their existence as strongholds of liberalism (even imperfect liberalism). A liberal, moreover, could rationally defend this fear as a ground for denying an outsider's claim. This provision has implications for foreign policy, including aid programs, which Ackerman holds must be extended only to "undeveloped countries of a liberal tendency."[30] It also means that immigration into a liberal, Western country must be permitted only up to the level of its "assimilative capacity," that is, a level that will preserve a sufficiently large "cadre of natives familiar with the operation of liberal institutions" to ensure that the liberal character of the country will be preserved.[31] This limit applies only to the migration of nonliberals (as perhaps many of those from non-Western countries would be), because a sudden influx of such people might jeopardize the very system under which they themselves would benefit. It justifies appeal only to po-

litical or civic assimilation (that is, absorption of liberal values) as a condition
of ongoing immigration, and not a requirement of broader, cultural assimilation that is sometimes invoked in immigration debates in political communities as they are.

These three arguments are, I believe, in essence the same. Jeffersonian
natural right, Mayo-Smith's Millian concern for the spread of liberal civilization, and Ackerman's conception of liberal social justice all tend to regard
political borders and civic distinctions as morally arbitrary and, when they
have the effect of perpetuating privilege, as illegitimate. All favor freedom
of individual movement and choice of civic membership, as a direct expression of individual rights, as a vehicle of equal opportunity, or as a practice
that facilitates the proliferation of liberal ideas and practices. All three theories, however, acknowledge that the principles they advocate are realized
imperfectly, and in only a few places, in the world as it is: republican,
civilized, or liberal regimes are scarce, while those who live under monarchical, barbarian, or illiberal regimes, and are presumably imbued with their
outlooks, are many. In these circumstances the citizens of liberal regimes
must be on their guard; the preservation of liberal institutions where they
exist must be the first priority, even if this means restricting some of the
operations that liberal principles would have in a more ideal world. Liberal
regimes must not only withstand aggression or deliberate subversion on the
part of competing types of regimes (such as monarchical ones) abroad; they
must also avoid being "swamped" by immigrants in such numbers or at such
a rate that the new residents cannot be assimilated into the liberal system,
with the consequence that it is undermined from within. (To this one might
add that immigration justified in liberal terms ought not to go so far as to
cause the native citizens to abandon their liberal convictions as a "backlash"
against its effects, on for example, their own living standards.)

What is envisaged here may be termed a "protectionist" policy, one that
is designed to protect and preserve a republican polity or a liberal society,
which are by hypothesis desirable in themselves for those who have them,
and that also indirectly sustain the material advantages that may accompany
this way of life. Such protectionism is, of course, the policy that one expects
the members of an advantaged community to enact, in the normal course
of things, by democratic procedures, whenever access to the advantages by
others appears to reduce their value to the present owners. Liberalism has
typically opposed protectionist policies, including restricted access to positions and careers. Protectionism with respect to liberal institutions themselves, however, in contrast to other forms, seems to be justifiable from the
universal or impartial viewpoint characteristic of liberal morality itself. The
policy is in the interest of humanity as a whole, including those who are not
currently so advantaged, if one makes the reasonable assumption that the
benefits of liberalism can only be more widely distributed by gradually
spreading from a secure base. Immigration into liberal countries (at some

point) may be restricted on the ground that more people (posterity included) would be harmed than benefited by unlimited entry, if the survival of the liberal base, as a liberal base, would be jeopardized by this practice.

The practical bearing of this argument, finally, depends on prevailing circumstances—on the actual number of potential immigrants and their political or cultural attitudes, and on the assimilative capacity of the liberal society. It is outlined here as a potentially restrictive argument with regard to immigration, since it qualifies the tendency of pure liberalism (from which it is derived) toward openness and free mobility in a restrictive direction, but given some actual state of affairs, it might turn out to justify rather extensive immigration. In fact, it might well be consistent with much higher volumes of immigration than the United States and other advanced countries presently experience. Indeed, arguments of the form suggested here might actually favor—even require—openness to immigration to the maximum level. Just as the preservation of republican government, civilization, or liberalism dictates that a society favored by its possession of any of these values not only *may* but *ought* to control immigration when it threatens the scarce value, so on the other hand the maximal diffusion of these values, or the conferral of their benefits on as many people as possible, might dictate the highest possible rate of absorption and assimilation of new members. Every immigrant, being a prospective new convert to liberal principles, represents a step toward the goal of their universal realization.

STATISM, DEMOCRACY, AND COMMUNITY

I turn now to several arguments against a requirement of open admissions derived from doctrines that could plausibly supplement liberalism, doctrines that are not liberal in themselves, but that have historically been associated with this viewpoint and that are presumably not deeply antagonistic to its most fundamental values. The preceding two sections presented arguments that appeared to require freedom of movement either in general, or especially between poor and rich countries today, except for the internal qualification relating to the preservation of the liberal character of the receiving country; these arguments are drawn from pure or abstract liberal doctrines. (Jefferson's republicanism and Mayo-Smith's conception of "civilization" no doubt contain other elements as well, but in this discussion they were considered as essentially liberal doctrines.) Few people, however, are in practice pure liberals—that is, liberals and nothing else. Most people, even those who are liberals, are hybrids of some sort, in the political as well as in other dimensions of their moral lives. In this section I offer some reflections on the implications for immigration of three familiar outlooks, one or another of which (or all in combination) captures the beliefs of actual liberal citizens more accurately than do some contemporary philosophical accounts of liberal principles. These outlooks are liberal statism, liberal democracy, and liberal

communitarianism, and the second element of each term also deserves examination.

Liberal Statism

Liberalism in some recently influential versions has been developed as a
branch of moral philosophy with little place for *political* content, if politics
refers to the organization of human beings into political units (*poleis*, or
states) and to the issues of rule and political activity that go on within and
among them. Liberalism was originally a more distinctly political doctrine,
one that addressed the question of the proper ends and structure of governmental authority and the proper distribution of civic rights within the
sovereign states that had taken shape in early modern Europe. One may
say that classical liberalism took for granted the existence of independent,
territorial states of the modern type, and, in so doing, tacitly gave its approval
to the existence of such states even while justifying some but not all the
political and social institutions and policies that might arise within them.
This association of liberal political philosophy with the sovereign state, and
thus with a world organized into a plurality of independent states of identical
juridical status, has continued largely unabated from the eighteenth century
to the present, although the underlying assumption in favor of the state has
been shaken by liberal dismay over the ferocity of twentieth-century interstate wars and by doubts about the continuing economic rationality of states
in view of transnational economic networks and interdependence. Since
liberal philosophers concentrated on the internal arrangements of the state—
especially the problem of securing individual liberty and limited government—they characteristically did not have much to say about the state system
and the state's sovereign powers as these are manifested in its external
relations. The standard statist assumptions of liberalism may therefore best
be seen by reading the liberal political theorists in conjunction with the
liberal international lawyers (Emer de Vattel and his successors) in whose
work these complementary matters are fully developed.

Nevertheless, liberalism and statism, although they have traditionally gone
together, may be in tension with each other; statism may be problematic in
light of liberal philosophical principles. The liberal commitment to individualism and universalism is evidently uncomfortable with national distinctions
and barriers; the liberal commitment to rational discussion and the peaceful
resolution of conflicts on the basis of underlying common interests or mutual
accommodation is uneasy with the threat of resort to arms that always seems
to be latent in interstate relations. Philosophical jurisprudence in the liberal
tradition (for example, Vattel) has tended to conceive of the state on the
model of the individual as a corporate "person" having a sovereign "will"
and interests that it may rightly pursue, with territorial sovereignty understood as analogous to private property.[32] This mode of thought is, however,

metaphorical, issuing in legal fictions that may be useful in grasping the nature of the sovereign powers that states actually claim and exercise, but inadequate to the problem of justifying them.[33] Similarly, drawing on the classical liberal account of the origins of civil society, one may think of the relations of states among themselves as resembling those of individuals in the state of nature; but then (from the liberal point of view) the question immediately arises why it is not rational, or even morally obligatory, for states like individuals to put an end to this condition by agreement on some kind of supra-state order.

The discomfort that liberalism experiences when its principles are brought to bear on the statist framework within which it has hitherto existed is thus clear. Whether or not liberals can do without the state, however, would seem to depend on the existence of a feasible alternative that is more consonant with liberal values. If there were no (realistic) alternative, liberals would have to live with the state—and, if they were political animals, give their support to it—as a simple given of modern political life. If there appeared to be some prospect of an alternative, but it was not feasible or safe to implement it now, then liberals could endorse the state system as a respectable second-best arrangement while prudently seeking to negotiate the transition to something preferable. The social contract model of liberal constitution making suggests the way to an alternative: states, in their own higher interests (and those of their citizens), ought to come to an agreement on a cosmopolitan civil order, either a more effective body of international law or, more strongly, a world state of some kind, as envisaged by Immanuel Kant. (A single world "state," of course, would mean the abolition of sovereign states as we know them, just as a one-class society would be, in Marxian terms, a classless society; many of the attributes of sovereignty concern the rights of states in their relations with other states.) Contemporary world politics, however, offers little reason to believe that such an event is imminent except insofar as one may entertain hopes for a gradual strengthening of international law, especially human rights law, through the work of the United Nations and related agencies. Liberals, therefore, may have no choice but to live in a world of states for the foreseeable future.

Apart from this argument from necessity, there are two main grounds (in a liberal perspective) for preferring a plurality of states to the alternative of a single world political order. The first pertains to the familiar specter of a "universal despotism," conceivably the worst of all possibilities.[34] In a world of many states, some may be despotisms, but it is unlikely that all will be despotic at the same time. The existence of nondespotic states offers the possibility of a refuge from the despotisms, and the possibility of the flight of skilled people from despotic to free societies (however much the despotic regime may try to prevent this) tends to temper despotic government. (This is an important liberal argument for free movement, especially emigration and asylum for refugees.) Moreover, the existence of the nondespotic states

stands as a constant reproach to the despotisms, offering a model of something
better and serving as a source of moral (and perhaps also material) support
for reformers, revolutionaries, and dissidents in the oppressed society. From
a world state, however, should it fall into the hands of a despotic government,
there would be no escape. The memory of nondespotic ways of life would
gradually fade away, and endogenous change in a liberal direction would be
difficult without external bases of support. A world of numerous independent
states with somewhat differing forms of government thus appears to offer
the means of correcting abuses that may appear here and there in the system
as a whole, much as a liberal constitution, with a separation of powers, is
supposed to offer the means of self-correction in the face of institutional
tendencies to corruption. If a world state could turn out to be the worst
case (in liberal terms), whatever its possible merits, a cautious liberal might
well choose to stick with the state system, whatever its actual defects, as a
framework within which the survival of liberal values seems more secure.

The second argument for a plurality of states arises from the typical liberal
(Millian) view of the sources of progress. Economic productivity and cultural
vitality flourish best when there is a large number of autonomous centers
of decision, each seeking opportunities for the (locally) optimal employment
of its particular set of resources and talents, their interactions with one
another coordinated only informally by markets, emulation, rational per-
suasion, and the like. Beneficial innovations (which outweigh the occasional
failures) are stimulated by the diversity that results when individuals are
free to choose their own "plans of life." Even conflicts among the competing
interests or ideals of independent agents are, to a point, healthy phenomena,
a theme Kant developed in terms of the "unsocial sociability" of human
beings. If this view is plausible with respect to a society of individuals, so
it may be also with respect to the society of states: each state follows, or
provides the political means by which its people follow, its own distinctive
genius or program of political experimentation, thereby not only attaining
the satisfaction that attends autonomy, but also making its own special contribution to the overall cultural resources of humanity.

If any of these arguments is plausible, liberals may have good reason to
support the continuing association of liberalism and statism. It remains only
to consider the implications of this for immigration or freedom of movement.
An acceptance of states implies the acceptance of sovereignty in some form.
The power of a state to distinguish between its nationals and aliens, to protect
the interests of its nationals over those of aliens, and in particular to restrict
the entry of aliens into its territory is traditionally one of the central and
undoubted elements of sovereignty. But is the power to exclude foreigners
essential to the existence of states, such as they must be for the arguments
just outlined to be valid? Could sovereign (nation-)states exist on the model
of the component units of a federation (like U.S. states), having stable territorial boundaries and jurisdiction over residents, but ever-fluctuating pop-

ulations? To defend the interal free movement of people (and the corresponding weakness of local citizenship) among, say, the U.S. states, but to reject international free movement is to assume that there is a relevant difference between the two cases. (Perhaps the historic loss of sovereignty by the U.S. states, contrary to the somewhat ambiguous intentions of the framers of the U.S. Constitution, is indicative.) The independence of small states would be jeopardized by the possibility of large-scale immigration (which might be deliberately encouraged) from larger neighboring states, with the ensuing domination of the local electorate by people with foreign allegiance. Even on a proportionally smaller scale, such a process could certainly destabilize the domestic political systems of states, or otherwise pose threats to national security, so long (as is likely) the international environment continued to harbor interstate distrust or hostilities. Such processes could indeed provoke international hostilities where none existed before, something that a proponent of states should be especially concerned to prevent, given that the prospect of war is the principal and admitted defect of the state system. These reflections, even fully developed, would probably not add up to a justification for completely closed borders, at least not in most real-world cases. On the contrary, the two arguments for states sketched above imply that states, especially liberal states, ought to be receptive to immigrants to some point; the interstate movement of people, perhaps especially of political refugees and bearers of ideas, helps ensure that the state system retains a liberal character. One who accepts these or other arguments for states, however, could probably feel justified in upholding *in principle* the sovereign power over immigration.

Liberal Democracy

This familiar phrase combines two distinct sets of elements (although there are some elements, such as the civil equality of individuals, that are common to both): the liberal dimension of a liberal democratic regime pertains to individuals' possession of the important civil rights, to latitude for individual choice of goals and life-styles, and to the maintenance of a restricted field for governmental activity and regulation; the democratic dimension refers to active citizenship and participation in public affairs, to majority rule, and in general to collective "self-determination" by a people with respect to what they take to be their common affairs. "Democracy" in this view pertains to the distinctively "political" part of human life to which such importance and dignity are attributed by Aristotle and by those who follow him to the present day in this, and which tends to be overlooked or discounted by the liberal philosophies to which I have alluded. For anyone, including liberals, for whom there is something to the Aristotelian view—for whom people are political animals—democracy and its conditions acquire a value apart from the liberal values with which they may fairly readily be combined.

Now while characteristic liberal activities, such as engaging in free speech or optional religious worship, entering into privately negotiated economic transactions, or pursuing one's own chosen "plan of life," can in principle be undertaken independently of boundaries or group membership, the practice of democracy logically presupposes that an individual is a member of a group—the *demos* or people that in some respects acts as a collectivity. Furthermore, although it is just barely conceivable that all humanity could constitute this group in a democratic world state, one can say that democracy practically requires the division of humanity into distinct, civically bounded groups that function as more or less independent political units. Democratic theorists of the past went so far as to argue that democracy was possible only in relatively small states, on the ground that only here was genuine or meaningful (participatory) citizenship possible. Although in the modern world democrats usually hold (sometimes with misgivings) that even large nation-states can be democratically organized, it is difficult to imagine that "world citizenship" could be the real thing, or that majority rule on such a scale, suitably informed by debate and deliberation, could be practicable or desirable. Hence democracy requires that *people* be divided into *peoples* (each people hopefully enjoying its own democratic insititutions), with each unit distinguishing between its own citizens—understood in a political sense as those eligible to exercise democratic political rights *here*—and others, who are regarded as aliens *here*, although (hopefully) citizens somewhere else. If we assume then the existence (and the value) of a number of democratic political units (and assume also that they are territorial units—democratic states, in fact), we then face the question whether the ideal of democracy implies any justification for a right on the part of the citizens to prohibit or control the admission of outsiders to their community. There are several arguments favoring this view.

First, democracy can be understood as a set of procedures (rules of debate and agenda setting, one-person-one-vote, periodic elections, majority rule, and so on) by which a group of people make collective or public decisions. Strong theories of democracy hold that democratic procedures (combined with the delegation of some powers to officials who are at least indirectly accountable to the majority) are the sole legitimate method of making such decisions; the operation of democratic institutions should amount to "self-determination," or control by the people over all matters that affect their common interests. The admission of new members into the democratic group, however, would appear to be such a matter, one that could not only affect various private interests of the current members, but that could also, in the aggregate, affect the quality of their public life and the character of their community. If power over this matter lay elsewhere than in the hands of the members, or if the matter (concerning which a number of alternative choices seem possible) were permanently removed from the agenda, the democracy that existed would be seriously attenuated; it would not amount to self-determination.

A democracy is an association of citizens, or a membership organization, above all; as such, as Michael Walzer has noted, it bears some resemblance to a club, one feature of which is that the present members have the power to determine the future membership, at least regarding the admission of new members.[35] It is true that democratic states differ from private clubs in certain respects that appear to restrict their procedural competence: clubs may frequently expel dissenting members, whereas the involuntary denationalization of citizens by a state (although it is done) is disapproved under international law; the membership of clubs may or may not be hereditary, whereas that of states normally is, so that the acquisition of citizenship is normally automatic; a state that failed to extend citizenship to all or nearly all residents, especially native residents, would hardly qualify as a democracy, whatever its governmental arrangements. These rules may be seen as widely accepted constitutional qualifications on democracy as practiced in territorial states; they are designed to ensure that everyone have citizenship in some state (by birth, if not by subsequent choice) and thus to remove one important obstacle to the universal realization of democracy, with its central institution of citizenship. These are qualifications on local majority rule, in other words, that can be defended in terms of democracy itself, as a value that ought to be universalized. This argument, however, does not apply to the migration of persons from one state to another. Reserving control over such movement to the present members of each state could still be consistent with a world in which democracy was realized for everyone. Democracy as a set of procedures for self-determination, then, appears to imply a power in the present citizen body to control immigration.

Second, there are a number of related arguments that understand democracy in a more substantive sense, as pertaining to or requiring a *democratic community* with a distinct identity and way of life that its members are entitled (and normally are expected) to maintain, if necessary by restricting the entry of outsiders who do not share the common identity or values. One common view, for example, holds that even for democracy (understood as a method of government) to work, its members must be united by mutual trust and capacity for communication, by similar styles of political behavior and familiarity with local norms, and by a consensus on basic goals, values, and common interests. Jefferson, for example, in his comments on immigration says, "It is for the happiness of those united in society to harmonize as much as possible in matters which they must of necessity transact together."[36] He worried that the civic harmony necessary for republican government (limited as its role was to be) could be threatened by the influx of foreigners, even quite apart from the lack of adherence to republican principles on the part of some of them.

Another view holds that democracy should be regarded not simply as the formal business of government, but as the larger process by which a determinate group of people develops, over time, its own distinctive "common life" or way of life, and it is to be justified in these terms. In this view democracy not only implies the power of a community to resist, but may actually *mean* resistance to, external pressures that could destroy its integrity or distort its development of its own inner resources and "shared understandings."[37] The politics of a democracy understood in this way might or might not, of course, lead to immigration restrictions (or to various qualitative kinds of immigration control). An ongoing tradition of diverse immigration is arguably part of the very identity of the democratic community of the United States, and the "common life" that is pursued here has long been heterogeneous in many respects. In other cases, however, it might appear that maintenance of ethnic or cultural uniformity against dilution by foreign influences could be a legitimate aspect of democratic practice. A policy of protectionism with respect to the local way of life (as in other matters) is often the natural expression of localized democracy as of other forms of localized political power; it is the democratic basis of such a policy that distinguishes and may justify it. Democracy in the substantive sense suggested here, at any rate, plausibly implies a power of the citizenry to resolve this matter as they see fit, and therefore a power in principle over immigration.

Citizenship in democratic states, as noted, is normally acquired by birth (although one may be free to leave); this practice is both cause and effect of the fact that democratic, like other, communities, with their distinctive ways of life, are communities or associations that persist through time, primarily on a hereditary basis. This fact seems troublesome from a certain philosophical perspective, especially in the case of an advantaged country that maintains a restrictive entry policy, since this seems to be a case of the hereditary maintenance of privilege—something that liberalism has historically always opposed (at least within the state). Democratic theory simply presupposes the existence of a group of citizens, but in the real world an individual is a citizen of a given (democratic) state either through the accident of birth there, or by having previously been admitted and naturalized, or as the result of the good fortune of descent from ancestors who were citizens by birth or previous admittance to that country. Should not democratic citizens then acknowledge the fortuitous character of the position they enjoy, and extend to others the same opportunity of admission of which they or their ancestors were beneficiaries, by a willingness to admit newcomers to their group? Ackerman's liberalism leads to a denial that the earlier comers to a country can legitimately deny residence and a share of the resources to late-comers.[38] Barry asks, "What is the merit of getting there first . . . or having an ancestor who got there first?"[39]

One can, however, accept the argument that the present members of a community cannot appeal to any merit of their own to justify their status without accepting the conclusion that they lack any right to maintain their restricted association, including the limited privilege of democratic citizenship that defines its political dimension. Any community, insofar as this concept is related to that of tradition, must sustain its coherence and identity to some degree through time; therefore, to uphold the value of community—including that of a democratic community with its civic traditions—entails defending the institutions that accomplish this end, even if this means fortuitous distinctions and privileges for some. Second, although liberal democrats obviously do not claim any merit from having particular ancestors, it is simplistic to suppose that present claims to citizenship arise from nothing more than the fact that one's ancestors "got there first." If there is anything morally relevant in the temporal perspective, it is not the priority of arrival of the ancestors, but rather the greater risks and difficulties encountered by the earlier settlers and their productive labors in creating the resources—civic and cultural as well as material—that their descendants now enjoy. A working democracy itself, although its procedures can perhaps be easily specified, is in concrete actuality built up gradually by the efforts of generations of members of a given society. Liberalism is uncomfortable with rights of inheritance, but much less so with the notion that those who have created goods by their labors should have the right to give or bequeath these goods to whom they please—whether descendants, adopted heirs, or outsiders whom they choose to favor. Might not this apply to civic goods like democratic membership as well as to property in the usual sense?

Furthermore, there is much good sense in Edmund Burke's idea that the moral health of a community (including, one may add, a specifically democratic one) depends on its members' regarding its resources as an inheritance or heritage that they have received from their predecessors and that they therefore have a duty to pass on intact or improved to their successors. The political expression of this sentiment is the "civic virtue" that in some form is doubtlessly necessary for the continued functioning of democratic institutions. Maintenance of exclusive citizenship by denying admission to foreigners appears to be an expression of group preference or group selfishness, illicit in liberal morality, from the point of view of the outsiders. From the point of view of the individual insider, however, national group preference in a healthy democracy is likely to be related to public-spiritedness and the subordination of private to common interests, a central element of civic morality. To the extent, then, that democracy as a mode of communal activity in practice requires these elements—in general, democratic *traditions* and their associated moral psychology—the fact that citizenship in democratic states is normally a hereditary institution would not seem to make restrictions on immigration unjustifiable.

Liberal Communitarianism

The discussion of liberal democracy has already brought us to the idea of a democratic *community* that preserves its character (of which its democratic

practices are a part) through time as a substantive ideal. I conclude this
section by reflecting a little further on the possible independent value of
community and community preservation as a ground for exclusion, taking
"community" to be constituted by any features, especially a culture and
traditions, that a people have "in common," that give them a common identity as a group, and are valued by them, other than commitments to liberalism
or democracy themselves. Although sometimes a newcomer can become a
member of a community through a process of assimilation, the most characteristic communal attributes are acquired by individuals involuntarily, by
birth and upbringing. It is thus misleading to think of them as the result of
choice, even of a hypothetical social contract, despite Rawls' efforts to portray
common agreement on the principles of liberal justice as the basis for a
psychologically satisfying community. This noncontractual quality most
clearly differentiates community, as a separate value, from the values of
liberalism. Some would go further: The fact that actual individuals acquire
a significant portion of their identity and character (including even their
liberal attitudes, if they have these) from their community life most clearly
reveals pure liberalism as a "myth," or (better), an abstraction. In any event,
it is an increasingly common view that liberalism—perhaps especially its
contemporary varieties—is deficient in its appreciation of both the formative
impact and the value of community, even though an alternative philosophical
account of community does not seem to be well developed.[40] Nevertheless,
I assume that liberalism can be combined with communitarianism in some
form, just as it can be with the state and democracy (liberalism, like democracy, could be the defining feature *of* a community, although it would
be in a sense conceptually subordinate to it), and that this conjunction might
have implications for the question of borders and immigration.

A defense of communitarianism could be developed along two different
lines. In either case the argument, if successful, would justify control over
entry, since the concept of community implies a reasonably stable distinction
between members and nonmembers (just as the concepts of the state and
democracy imply distinctions between nationals and aliens, citizens and
noncitizens) and a collective identity that could be vulnerable to destruction
by excessive foreign influences. (The identity of a community, however, like
that of an individual, can change gradually, by "growth" and adaptation and
sometimes even by deliberate choices without being destroyed, and a certain
amount of permitted immigration could be part of this process.)

First, relying on theories of human nature or on the findings of psychology,
one could uphold the value of community membership for each individual
as a necessary component of a fully satisfactory human life, as a necessary
vehicle for some aspects of self-realization, or perhaps even as the necessary
context for those aspects of the moral life that involve personal relations and
special commitments to others. The importance of these matters is of course
disputable (and may well vary from one individual to another). Although

liberal theory does not emphasize them, liberal thinkers have naturally been aware of them and sensed the need to accommodate them. Singer, for example, acknowledges the great strength of group preference (and group altruism) among human beings, even accepting the claim of sociobiology that such tendencies are rooted in our genetic nature. His conclusion is that the very recognition of these "relics of our evolutionary history" should help us to overcome them in favor of the universalist ethic of border-less sharing of resources mentioned above.[41] But it is not clear why the naturalistic perspective that he espouses here could not just as well lead to a kind of ethical naturalism that would accord value to sentiments that are deeply rooted in us, especially those that give rise subjectively to evaluative attitudes.[42] Moreover, the preference utilitarianism embraced by Singer and some other contemporary liberal moralists would yield practical conclusions more favorable to the maintenance of communities and the main elements of their accustomed ways of life if more weight were given to the satisfactions (perhaps often of a background sort, and therefore not salient except when threatened) that people derive from this source.

Earlier liberals, of course, frequently assumed that the nation was the natural or historically destined community for human beings, and therefore embraced a doctrine of liberal nationalism. This project proved to be seriously flawed by the difficulties of universally applying the "principle of nationality" (as Mill termed it), and it was undermined to some extent by the excesses of illiberal nationalism. But it generated the ideal of the liberal nation-state, the maintenance of which still provides the popular justification for restrictions on immigration in most of the relatively liberal parts of the world. Whether a "nation of immigrants" like the United States, which lacks a homogeneous nationality, can invoke this argument (without significant qualification) is questionable. It seems overly cynical to hold that appeals to maintaining a "way of life" in the United States are fraudulent pretexts for maintaining affluence, since most economists agree that immigration (at past and current levels, anyway) is materially beneficial for most of the native population.[43] Perhaps the apparently growing movement in favor of English-language dominance expresses a genuine communitarian sentiment of nationality (as well as fears like Jefferson's about the prerequisites of stable republicanism). In any case, arguments for preserving national communities are more plausible in countries—say, Japan or Iceland—where such communities exist more unambiguously, along with the case for restricting immigration on this ground.

Communitarianism (including its national form) can finally be defended in a liberal spirit from a more general perspective, by an argument that parallels the one for states. Just as (according to Mill) cultural vitality and progress are the result of many individuals pursuing their own ideas and freely conducting their "experiments in living," so the same goals are advanced, on a larger scale, by the existence of a number of independent communities, each developing its own distinct way of life. This would be plausible anyway, so long as each shared some of its fruits with outsiders, if only by offering an example for contemplation. Humanity as a whole benefits (at least in the long run) from the diversity that manifests itself when many discrete communities are able to go their own way; even a few illiberal communal experiments (a Saudi Arabia or an Albania here and there) may add flavor to the overall mix, if only by providing a salutary warning to others, so long as they do not involve aggression against others. Some movement of people among communities is of course desirable in this scheme disseminating valuable new ideas and adding a little spice to stodgier societies. But universal free movement would mean universal homogenization; life would be less interesting as well as devoid of the sources of continued movement and change. Again, this argument applies to the present question insofar as community control over the admission of new members is in fact—as it would often appear to be—a requisite institution for community preservation.

Three doctrines—statism, democracy, and communitarianism—if defensible, can thus generate arguments for borders, member-nonmember distinctions, and immigration restrictions that appear to be unavailable to some abstract theories of liberal society and liberal morality. These themes, although not liberal themselves, can in various ways be combined with liberalism in composite theories that perhaps come closer to ordinary beliefs and lead to policy conclusions that are less paradoxical than does liberalism alone. The first two (and communitarianism too in some forms, such as nationalism) have the merit of contributing a needed political dimension to relatively apolitical forms of liberal philosophy. On the matter of their compatibility, I conclude by noting that, while these doctrines depart from liberal morality's equal consideration of the interests of all (undifferentiated) individuals as such, they are not entirely opposed to characteristic liberal universalism. To act out of loyalty to one's own state, fellow citizens, or community, is indeed in a sense to exhibit a kind of preference for the interests of one's own group over those of outsiders. But statism, democracy, and community are themselves universal principles: no one should be stateless; everyone can and should enjoy democratic citizenship and community membership, somewhere. This proviso might suggest a special solicitude for stateless refugees and victims of tyranny. But in general one's own participation in the life of a group need not preclude, and ought not to be pursued at the expense of, other people's doing the same.

NOTES

1. See Frederick G. Whelan, "Principles of U.S. Immigration Policy," *University of Pittsburgh Law Review* 44:2 (1983): 447–484, for a review of U.S. policy in light

of the "national interest" standard that is taken for granted in the 1981 Select Commission Report and in most debates on immigration policy.

2. John Rawls, *A Theory of Justice* (Cambridge, Mass.: Harvard University Press, 1971).

3. Charles R. Beitz, *Political Theory and International Relations* (Princeton, N.J.: Princeton University Press, 1979), part III.

4. John Rawls, "Constitutional Liberty and the Concept of Justice," in *Justice: Nomos VI* ed. C. J. Friedrich and J. W. Chapman (New York: Atherton, 1963). This item is not listed among the basic liberties in *A Theory of Justice*, however; it may be implicit in the notion of "freedom of the person" in sec. 11, p. 61.

5. This of course is not a specifically liberal moral intuition, although it has been adopted by some liberal moralists. The view that a rich person's surplus should be shared, as a matter of right, with the needy is a clear component of Christian (e.g., Thomist) teaching on private property—one that was accepted by early liberals such as John Locke, though perhaps sometimes omitted in the nineteenth century.

6. Peter Singer, "Famine, Affluence, and Morality," in *International Ethics* ed. Charles R. Beitz, Marshall Cohen, Thomas Scanlon, and A. John Simmons. (Princeton, N.J.: Princeton University Press, 1985), pp. 247–261; Brian Barry, "Humanity and Justice in Global Perspective," in *Ethics, Economics, and the Law; Nomos XXIV*, ed. J. R. Pennock and J. W. Chapman (New York and London: New York University Press, 1982), pp. 219–252.

7 Peter Singer, *Practical Ethics* (Cambridge: Cambridge University Press, 1979), chapter 8. The marginal utility formula is used by Singer, "Famine, Affluence, and Morality," p. 259, and in his discussion of this argument by James Fishkin. *The Limits of Obligation* (New Haven, Conn.: Yale University Press, 1982), chapter 9.

8. Cf. James S. Fishkin, "The Boundaries of Justice," *Journal of Conflict Resolution* 27:2 (1983); pp. 356–358.

9. Singer, *Practical Ethics*, p. 158, citing Robert McNamara.

10. The equivalence of foreign aid and the admission of needy immigrants is expressed in the view that "Japan's refusal to admit outsiders would seem less troublesome if Japan contributed a more significant proportion of its resources to poorer countries." Joseph H. Carens, "Migration, Morality and the Nation-State," paper presented at the meeting of the American Political Science Association, New Orleans, 1985, p. 35.

11. On the latter point, see Richard R. Hofstetter, "Economic Underdevelopment and the Population Explosion: Implications for U.S. Immigration Policy," in *U.S. Immigration Policy*, ed. Richard R. Hofstetter (Durham, N.C.: Duke University Press, 1984), pp. 55–79. Hofstetter argues that aid programs and investment would be preferable to migration for the people of poor countries, since they would contribute to economic development and an eventual "demographic transition." He also argues that they would be better for *us*, since, although on a simple analysis the investment of capital abroad is equivalent to the migration of labor from a capital-poor to a capital-rich country, there are hidden costs connected with the assimilation of immigrants in the receiving country that make the two asymmetrical.

12. Foreign aid and opportunities for immigration seem equivalent from the point of view of "assisting the needy." They are not, of course, equally obligatory in all theories of justice. Nozick's theory in *Anarchy, State, and Utopia*, for example, would appear to lack any grounds for justifying closed borders and immigration

control, while at the same time its strong theory of property rights would deny claims for redistribution. On the other hand, statist theories of international justice, such as Beitz's, call for redistribution of wealth while apparently, through their acceptance of sovereign states, upholding the permissibility of restrictive immigration. The problems attending state-to-state aid programs pose problems for statist theories.

13. Singer, *Practical Ethics*, p. 160.

14. See Michael Piore, *Birds of Passage: Migrant Labor and Industrial Society* (Cambridge: Cambridge University Press, 1979).

15. As does Hofstetter, "Economic Underdevelopment and the Population Explosion."

16. Singer poses this question. So, too, addressing advocates of redistribution, does Robert Nozick, *Anarchy, State, and Utopia* (New York: Basic Books, 1974), pp. 265ff.

17. Fishkin, *Limits of Obligation.*

18. But if this is the case, it is not likely that they have reached this conclusion as the result of reasoning from liberal principles.

19. *International Covenant on Economic, Social, and Cultural Rights* (1966), art. 1; and *International Covenant on Civil and Political Rights* (1966), art. 1; in *Basic Documents on Human Rights* ed. Ian Brownlie (Oxford: Clarendon Press, 1971), pp. 199, 212.

20. Art. 2 of both covenants states: "All peoples may, for their own ends, freely dispose of their natural wealth and resources." Ibid., pp. 200–212.

21. See Frederick G. Whelan, "Citizenship and the Right to Leave," *American Political Science Review* 75:3 (1981); 649–650.

22. The question as it was debated in early American history usually pertained to naturalization (civic admission) rather than immigration as such, perhaps because the U.S. Constitution explicitly grants power over naturalization but not immigration to the federal government. Even the Know-Nothing party in the 1840s seems mainly to have called for more severe restrictions on the eligibility of the foreign-born to be naturalized, vote, and hold office; proposals for restricting the physical entry of foreigners were advanced and acted on only later in the nineteenth century. Even in the earlier period, however, it was recognized that easy naturalization encouraged immigration and that obstacles to naturalization deterred it.

23. Thomas Jefferson, *Notes on the State of Virginia*, Query VIII, in *The Portable Thomas Jefferson*, ed. Merrill D. Peterson (Harmondsworth, England: Penguin, 1975), pp. 124–125.

24. Jefferson actually appears to make a general, not a specifically republican, argument here: He invites his readers to reflect that France too would be "more turbulent, less happy, less strong" if 20 million republican Americans were suddenly thrown into that kingdom. Ibid., p. 125.

25. Ibid.

26. Richmond Mayo-Smith, *Emigration and Immigration* (New York: Charles Scribner's Sons, 1912 [1890]), pp. 290–292.

27. Ibid., p. 293.

28. Bruce A. Ackerman, *Social Justice in the Liberal State* (New Haven, Conn., and London: Yale University Press, 1980), p. 93.

29. Ibid., p. 90. Ackerman's otherwise vivid imagination fails him when it comes to composing arguments that the more advantaged might employ in their dialogues. He supposes that they would be forced to mutter the unacceptable "Because I'm better than you!" But why couldn't they say (as seems more natural) "Because I was *lucky* in the genetic (or the nationality) lottery." Good fortune seems a noninvidious, neutral reason why some people are or have something that others lack; Ackerman does not explain why this will not do.

30. Ibid., p. 257.

31. Ibid., p. 94.

32. Frederick G. Whelan, "Vattel's Doctrine of the State," *History of Political Thought* (Spring, 1988). The analogy between the sovereign state and the private property owner is mentioned also by Peter H. Schuck, "The Transformation of Immigration Law," *Columbia Law Review* 84:1 (1984): 6–7; and Charles R. Beitz, "Bounded Morality: Justice and the State in World Politics," *International Organization* 33:3 (1979): 409.

33. See, however, the argument of Benn and Gaus that "organic" models of society supplement "individualist" ones in liberal thought, or at least are implied in liberal discourse about the "public interest" and related matters. Stanley I. Benn and Gerald F. Gaus, "The Liberal Conception of the Public and the Private," in *Public and Private in Social Life*, ed. Benn and Gaus (London and Canberra: Croom Helm, 1983), pp. 48–58.

34. All political possibilities, that is. General extinction resulting from an interstate nuclear war would no doubt be worse, so far as we can imagine it.

35. Michael Walzer, *Spheres of Justice: A Defense of Pluralism and Equality* (New York: Basic Books, 1983), pp. 35ff.

36. Jefferson, *Notes on Virginia*, p. 124.

37. Walzer has developed the theory underlying this view most extensively in *Spheres of Justice*; but see also important earlier statements in parts of his *Just and Unjust Wars* and "The Moral Standing of States: A Response to Four Critics," reprinted in *International Ethics*, ed. Beitz et al., pp. 165–194, 217–237. In this view, the most clear-cut opposite of democracy would be imperialism, but informal pressures from abroad that tend to alter local conditions in an unwanted fashion, including unwanted immigration, would also attenuate democracy.

38. Ackerman, *Social Justice in the Liberal State*, p. 90.

39. Barry, "Humanity and Justice in Global Perspective," p. 235. Barry here is criticizing the claim of the state to sovereignty over natural resources; but the argument applies just as well to its sovereignty over its territory and thus its power over border control and immigration.

40. See Amy Gutmann, "Communitarian Critics of Liberalism," *Philosophy and Public Affairs* 14:3 (1985): 308–322, with reference especially to MacIntyre and Sandel.

41. Peter Singer, *The Expanding Circle: Ethics and Sociobiology* (New York: New American Library, 1981), p. 71 and passim.

42. Singer appears to be a naturalist with respect to his arguments for the moral status of animals, attributing moral significance to their capacity for pain and fear, and to the natural (biological) unity of the human and animal worlds.

43. Joseph H. Carens, "Migration, Morality, and the Nation-State," p. 32.

BIBLIOGRAPHY

Ackerman, Bruce A. *Social Justice in the Liberal State.* New Haven, Conn., and London: Yale University Press, 1980.

Barry, Brian. "Humanity and Justice in Global Perspective." In *Ethics, Economics, and the Law: Nomos XXIV,* edited by J. R. Pennock and John W. Chapman. New York and London: New York University Press, 1982.

Beitz, Charles, R. "Bounded Morality: Justice and the State in World Politics." *International Organization* 33:3 (1979).

———. *Political Theory and International Relations.* Princeton, N.J.: Princeton University Press, 1979.

Benn, Stanley I., and Gerald F. Gaus. "The Liberal Conception of the Public and the Private." In *Public and Private in Social Life,* edited by Stanley I. Benn and Gerald F. Gaus. London and Canberra: Croom Helm, 1983.

Brownlie, Ian, ed. *Basic Documents on Human Rights.* Oxford: Clarendon Press, 1971.

Carens, Joseph H. "Migration, Morality, and the Nation-State." Paper presented at the American Political Science Association meeting, New Orleans, 1985.

Fishkin, James S. "The Boundaries of Justice." *Journal of Conflict Resolution* 27:2 (1983).

———. *The Limits of Obligation.* New Haven, Conn: Yale University Press, 1982.

Gutmann, Amy. "Communitarian Critics of Liberalism." *Philosophy and Public Affairs* 14:3 (1985).

Hofstetter, Richard R. "Economic Underdevelopment and the Population Explosion: Implications for U.S. Immigration Policy." In *U.S. Immigration Policy,* edited by Richard R. Hofstetter. (Durham, N.C.: Duke University Press, 1984).

Jefferson, Thomas. *Notes on the State of Virginia.* In *The Portable Thomas Jefferson,* edited by Merrill D. Peterson. Harmondsworth, England: Penguin, 1975.

Mayo-Smith, Richmond. *Emigration and Immigration.* New York: Charles Scribner's Sons, 1912.

Nozick, Robert. *Anarchy, State, and Utopia.* New York: Basic Books, 1974.

Piore, Michael. *Birds of Passage: Migrant Labor and Industrial Society.* Cambridge: Cambridge University Press, 1979.

Rawls, John. "Constitutional Liberty and the Concept of Justice." In *Justice: Nomos VI,* edited by C. J. Friedrich and John W. Chapman. New York: Atherton, 1963.

———. *A Theory of Justice.* Cambridge, Mass.: Harvard University Press, 1971.

Schuck, Peter H. "The Transformation of Immigration Law." *Columbia Law Review* 84:1 (1984).

Singer, Peter. *The Expanding Circle: Ethics and Sociobiology.* New York: New American Library, 1981.

———. "Famine, Affluence, and Morality." In *International Ethics,* edited by Charles R. Beitz, Marshall Cohen, Thomas Scanlon, and A. John Simmons. Princeton, N.J.: Princeton University Press, 1985.

———. *Practical Ethics.* Cambridge: Cambridge University Press, 1979.

Walzer, Michael. "The Moral Standing of States: A Response to Four Critics." In *International Ethics,* edited by Charles R. Beitz, Marshall Cohen, Thomas

Scanlon, and A. John Simmons. Princeton, N.J.: Princeton University Press, 1985.
————. *Spheres of Justice: A Defense of Pluralism and Equality.* New York: Basic Books, 1983.
Whelan, Frederick G. "Citizenship and the Right to Leave." *American Political Science Review* 75 (1981): 636–653.
————. "Principles of U.S. Immigration Policy." *University of Pittsburgh Law Review* 44 (1983): 447–684.
————. "Vattel's Doctrine of the State." *History of Political Thought* (Spring, 1988).

2

Nationalism and the Exclusion of Immigrants

LESSONS FROM AUSTRALIAN IMMIGRATION POLICY

Joseph H. Carens

In the world today armed force is the primary means for keeping millions of impoverished and oppressed people in the Third World from coming to affluent Western countries in search of better conditions of life. We get some inkling of how many might come from the long queues waiting for admittance to the few industrial countries that welcome immigrants, from the growing number of illegal aliens in many Western countries, and from the desperate ploys that some adopt to gain admittance through cracks and loopholes— Tamils paying to be set adrift in lifeboats off the Canadian coast; Portuguese claiming to be persecuted Jehovah's Witnesses in order to qualify for refugee status; Africans and Asians flying to East Berlin to cross into West Berlin where no border checks are imposed for complex diplomatic reasons.

One way to respond to this situation is to ask whether the exclusion of peaceful immigrants can be justified in the light of fundamental principles of justice and morality. I took this approach in an earlier essay and concluded, in general, that exclusion is not justified, at least not under current conditions.[1] Frederick G. Whelan takes the same approach in his contribution to this volume but comes to the opposite conclusion. In his view, a justifiable concern for the independence of states, democratic autonomy, and communal integrity all warrant the state's right to limit the admission of aliens.

One problem with this approach (regardless of the conclusion one reaches) is that it may lead one to neglect the moral discourse that emerges from actual debates over policy. In policy debates questions of fundamental principle are often taken for granted, but moral issues nevertheless arise. For example, actual debates over immigration policy often start from the assumption that states normally have a moral right to exclude aliens and then go on to focus on the ways in which that right to exclude ought (or ought not) to be exercised by particular countries in particular circumstances.

This suggests that a different approach might be more fruitful. To argue for or against open borders on the basis of fundamental principles is perhaps to go too deep too soon. We may learn more about the ethics of immigration by trying to explore the moral views embedded in the political practices and policies of different states. The assumption behind this second approach is not that morality always determines policy or that the best moral view always triumphs, but that we can understand these issues in politics best by being sensitive to the moral understandings of the participants themselves as reflected in debate and in action. In this view, any important question of political morality is bound to have complex, local dimensions tied to the history and culture of particular communities. We need not accept local understandings uncritically, but we should begin with these understandings if we wish to inhabit the same moral world as those about whom we write.[2]

This second approach has much in common with the critique of foundationalism in political theory.[3] I borrow here a story recounted by Clifford Geertz in his famous essay on "thick description":

> There is an Indian story—at least I heard it as an Indian story—about an Englishman who, having been told that the world rested on a platform which rested on the back of an elephant which rested in turn on the back of a turtle, asked (perhaps he was an ethnographer; it is the way they behave) what did the turtle rest on? Another turtle. And that turtle? "Ah, Sahib, after that it is turtles all the way down."[4]

It is fitting—given Geertz's emphasis on the contestability of interpretation, that the story can be read in many ways. For my purposes, the Englishman asking the questions is not an ethnographer but a foundationalist philosopher. Foundationalists want to rush right to the turtle at the very bottom. From there they will work their way up, studying the characteristics of each turtle along the way—what it looks like, how it supports the turtle above it and is supported by the one below, and so on. Eventually they will get back to the elephant, the platform, and the world. The critics of foundationalism—call them contextualists, to give them a positive name—think that starting with the bottom turtle is a mistaken enterprise, and probably a doomed one. It's very dark down there in the nether regions. All the turtles are apt to look alike. It will be hard to tell whether you even managed to get all the way down. Whenever you think you have identified the turtle at the bottom, someone else will point out one below that. More importantly, this search for lower turtles misses the point of the original story about the platform, the elephant, and the turtle. (At least, this is the way I interpret the Indian's response to the Englishman.) It is wiser, from the contextualist perspective, to study the platform, the elephant, and the (first) turtle (or at most the first couple of turtles) and to consider their relations with one another and the world.

To return explicitly to the context of immigration, the contextualist approach is to treat the nation-state as a turtle. There is not much point in looking too far beneath it. For the present and the foreseeable future the nation-state is here to stay, and every state regards the right to control the admission of aliens as essential to its political sovereignty and territorial integrity, the two hallmarks of the modern nation-state. The important questions to ask are not whether all borders should be open, but whether there are any limits to the right of states to admit or exclude whomever they choose, why some states open their borders more than others or differently from others, what sorts of reasons they offer for (or we infer from) their policies, and whether their reasons are good reasons from a moral perspective. In exploring these questions, we should be sensitive to the different circumstances, norms, and aspirations of different political communities. We should ask what they think membership means, what justice or other values require in the distribution of membership, and whether their policies conform to their ideals.

I'm not sure whether the contextualist approach is ultimately satisfactory. Like the Englishman, I keep wanting to ask what's beneath the turtle. In the world today, for the problem of immigration, that's not just a philosophical itch. It's a question prompted—to change metaphors—by the pounding on the door. But perhaps the contextualist approach will take us a long way. In any event that's what this essay explores.

The essay focuses on one of the few cases in which a country's immigration policy acquired a famous (or infamous) name: the White Australia policy. The case is particularly interesting because the White Australia policy was widely criticized even by people who lived outside Australia and did not advocate open borders as a general rule. Thus, the case enables us to see how contextually specific moral considerations may limit the claims of state sovereignty, democratic autonomy, and communal integrity. Of course, Australia was not the only country to place racial and ethnic restrictions on the admission of new members. Canada and the United States, for example, both pursued policies of overt discrimination against nonwhites well into the twentieth century. Much, but not all, of what I have to say about the morality of Australian immigration policy is relevant to these cases as well. One of the challenges for a contextualist moral inquiry is to show how and why wider lessons may be drawn from a case without violating the specificity that is central to the contextualist enterprise. The discussion draws attention to the ways in which the specific and the general are interwoven.

Since the initial British occupation in 1788, immigration has played a major role in Australian history. From its time as colony through federation and independence, Australia not only welcomed but actively promoted permanent immigration from Britain. Immigration from northwestern Europe was also welcomed, though not as actively encouraged, while immigration from southern and eastern Europe was limited, and immigration of nonwhites from neighboring Asian lands (or elsewhere) sharply restricted. The result, by 1947, was a population of about 7,620,000 that could be divided along ethnic origins as follows: British 87.8 percent, northwestern Europeans 7.2 percent, southern Europeans 1.7 percent, eastern Europeans 0.8 percent, other whites 1.2 percent, nonwhites 1.3 percent of which most (0.9 percent of the total) were at least part Aborigine. The goal of immigration policy had been to create a homogeneous, British-like population in Australia. As these figures indicate, the policy until 1947 was remarkably successful in achieving this goal.[5]

From World War II to the early 1970s, Australian policy continued to promote large-scale immigration, aiming at a population increase of 2 percent a year, of which half was to come from immigration. The White Australia policy was gradually modified. First, greater assistance was provided to continental European immigrants, although British immigrants continued to be treated more favorably than others. More significantly, the racial restrictions were gradually reduced, so that by 1972, approximately 12,000 non-European settlers a year were arriving as compared with the handful thirty years earlier. (Overall settler arrivals ranged from over 180,000 in 1969 to 112,000 in 1972.) Despite this change, non-Europeans continued to be disadvantaged compared with Europeans in terms of eligibility for naturalization, assistance with transportation costs, access to temporary visas, rights to stay after completing an education in Australia, and other areas.[6]

At the end of 1972, the White Australia policy was formally abolished. Immigration policy was to be based on the "avoidance of discrimination on any ground of race, color of skin, or nationality."[7] At the same time, the special preferences historically granted to British immigrants in visa procedures and naturalization were eliminated.

What can we learn about the ethics of immigration from the patterns and changes in Australian policy? Obviously, we cannot assume that policy changes reflected changes in moral views in any simple way. Policies normally change because of changes in power, in circumstances, and in goals and interests (or perceptions of these), much more than because of changes in moral views. Still, there can be moral elements in each of these factors. In the case of the changes in immigration policy in Australia, moreover, it is clear that views about the moral legitimacy of the White Australia policy were changing. Its final abolition came about as a result of a change in ruling parties. The Labor party came to power in 1972, and it had made the elimination of racial discrimination in immigration an important plank in its platform. Since there were relatively few nonwhite voters, this campaign cannot be construed as an appeal to the interests of the voters but rather to their moral judgments. (On the other hand, there were more salient issues in the election, especially economic ones, so it would be a mistake to read the Labor victory as simply an endorsement of the party's position on immigration.) Of equal importance is the fact that the White Australia policy had already been eroding under the Liberal party. The trend toward abolition was clear.

But why does this matter? Do we want to say that the White Australia policy was right when a majority of Australians thought it was right and wrong when enough of them changed their minds? This sounds like a version of morality by referendum. It does not respect the way in which we articulate our deepest moral views about right and wrong. On the other hand, we cannot simply assume that if the White Australia policy was wrong in 1972, it was equally wrong in 1902 or in 1872. Circumstances change, and sometimes these changes affect our moral judgments. The brief history of immigration provided here gives us a context for moral analysis, no more. We cannot avoid making our own moral judgments and defending them. What follows is an articulation of the arguments that were offered, or could have been offered, in debate over Australia's immigration policy and to evaluate these arguments on their merits. One of the points to make in the process is that there are several different kinds of moral considerations (for example, principles, ideals, interests) relevant to immigration policy. Because a proper understanding of the issues in this case requires much more than a simple condemnation of the White Australia policy as racist, the ways in which moral considerations conflict with or complement each other also merit exploration. Three aspects of the policy will be the focus of this essay: (1) the exclusion of non-Europeans as permanent immigrants until relatively recently, (2) the preferences granted settlers from Britain until relatively recently, and (3) the question of Australia's obligation to permit substantial permanent immigration.

What (if anything) can be said in defense of the White Australia policy? More than might be thought (though, in the end, not enough). An Australian minister of immigration defended it, "We seek to create a homogeneous nation. Can anyone reasonably object to that? Is not this the elementary right of every government, to decide the composition of the nation? It is the same prerogative as the head of a family exercises as to who is to live in his own house."[8]

One way Australians went about creating a homogeneous nation was by killing off the original inhabitants of the land. And that was not their elementary right, however common a practice it may have been in other places as well, including America. But in fairness to the minister, the issue here is not killing but keeping out.

Let's elaborate the minister's case further, trying to cast it in the most favorable light, even if that involves altering some historical details. He might say something like this: Immigration policy is clearly the sort of issue that states have a right to decide for themselves. That is conceded by all except a few fanatics or dreamers who think we should live in a world of open borders or a world without borders. Everyone else recognizes that states have a right to decide whom to admit—at least in normal cases. (The problem of refugees is, for now, left aside, along with the question of temporary admissions in the form of guest workers.) I'm talking about permanent, voluntary immigrants. Many states—most of the western European ones—say they are simply not countries of immigration. They do not accept new settlers in normal circumstances. No one criticizes them for that. In the countries that do admit immigrants, the criteria vary considerably from one to another. Some emphasize family reunification (in other words, blood ties to people already living in the country). Others emphasize job skills, or education, or knowledge of the local language(s). Almost no one criticizes them for using these criteria—at least, not the way we have been criticized by outsiders. There are, of course, internal debates within these other countries as to which criteria are the best to use, just as there are internal debates in our own country. That is perfectly proper. But we have come to the conclusion—at least a majority of our elected representatives have—that race is a useful criterion in our admissions policy.

You see, we want to recreate Britain as much as possible here in Australia. In some ways, that's just a matter of taste, rather like the kind of housing one likes. Some people like Victorian houses and some like colonials. There's no accounting for taste. But we don't try to tell other people what kind of house they should live in, and we don't think they should tell us what kind of house we should live in. We want a British way of life. It suits us.

There is more to it than that, however. In the first place, the homogeneity we seek has important benefits for our collective political life. If people share the same cultural background, they're more likely to understand each other and thus to trust each other. They're more likely to want the same things and thus to be able to cooperate on common projects and to provide collective benefits without creating the sense that one part of the community has unfair advantages or disadvantages. If people have a sense of fellow feeling and attachment, they are also more likely to agree to programs that do help certain regions or groups or individuals more than others, either because they're confident that their turn will come later or because they're sympathetic to their fellow members in need. All these reasons are sometimes used to justify drawing political boundaries along national lines (where nationality is defined in terms of this sense of fellow feeling and mutual attachment). They would seem to offer equally good reasons for drawing immigration policy along national lines, as we have done.

There is a further point still. We believe in British culture and civilization. We think of it as one of the great achievements in human history. We want to help preserve and perpetuate that form of civilization. We don't claim that it is better than, say, the Chinese or Indian cultures and civilizations. These are great achievements, too. But they are quite different from British culture and civilization. If one tried to preserve and perpetuate all three in one society, the result would be a hodgepodge, far inferior to any of the originals. Or, let me be more cautious. The result would be a mixture, quite different from any of the originals, in ways that might be good and might be bad. Now, all that we are claiming is that our dedication to the preservation and perpetuation of British culture and civilization in Australia is a worthy ideal for us to pursue. So, our commitment to recreating Britain is more than simply a matter of taste or even of our common interests. But the pursuit of that particular ideal and way of life inevitably precludes the pursuit of other (worthy) ideals and ways of life. That is true of any culture and civilization, including those that value diversity.

To recreate Britain, we need to admit as immigrants people who are as much like the British as possible. Of course, the best are those who have been born and brought up in Britain, and we take special steps to encourage them to come and to make it easier for them to stay. The next best are other British colonials, people from Canada and the United States. After all, they speak the same language (as their native tongue) and they share a lot of the same history, culture, law, and politics. The northern Europeans have a lot in common with us, too, so they're all right. We don't really like to admit the southern and eastern Europeans, because they're too different. And this shows we're not really racist by the way. It's fundamentally a question of culture, not race. But we have found that nonwhites just don't fit in with the kind of society we want to create. They have different backgrounds, different values, different cultural ideals. In fact, it really would not be fair to such immigrants to expect them to assimilate as thoroughly to our culture and way of life as we want. To do that, they'd have to deny their own heritages and identities. That's not reasonable or realistic. It's sowing the seeds of trouble for later on. If a country is going to admit immigrants of diverse backgrounds, then it ought to recognize the inevitable consequences, and accept cultural mixing and cultural diversity as Canada and the United States have. You can't expect the immigrants to give up everything of their origins. So, if you do want cultural homogeneity, as we do, it's better for everyone if you keep out people who don't fit. That's why we don't admit nonwhites. There is really no offense intended.

It's important to add that we do not practice racial discrimination internally. We're liberals, too. We accept the principle of equal citizenship. For various reasons there are some nonwhites who have become members of Australian society. We accept them and we treat them equally. We're not at all like the South Africans, pretending that nonwhites who clearly are members of their society are not entitled to full citizenship. But there is a big difference between someone who is born and brought up in a society and someone who wants to join it from outside, leaving his or her community of origin. People who are born and brought up within Australian territory normally have a right to Australian citizenship and the equal treatment that goes with it. And we respect that right, regardless of race or color. But there is a big difference between racial discrimination internally and the use of race as a criterion in the selection of new members. Avoiding internal racial discrimination does not require racial neutrality in the selection of new members. We want to maintain a particular kind of society while still growing through immigration. Neutral selection of new members will not permit us to do that.

No doubt someone will object that it is wrong to use race as a criterion because race is determined by birth and one can't change the color of one's skin. And further, that some nonwhites can assimilate in the ways we want, so it is unfair to exclude them on the basis of race. As to the first point, there are many sorts of factors determined by birth that are used to assign membership in political communities and that no one challenges. The most obvious is that the initial assignment of membership is normally determined by place of birth or parentage or some combination of the two. You can't choose your place of birth or who your parents are, but almost no one argues that it is wrong to assign citizenship at birth on these bases. Moreover, other apparently acceptable criteria for citizenship are linked to factors determined by birth. For example, family reunification is widely accepted as an appropriate criterion for immigration policy. This obviously discriminates against those unlucky enough not to have a blood relative in the country into which they wish to immigrate. If the use of race as a criterion is racism, why isn't the use of family ties nepotism? As to the second point, it is undoubtedly true that some nonwhites could assimilate in the ways we want. But no criterion is a perfect indicator. The same point could be made about people who don't meet our criteria for education or job skills. Many of them would do well, too. But many wouldn't, and it is far too difficult and costly to get more precise indicators. Race is a relatively reliable screening factor. Perhaps we exclude a few we don't need to exclude, but from our perspective that's a better mistake to make than admitting ones who don't fit in. This approach might be inappropriate in domestic policy. But again we do not owe equal treatment to potential immigrants in the way that we do to our fellow citizens.

I have said something about why we have chosen this policy and more than I need to. The bottom line is the one with which I began. This is our business and no one else's. We're not saying that any other community should follow our pattern. Let others decide for themselves. Australians won't criticize the United States or Canada for choosing racial and cultural diversity. We won't criticize Japan or China or any of the African states if they decide to keep out whites. Other states have a right to make their choices on immigration, and we have a right to make ours. We don't criticize anyone else's policy, and no outsider should criticize us. Inside Australia, there is a healthy debate on this issue. Australians criticize one another. That's part of the democratic process. But those who are not Australians have no right to try to get involved in our internal debate. I don't say outsiders have no right to their own opinions on the issues. People are entitled to form their own opinions, and we're all inclined to draw comparisons with others in thinking through the problems and issues we ourselves face. But in the end, others should recognize that Australian immigration policy is a matter for Australians to decide. They should respect our right to make that choice by not criticizing our policy.

In putting this speech in the minister's mouth, I have tried to articulate the strongest and most persuasive defense of the White Australia policy that I could imagine, given our contemporary moral views. Thus, the case I have offered does not accurately reflect all the actual historical arguments on behalf of the White Australia policy. Those arguments were often quite explicit in their claims about the superiority of the white race. I am assuming, however, that overt racism of that sort has been discredited. (I will defend this assumption more fully below.) By contrast, I think that the arguments I've just presented have considerable force for us today even though I will try to refute them in a few moments.

It is tempting to divide the arguments on behalf of the White Australia policy into two categories: a procedural argument on behalf of democratic autonomy and a substantive argument on behalf of the ideal of a homogeneous British Australia. The distinction has merit, but it is also misleading. Analytically, the distinction is important. If the democratic autonomy argument succeeds, then the substantive argument becomes much less relevant. Indeed, if the democratic autonomy argument worked fully, it would defend even an overtly racist policy against external criticism, not just the sanitized version I have presented. In practice, however, the two arguments interact. There is always some question about the proper scope of democratic autonomy. So, if it can be shown that the ideal pursued by the White Australia policy is reasonable (even if everyone would not endorse it), it strengthens the case for regarding this policy as being within the scope of democratic autonomy and thus immune from external criticism.

It is important to see that the argument about democratic autonomy is an argument about the proper location of social criticism, not about sovereignty. The question of sovereignty is not in dispute here. No one is arguing that the White Australia policy would justify foreign intervention. The question is whether it merits foreign, as well as domestic, criticism. The minister's arguments appeal to that familiar rule of our moral world "Mind your own business." I want to endorse that rule without trying to construct an elaborate defense here. The rule applies not only to relations among individuals but also to relations among institutions (such as universities or departments) and political communities at all levels (cities and provinces as well as nation-states). Of course, there is often dispute about whether an issue is or is not someone's business, but (given the nation-state as turtle context), there can be little doubt that immigration policy would normally be regarded as the business only of the state whose policy it was (unless this policy directly affected the interests of another state and perhaps not even then). This view is reflected in practice by the fact that immigration policies are rarely the subject of external debate or criticism, apart from occasional appeals to generosity. This has two implications here. First, external critics of the White Australia policy have to show that this issue is an exception to the general rule of "Mind your own business." Second, the arguments available to external critics are more limited than those available to internal critics. As it turns out, criticism of the policy can be quite effective even within these constraints.

The first point to be noted in response to the minister's arguments is that many outsiders did, in fact, feel justified in criticizing the White Australia policy, even though they did not feel entitled to criticize most aspects of immigration policy in Australia or elsewhere and did not do so. This fact alone does not prove that they were right. We still have to see what arguments can be offered for their position. But if one thinks that moral practice counts for something (and I do), it is striking that so many people (including public officials) accepted the general claims about democratic autonomy and its application to immigration policy but thought that this principle should not prevent criticism of the White Australia policy. Why?

One answer is that Australia claimed sovereignty over a vast territory whose land and resources remained relatively undeveloped in an area of the world where other lands were densely populated and famines were common. I will return to this element in the criticism later. It was not the most important part of the criticism, however, as is illustrated by the fact that under the Labor party, which formally abolished the White Australia policy, the flow of nonwhite immigrants increased only slightly, in part because of cutbacks in total numbers admitted. These cutbacks did not provoke the same sort of criticism as the White Australia policy had.

Most criticisms focused on the "white" in the White Australia policy. They argued that the policy was racist and that a racist immigration policy was not a legitimate exercise of democratic autonomy. Again, there was no question of actual intervention. The issue was the "Mind your own business" threshold. The critics claimed that they were entitled to ignore the normal constraints on criticism of others because this was a racist policy. Were they right?

Note first that the minister's defense of the White Australia policy denied that it was a racist policy in any morally objectionable sense. To recall the main points, the minister argued that race served only as an indicator of cultural similarity and assimilability, that the Australians were not choosing *against* nonwhites but *for* a particular kind of society, that the policies entailed no claim of racial superiority, and that no offense was intended to nonwhites.

In response, the critics could say something like this: The moral meaning of the White Australia policy cannot be detached from its history. It emerged in the context of British colonialism and imperialism, and it explicitly expressed and embodied the concepts of racial superiority and racial domination that were part of that context. Given that history, it is not persuasive to claim that the policy no longer carries the same connotations and associations. The meaning of a public distinction such as the one drawn between whites and nonwhites in the White Australia policy cannot be established on the basis of analytic possibilities or the will and intent of one particular person, such as the minister of immigration. It must be found in the history and social practices in which that distinction has been used. That context makes clear that the distinction between whites and nonwhites drawn by the White Australia policy is not merely the benign expression of a cultural preference. It inevitably endorses the history of oppression from which it emerged. That is why it is morally objectionable to outsiders as well as to those inside Australia who wish to repudiate that history.

The claim that the White Australia policy need not carry any implication of racial superiority resembles the claim that "separate but equal" need not be discriminatory in the context of American race relations. In *Plessy v. Ferguson*, the Supreme Court majority who upheld the "separate but equal" doctrine contended that, if blacks found their separate treatment stigmatizing or degrading, that was their problem. Separation alone carried no implication of inferiority, so long as the treatment was equal (for example, comparable facilities). Given the *actual* disparity between the treatment of blacks and the treatment of whites at the time, it would be kind to call this argument disingenuous. But later, in an attempt to maintain segregation, some communities did upgrade the facilities available to blacks (physical plants, money spent on educational resources, and so on), so that the claim that the treatment was separate but equal was not absurd on its face, as it had been in the past. Still, everyone knew what segregation was all about. Whites regarded blacks as inferior. That is why the whites wanted them kept separate. Given the history of American race relations, for whites to keep blacks apart was inevitably stigmatizing and degrading. That is why the later Supreme Court was correct to rule in *Brown v. Board of Education* that separate treatment of blacks was inherently unequal. What is, or is not, stigmatizing is not merely a matter of the subjective perceptions of individuals. It is a social construction and a cultural reality. Particular claims about what is stigmatizing may be contestable, but some claims are clear beyond a rea-

sonable doubt. That the segregation of blacks was stigmatizing is clear in
that way. That the White Australia policy was stigmatizing to nonwhites is
comparably clear.

The claim that separate but equal is inherently unequal is not an analytic
truth. Take the famous case of equal toilets for men and women. Opponents
of the Equal Rights Amendment (ERA) argued that equal treatment of the
sexes would require the elimination of separate toilet facilities for men and
women, on the "separate is inherently unequal" hypothesis. But there is
nothing stigmatizing in having separate public toilet facilities. It reflects a
particular cultural norm about privacy. It is perhaps an odd norm—as anyone
who has seen *The Discreet Charm of the Bourgeosie* can recognize. (Buñuel
has a scene in which people retreat quietly to locked rooms to eat and sit
on toilets around a common table to talk.) It may also be an incoherent
norm, as many people suggested in noting that men and women normally
use the same bathrooms in private homes. But no one, as far as I know,
supposes that the separation of public facilities is in itself stigmatizing, or
degrading, or disadvantaging to one sex over another. Now what counts as
equal treatment is another matter. If one measured equal treatment not by,
say, equal footage of lavatory space but by time spent waiting in line to use
the facilities, I suspect we would indeed conclude that women are disadvantaged (though still not stigmatized—that's not part of the cultural mes-
sage) by the "separate but equal" treatment. There simply is no comparable
argument about separate toilets for blacks. Its social meaning is clear, at
least in every society that I know of.

So, for advocates of the White Australia policy to say that no offense is
intended is not enough. Given Australian history, offense to nonwhites is
unavoidable. Any nonwhite outside Australia can say to the Australian minister of immigration: "You can't fly a flag that clearly insults me and then
expect me not to be angry about it and to criticize you for it. The White
Australia policy is just such a flag. And let's not quibble about how to interpret
the flag. The symbol on it is clear enough. Everyone knows what that symbol
means." And whites outside Australia have a right to feel outraged, too,
because the White Australia policy insults people who are entitled to equal
moral respect as human beings, often people who are their fellow citizens,
friends, neighbors, or relatives.

The line of argument presented in the last paragraph shows why the appeal
to democratic autonomy won't work in the end. Racism is not protected
from external criticism by democratic autonomy. (Remember that I am not
talking about intervention here.) But perhaps that conclusion is just an
artifact of the way I have constructed the argument.

Some people might feel I've sabotaged the White Australia policy by
dressing it up first in nonracist garb, which I then stripped off to reveal the
racism underneath. Why couldn't defenders of the White Australia policy
openly acknowledge it as a racist policy and claim simply that they have a

right to be racist within their own community and in their own immigration policy? Perhaps they could have a hundred years ago, but I don't think they could today. Prime Minister Pieter Botha of South Africa took great pleasure recently in quoting a speech from Abraham Lincoln in which Lincoln said he believed the white man was superior to the colored race and he (Lincoln) was opposed to intermarriage, social mixing, suffrage for blacks, and so on. Botha apparently thinks this should give Americans pause before they criticize South Africa. Instead it merely confirms the view that he is a century out of date. This bit of information might change some views about Lincoln. Botha probably found it in one of the books written by radical American historians aimed at challenging the myth of Lincoln as the Great Emancipator. But it will not change anyone's views about moral equality.

Western moral views on race have changed in the past century. (Remember this is a contextualist, not a foundationalist inquiry.) One hundred years ago there would have been some point to arguing that racial discrimination was wrong, because so many people thought it was right. Today it is almost pointless to argue against overt racial discrimination, not because racism has been eliminated but because almost no one will defend it openly. People who practice racism today normally take pains to conceal it—the tribute vice pays to virtue. Even the South Africans try to deny that apartheid is racially discriminatory. It's separate but equal. There are exceptions, to be sure, overt racists such as the Ku Klux Klan in the United States and neo-Nazis in Europe. But racism of a kind that was commonplace even thirty or forty years ago is no longer acceptable in polite society. It is simply no longer possible (as it once was) to claim to accept Western, liberal values and to defend racism at the same time. The case of South Africa merely confirms my point, given the overwhelming public criticism of South African policies. Botha is undoubtedly right that their views would not have suffered this opprobium a century ago.

I am not sure why this change has occurred. Perhaps it has something to do with scientific critiques of pseudo-scientific claims about race. I suspect it has more to do with power: the struggle against Adolph Hitler and the end of colonialism. But ideas played some role in these struggles, and ideas shape power as well as serve it. In any event, it ill behooves a contextualist moral philosopher to ask why turtles move. (Acceptance of firmly rooted turtles is the strength—and the weakness—of this approach.) In the modern Western world, at least, repudiation of overt racism is as much a firmly rooted turtle as acceptance of the nation-state. There are fringe critics of both but no one takes them too seriously or expects them to persuade many others. That is why it would be a losing strategy to try to defend the White Australia policy by openly acknowledging its racist character. Once that is acknowledged, it no longer counts as a reasonable choice. And the scope for democratic autonomy does not extend to protection from external criticism of clearly unreasonable choices.

So far, I have focused on the external critics—people outside Australia who might object to the White Australia policy. I have tried to show that they have powerful arguments at their disposal, arguments that I find persuasive in rebutting the defense of the White Australia policy. But this is not yet a full exploration of the morality of Australian immigration policy. The external critics are largely confined to negative arguments. They can say what the Australians ought not to do. A racist immigration policy is unacceptable, but there are many different nonracist immigration policies. Which one should the Australians adopt? That must be up to them, not outsiders, to decide. Australian opponents of the White Australia policy should be able to challenge it more effectively than the external critics. As insiders, their right to participate in the debate is not in question. Equally important they can offer positive alternatives to the White Australia policy, so that rejecting it can seem like a positive step forward not merely a concession to external pressures.

I do not have the actual Labor party statements on immigration, but it is clear that the Labor position involved a repudiation of both racial discrimination and Australia's traditional ties to Britain.[9] They could have defended their position like this: We live in a postcolonial age. Leave aside the question of whether or not the White Australia policy was right or wrong in the past; it is clearly no longer appropriate today. We can't have a White Australia policy without being seen as trying to perpetuate white domination, and that can't be defended today. We have to get along with our neighbors, including many newly independent states, and they're all insulted by this policy. Moreover, we shouldn't even try to defend it. We don't want to be apologetic about our country and constantly on the defensive. We want to be proud of what we stand for and admired for our principles and our way of life. And we should be proud of Australia, but that's hard to do when people keep talking about the preservation of *British* culture and civilization. Some people want to be more British than the British themselves. But the Brits still look down their noses at us and regard us as colonials. Well, imitations are always second rate. So, let's be Australian and proud of it. Let's drop all these special ties to Britain, with special immigration preferences for those of British origin. Of course, a lot of us come from Britain or our parents or their parents did. And we can feel proud of that. But Britain is a long way away. We're Australians now, first and foremost. And lots of our fellow Australians didn't come from Britain. They shouldn't be made to feel like second-class citizens. An Australian is an Australian, period. Let's stand on our own two feet. We've got a great country here, a new land full of possibilities. Immigration is vital to Australia's future. We should make sure immigration is orderly, so that we don't bring people in who can't get decent jobs, and we should use sensible criteria, paying attention to the skills we need, to family ties, and so on. But we should welcome anyone who wants to help us build this country, regardless of race or color or nationality. Australia is the the new land of opportunity.

This rhetoric is probably a bit overblown, but the line of argument should be clear. Is it a moral argument? It certainly illustrates one of the ways moral elements can enter political discourse. When we think of "morality," we sometimes think first and foremost of fundamental principles of right and wrong, such as those illustrated by the criticism that racism fails to respect the equal moral worth of all human beings. But morality has other dimensions as well. Morality is concerned with ideals and ways of life. This argument recommends a particular self-understanding to Australians that is (in part) an ideal and a way of life. The argument blends appeals to principles and ideals with appeals to interests and makes claims about the consequences of alternative courses and about the direction of history. A good politician will manage to blend these sorts of things together, so that virtuous actions seem advantageous and advantageous ones virtuous, so that inevitable outcomes seem like choices and choices seem obvious. A bad politician does the reverse. In either case, it is often difficult to get a clear fix on what parts of a political argument are moral and what parts are something else. I would not want to try to disentangle the elements here. What would be the point of doing so anyway?

The minister's argument used nationalism to justify the exclusion of nonwhites and to embrace the preferences granted to settlers of British origin. The argument I have just offered uses a different version of nationalism to justify the inclusion of nonwhites and to reject preferences for those of British origin. In taking this approach, the argument implicitly confronts and helps to solve one of the problems that the minister pointed out but is not resolved simply by the rejection of racism.

The question is how much assimilation a country of immigration may legitimately demand of its new entrants. All countries of immigration must face this question. As a general principle, I think that the argument I constructed for the minister was correct. It is unreasonable for any state to expect new immigrants to abandon their previous cultural identity altogether. Consequently, diversity of immigrants will lead to diversity of culture, and it would be wrong to try to curtail this too sharply. On the other hand, the country of immigration seems entitled to expect some sort of assimilation from those it admits. How much assimilation it is reasonable to expect will depend in part on how great the differences are between the country of origin and the country of immigration. The closer the culture of the immigrants to the culture of the new country, the more homogeneity it is possible to obtain, if that is the goal. That was precisely the virtue of the strong preference for immigrants from Britain, according to the minister. They made possible *both* large-scale immigration *and* cultural homogeneity. The elimination of racial restrictions was going to make it harder to achieve the goal of cultural homogeneity. There were at least two possible responses to this.

The first was to continue to endorse the goal of cultural homogeneity and to try to approximate it within the constraints of a nonracist immigration policy. What would that have entailed? One strategy would have been to give priority in admissions to the most Europeanized, indeed the most British among the nonwhites (as well as among the whites). There might have been several ways to do this. Until the 1960s, Canada excluded blacks *unless* they were from the United States or Britain or in one or two other "preferred" categories. This might reasonably have been rejected as racist, however, and Canada did drop the policy as part of a move to end discrimination in its own immigration policy. Another possible strategy would have been to give preference in immigration to the citizens of Commonwealth countries. There is enough racial diversity among the Commonwealth countries that the policy could reasonably have been defended as a nonracist way of preserving the British character of Australia. All these countries are former British colonies (like Australia). Immigrants from any of them would be likely to speak English, to be familiar with at least some British institutions and some aspects of British culture. Presumably Australia could have even developed a point system, giving higher priority to those who had been educated in Britain or had lived there. So long as such a point system was not merely a disguised form of reintroducing racial restrictions, it would have been immune to significant moral criticism from those outside Australia. Neighboring Asian states without British connections might have grumbled, but it would have been hard for them to make the case that such a policy was illegitimate in the way the White Australia policy had been.

The second response was the one Australia actually adopted under the Labor government: Abandon the goal of cultural homogeneity and embrace greater cultural diversity as an ideal. Ironically, the minister's argument about assimilation would have encouraged this second choice once racial restrictions on immigration were dropped. According to that argument, racial diversity would inevitably lead to cultural diversity and make the British way of life (relatively) less attractive because it would be less feasible. It would also have made the acceptance of cultural diversity seem (relatively) more attractive because it would be inevitable. Those who wanted to argue for a more diverse culture and way of life could suggest that the Anglophile approach was doomed anyway.

Note that this line of argument does not suggest that it is always wrong for a nation-state to maintain cultural or even racial homogeneity. Some states can do so simply by refusing to admit immigrants. Japan is a good example. But Japan has a relatively large number of people living on a relatively small landmass. It has at least a prima facie case for not letting immigrants in. Australia has a relatively large landmass and a relatively small population. Moreover, Australia had a long history of admitting immigrants (whereas Japan has a long history of excluding them). If Australia had tried to maintain its cultural homogeneity simply by refusing to admit anymore immigrants at all, that would have been perceived to be almost as racist as maintaining an explicit White Australia policy. In other words, Australia found itself in a set of circumstances in which it was very difficult to pursue cultural homogeneity ethically and effectively. This greatly affected the relative power of the competing social ideals.

The Labor government abandoned a variety of special immigration preferences that had traditionally been granted to the British in Australia. Would it have been wrong for them not to have abandoned these preferences? I think not, at least not from an outsider's perspective.

Consider an analogy with university admissions. There is a fundamental difference between discrimination against applicants on the basis of race and granting preference to some applicants because, let us say, they are the children of alumni. No university may legitimately discriminate *against* people on the basis of race (regardless of whether such discrimination is against the law or not). This violates a fundamental moral norm. On the other hand, universities do (and should) have a good deal of discretion in selecting among applicants. Being the child of an alumnus is not the sort of criterion on which I would put much weight, but some universities do. They have a right to do so, because the universities ought to be free (within some broad limits) to shape their own institutional characters, and the selection of a student body is an important part of that shaping. (This argument presupposes that the alumni themselves are racially diverse or that the number of alumni children admitted is small enough relative to the total number of students admitted that the policy of favoring alumni children does not create a *de facto* pattern of discrimination. It also presupposes a good deal about the value of institutional autonomy that I will not defend here.)

Analogously, Australia would have been entitled to continue the preferences for British over other potential immigrants, if the Australian government had chosen to do so, as part of the process of shaping the character of Australian society, so long as this was not used as a device for covertly maintaining the White Australia policy. To favor British immigrants over other white immigrants was not racist, nor was it the moral equivalent of racism because there was no history of oppression and degradation of other whites by the British that is remotely comparable to the oppression and degradation of nonwhites by whites. The absence of such a social context made the distinction much less insidious, even though it clearly favored British over non-British whites. Such a policy might have been unwise and even morally objectionable from the perspective of other Australians, but it would have given an outsider no grounds for moral criticism.

Finally, what about the claim that Australia was or is morally obliged to take in nonwhite immigrants because its land was so sparsely populated (and still is) in relative terms? This claim had more merit fifty or a hundred years ago than it does today.

The debate about the moral significance of Australia's vast land and resources is filled with ironic developments. There is no doubt that relative underdevelopment was part of what shaped the negative response to the White Australia policy, especially in the first part of the twentieth century. But Australia's response after World War II was to increase the pace of *white* immigration. The goal was to develop the land and resources with *white* settlers, so that people would stop complaining that the territory was underused and underpopulated. To some extent, that policy seems to have succeeded. The pressures for more immigration from the surrounding area have eased. During its term in office in the 1970s, the same Labor government that abolished the White Australia policy actually reduced the overall flow of immigration without apparently evoking much hostile external criticism. The Labor government took this action partly in response to a downturn in economic conditions—and Australian immigration has always responded to cyclical economic effects—and partly in response to the growing demand among some Australians for conservation of wilderness and natural resources, greater ecological sensitivity, and a growing belief in the virtues of limiting population.

The emphasis on Australia's landmass and natural resources and its proximity to densely populated neighbors made much more sense in the nineteenth and early twentieth centuries when most people lived on the land and needed land to live, when people were needed to develop the land and its resources, and when long-distance transportation was expensive and dangerous. All these conditions have changed drastically. In an industrial age, agricultural production is only one part—and a constantly declining part— of economic production. A society's capacity to support its population depends not primarily on its landmass but on its overall capacity to create jobs. The point is illustrated by a 1966 official statement on immigration in Canada, another country with a huge landmass and a relatively low population density: "We do not have a frontier open to new agricultural settlement. . . . Despite its low population density, Canada has become a highly complex, industrialized and urbanized society. And such a society is increasingly demanding of the quality of its work force."[10]

Australia could make the same point. It is an industrialized country. It could not admit large numbers of peasants to engage in subsistence farming without major social dislocations. And the Australians would undoubtedly ask, "Why should we be expected to undergo these social dislocations if other Western countries don't." After all, transportation from Asia to Europe and North America is now relatively easy and inexpensive. All developed countries should have as great a capacity to create new jobs as Australia does. Yet many of these countries simply declare that they are not countries of immigration. They don't accept any permanent new immigrants, apart perhaps from refugees. But if they can get away with that, why should the Australians admit more than they can comfortably manage and fit in without disrupting their current way of life? For that matter, there are other places with relatively low population densities—Canada, some of the Scandinavian countries, some of the western and midwestern states in the United States. Are these places willing to admit large numbers of new settlers, many of them peasants who do not speak the language and know only subsistence farming? If not, why ask Australia to do it? Proximity simply does not carry *that* much more weight.

Even if Australia's land is relatively underused, it is far from clear that the solution is to admit thousands of Asian peasants. (Or hundreds of thousands? millions?—anything less than millions would have no noticeable impact on the population problems of Indonesia or the Philippines.) Subsistence farming may not be the best way to use the land. On the one hand, it might be possible to produce more through mechanization of farming. On the other hand, given the overexploitation of land in many countries, it might be good for the future of the human race to have some relatively underused agricultural land somewhere. And it's also crucial to preserve wilderness and mineral resources for future generations. Australia is in a position to do that now, because the population is small enough to contain the demands for overdevelopment. If the population grows too large, the demands won't be able to be contained.

I find all these arguments on behalf of Australia to be persuasive. I don't mean to say that Australia has no obligation to accept immigrants. It clearly has the capacity to absorb a regular flow without serious disruption, and the proximity of the overpopulated states is not totally irrelevant. But, on the whole, it's not clear why we should regard Australia as having a special obligation to take in a larger number of immigrants than it presently does. Perhaps we should challenge the right of every state to keep people out. But that is the turtle I promised not to turn over.

NOTES

1. Joseph H. Carens, "Aliens and Citizens: The Case for Open Borders," *The Review of Politics* 49 (1987): 251–273.

2. For this approach in political theory, see Michael Walzer, *Spheres of Justice: A Defense of Pluralism and Equality* (New York: Basic Books, 1983).

3. See, for example, Donald Herzog, *Without Foundations* (Ithaca, N.Y.: Cornell University Press, 1985).

4. Clifford Geertz, "Thick Description: Toward an Interpretive Theory of Culture," in *The Interpretation of Cultures* (New York: Basic Books, 1973), pp. 28–29.

5. For the information in this paragraph and on Australian immigration policy generally, I rely primarily upon Charles Price, "Australia," in *The Politics of Migration Policies*, ed. Daniel Kubat (New York: Center for Migration Studies, 1979).

6. Ibid.

7. Ibid., p. 8.

8. Quoted in H. I. London, *Non-White Immigration and the "White Australia" Policy* (New York: New York University Press, 1970), p. 98.

9. Price, "Australia," p. 11.

10. Quoted in Daniel Kubat, "Canada," in *Migration Policies*, ed. Kubat, p. 24.

BIBLIOGRAPHY

Carens, Joseph. "Aliens and Citizens: The Case for Open Borders." *The Review of Politics* 49 (1987): 251–273.

Geertz, Clifford. *The Interpretation of Cultures*. New York: Basic Books, 1973.

Herzog, Donald. *Without Foundations*. Ithaca, N.Y.: Cornell University Press, 1985.

Kubat, Daniel, "Canada." In *The Politics of Migration Policies*, edited by Daniel Kubat, pp. 19–36. New York: Center for Migration Studies, 1979.

London, H. I. *Non-White Immigration and the "White Australia" Policy*. New York: New York University Press, 1970.

Price, Charles. "Australia." In *The Politics of Migration Policies*, edited by Daniel Kubat, pp. 3–18. New York: Center for Migration Studies, 1979.

Walzer, Michael. *Spheres of Justice: A Defense of Pluralism and Equality*. New York: Basic Books, 1983.

3

The Force of Moral Arguments for a Just Immigration Policy in a Hobbesian Universe

THE CONTEMPORARY AMERICAN EXAMPLE

John A. Scanlan
and
O. T. Kent

I

We begin with the assumption that those making U.S. immigration policy can and should take moral considerations explicitly into account in determining which migrants will be permitted to enter the United States, and under what conditions. By moral considerations, we mean considerations that are based on theories of justice and social obligation, and are not reducible to a utilitarian calculus of value.[1] Thus, we do not deny that society as a whole may, as measured by economic or sociological standards, be "improved" if certain morally defensible immigration choices are made. But we also recognize that there is a variety of immigration choices that can be made that have arguably positive moral implications (such as accepting a substantial number of refugees for admission, or requiring that so-called "migrant workers" be afforded a full panoply of civil rights), yet have utilitarian consequences that are at best uncertain and may in fact contribute to a decline in the "quality" of American life. We contend that adequate moral consideration must include a recognition that the costs of doing good are frequently difficult to determine and might outweigh the measurable social benefits that could accrue from particular immigration choices. We argue that a commitment to a "just" immigration policy must include a willingness to require—or persuade—the nation, under some circumstances, to bear those costs.

However, we also believe that the modern state is not a fundamentally altruistic institution. We acknowledge that states have more than instrumental or political coherence (the coherence perhaps can be explained in economic, linguistic, or mytho-historic terms). But we are not persuaded by the implicit analogies between the state and the family, clan, neighborhood, or ethnic enclave that appear to lie behind much of the "communitarian" political theory and moral philosophy that has emerged in the last decade. Consequently we reject the idea that principles of moral obligation that derive from postulated or idealized relationships in smaller, more unified social units have direct relevance to a discussion of how national policy is or should be made. Instead, we contend that the Hobbesian view of the state, as modified by more recent realist, utilitarian, bureaucratic, and consensus/coercion theories, more accurately reflects its essential nature as a battleground of competing interests (which may include, but are not limited to, competing social classes and elites). Under such a view, political choices reflect the dominance of particular interests or coalitions and also reveal the extent to which accomodation, compromise, or ideological manipulation dominate the political process. We also recognize that immigration policies implicate not only the structures of power and influence *within* particular states, but also the *external* relations of such states. In the international arena, we acknowledge the dominance of *realpolitik* decision making as relationships between countries are actually played out. Thus, we are fully aware of the practical limits to the realization of any broad commitment by the world community (or indeed, by any state) to an immigration policy that is perfectly just according to the requirements of *any* philosophical system.

Nevertheless, the central premise of our argument is that political systems in general—and the American political system in particular—still leave room for moral considerations in shaping and implementing immigration policies. One reason that moral discourse remains possible derives from the nature of the interests participating in the political process. Thus, the United States, like most modern states that have not unconditionally shut their doors to all immigrants, is a constitutional democracy.[2] A broad range of interests is given formal access to political power. As advocates of policy in any field—including the field of immigration—those interests frequently structure their demands in moral terms. To offer one example, churches have been particularly active in promoting the cause of refugees and asylum seekers in the United States. As an interest group, they have to be taken into account when considering what shape America's immigration policy is likely to assume. Yet in taking them into account, the government is forced to confront the arguments of ethical obligation that they frequently use.

It could, of course, be argued that the political "clout" of the churches, even in conjunction with other interests that might share their views on refugee admissions, will probably be sufficient to overcome deeply entrenched restrictionist forces within government and society as a whole. At some level, this is self-evident. No politically conceivable constellation of interests, for example, could ever overturn restrictionist sentiment to the extent of permitting unlimited immigration to the United States, or even the unlimited admission of refugees. Interests, nevertheless, sometimes have the institutional capability of promulgating ideas that have considerable practical impact. Thus, the second reason why (within certain limits) moral discourse remains a viable influence on the immigration process relates to the role that ideological and symbolic modes of representation play in government. As Antonio Gramsci made clear, the ability to govern without overt coercion depends largely on the ability of those in power to exploit systems of belief that the larger population shares.[3] The nature of that system of belief is to some extent determinable by policymakers, since in the modern state they possess a significant ability to propagandize for their views. Yet ideologies are as much unconscious as they are conscious constructs and depend to a significant extent on the systems of belief that are already implicit in social organization.[4] Those beliefs, emerging in the United States out of a "liberal" political tradition, the practice of receiving immigrants for more than two centuries, and traditional rhetoric characterizing the United States as a land of opportunity and freedom, run counter to, and to some extent transcend, quotidian restrictionist concerns.[5] The myth of American generosity is well established where immigration is concerned and affords considerable collateral support to those who argue that justice demands a more equitable and open immigration policy.

We have set ourselves a dual task. First and most important, we will set forth in general terms the basic moral arguments for a just immigration policy that we believe can subsist within a political universe dominated by Hobbesian concerns about "national security." We will delineate the fundamental Hobbesian perception as it relates to national and international political order and the threats to that order that population growth and migration pose. That perception, we will argue, cannot be refuted by any appeal to general principles of international cooperation or any specific invocation of a "successful" international regime governing the movement of persons. Whatever its demerits from a "liberal" perspective on distributive justice, the Hobbesian view is thus likely to prove persuasive in putting at least some limits on the nation's willingness to open its borders. In practical terms, we will concede, the exercise of national generosity is always likely to fall short of what moral aruguments demands.

What we will not concede, however, is that the Hobbesian perspective precludes moral arguments altogether. Such arguments, we contend, are grounded in certain intersubjective values (including a belief in racial equality and in fundamental human rights) that are rooted in the "liberal" tradition, are widely shared in the United States, and have been incorporated into the prevailing American political ideology. These values, we argue, establish general norms of "acceptable" political behavior, which transcend individual preference and are not reducible to utilitarian terms. Taking at least partial issue with Michael Walzer, we believe that these values (and their resultant norms) impose *general* obligations on the "liberal" state to deal generously *and* impartially with broad classes of aliens seeking immigration benefits.

Second, we will attempt to evaluate more concretely the significance of these general obligations as they manifest themselves within the "Hobbesian universe." We will look at the situation of several groups of actual and potential immigrants, and delineate the ways that those situations intersect with "liberal" values and elicit specific, morally based political responses. We will focus primarily on two types of immigration restriction: one affecting political refugees seeking asylum in the United States, and the other affecting people "of color" and members of other disfavored minority groups. We will argue that America's discriminatory asylum policy, which continues to select those to be aided primarily on the grounds of the geopolitical benefits they will afford the United States rather than on the basis of their suffering, demands to be evaluated on moral rather than Hobbesian terms. Although racial and ethnic discrimination in the selection of aliens is no longer specifically authorized by statute, both appear from time to time in administrative practice. More important, the courts still regard both as permissible under a broad theory of "national security." That theory, we will argue, *can* be validly used to bar aliens from unfriendly nations, but we will contend that it does not provide any moral justification for invidious discrimination.

We will devote less attention to other immigration matters. However, we will draw a contrast between situations like the foregoing, which we believe are paradigmatic of those giving rise to a "strong" sense of obligation, and others that do not raise clear moral issues. Thus, we also will examine, albeit in a more summary fashion, the morality of numerical limitations on immigration, and of establishing special admissions criteria for so-called "guest workers." In each instance, a discussion of the moral foundations of policy will be linked to the specific political environment in which particular immigration choices are made. For example, we will argue that the moral basis for establishing a restrictive immigration ceiling is, at best, problematical. But we will suggest that the dominance of realpolitik concerns about jobs, housing, environment, and standard of living make it impossible in any practical way to bring this moral insight to bear on the political process. On the other hand, we will show that other questions, including those involving the rights of racial minorities and political asylum applicants are more amenable to policitically effective moral advocacy, in part because of their different effects on "native" interests, but, more important, because they are so closely connected to fundamental American political and social concepts of liberty and equality.

II

Human migration is a phenomenon probably as old as humankind. There have always been mass population movements, and they have always brought with them the threat of massive social dislocation. Yet the characteristic political, legal, and moral problems associated with large-scale "immigration" to developed countries are comparatively recent. Although the flight from hunger, hardship, or persecution sometimes resembles the disorganized influx of nomadic hordes, the modern state, though seldom capable of fully policing its borders, ordinarily possesses enough bureaucratic and military sophistication to stop most uninvited migrants.[6] Nor does immigration ordinarily pose the same direct threat to the modern state and its political organization as a military invasion. Despite the fact that warfare is one of the principal contemporary causes of population movement, and it is sometimes in the perceived interest of a warring party to drive its opponents across a national border, the threat or danger ordinarily posed by immigrants—or at least perceived by those empowered to keep them out—is not that they will promote the specific goals of an identifiable enemy power.[7] Instead, the fear is that their presence, particularly in large numbers, will lead to increased racial or ethnic conflict, or exhaust limited resources (or at least increase competition for those resources), and in extreme cases have the consequence of threatening the government in power and indeed the survivability of basic political institutions.[8]

These fears are quite widespread. Even the world's poorer countries, places like Zaire and Rwanda, Pakistan and Thailand, Honduras and Mexico, are frequently subject to pressures on their borders. Yet in a world characterized by great disparities in national wealth, the control of disease and life expectancy, and the amount of political freedom and social equality afforded to various classes of citizens and residents, the Western democracies, which are comparatively wealthy, healthy, and free, are natural magnets. Not all who are disadvantaged or fearful, it is true, have the means to travel to Western Europe, North America, Australia, or New Zealand. But the physical barriers to movement in the last decades of the twentieth century are less extensive than ever before in human history. Ships still carry migrants, but most no longer depend on the vagaries of the sea. The same airliners that take tourists to the far corners of the world often bring immigrants back. The same roads and railways that have expanded the network of global trade carry people as well as commodities. A large percentage of those who move—and a larger percentage of those who express interest in migrating in the future—head for the great immigrant-receiving nations of the nineteenth and twentieth centuries. If immigration opportunities were unlimited, it is indisputable that the United States, like Canada and Australia, would quickly gain millions of new residents.[9]

In fact, however, the United States has long taken steps to limit admis-

sion.[10] Even in the colonial and the antebellum era, individual colonies and
states took measures to control immigration. Federal controls were initiated
in 1875, and Congress adopted the first national quota system in 1921. Today,
the number of immigrants permitted to enter the United States legally each
year is quite strictly limited.[11] Admissibility is determined on an individual
basis. Each potential immigrant is screened with reference to three inter-
related, yet analytically distinct criteria.

The first criterion is number. Not counting refugees and certain close
relatives of American citizens, a maximum of 270,000 immigrants are permitted to enter the United States each year, no more than 20,000 of whom
can come from any particular country. Refugees are afforded a separate,
flexible quota (termed an "allocation" in U.S. refugee law), which is set by
the president each year after consultation with key members of Congress.
The near relatives specified by statute (spouses, parents,[12] and unmarried
minor children) are subject to no quota at all.

The exception for near relatives is a special instance of the second criterion
for admission, membership in a specially favored group. As American immigration law is written, first claim on all quota numbers goes to intending
migrants whom the nation would *prefer* to have as residents or citizens and
who are therefore accorded statutory "preferences." In recent years, *every*
available visa has in fact been claimed by preference immigrants. Thus, 80
percent of those admitted under the quota system have been relatives of
American citizens and permanent resident aliens who are not eligible for
nonquota visas, but are statutorily designated preference migrants. The remaining 20 percent have been people with special job skills, who are also
accorded special statutory preference. (Refugees do not fall within the statutory preference framework; however, when—as in Indochina—demand
for visas has outstripped the annual refugee allocation, an administrative
preference system has been adopted that tends to place special emphasis on
relationship to American citizens and residents, past association with the
U.S. government, and matters of special humanitarian concern.)

The third criterion for admission, which operates negatively rather than
positively, is the reverse of membership in a particularly favored group. It
identifies characteristics or conduct that the government regards as socially
or politically unacceptable and *excludes* any alien who possesses those characteristics or has indulged in that conduct. Determining when an alien is
excludable involves both statutory interpretation and the exercise of considerable administrative discretion. At present, there are thirty-three statutory
grounds for exclusion, which deny admission to those who were convicted
of or admit to certain crimes, or who have been involved in activities that
the state regards as immoral or deviant, or who espouse causes that the state
regards as politically subversive, or who give evidence of being afflicted with
various mental and physical diseases. This list is less comprehensive than it
once was. Thus, between 1882, when Chinese exclusion began, and 1965,

when the National Origins Quota System was abolished and the last clear vestige of racial discrimination was removed from American statutory immigration law, a principal factor determining admissibility was ethnic or racial identity. Today, no statutory authority exists to exclude anyone on the basis of ethnic or racial origins. Yet the courts have been remarkably deferential to the executive branch in its administration of immigration law, granting it broad discretion to interpret the reach of exclusionary statutes and to waive the provisions of those statutes,[13] and sometimes suggesting that the president possesses power independent of those statutes to exclude aliens whom he regards as a threat to the nation.[14] It is by no means settled that the president lacks the power to exclude aliens solely on the basis of their race.[15]

The legal possibility that the United States *can* select its immigrants on the basis of their race or nationality is matched by other possibilities and other practices long countenanced by the law. In some important respects, American immigration law has become more "liberal" over the past two decades. The abolition of the national origins quota system has been followed by the repeal or the administrative tempering of some of the other traditional grounds for exclusion. Widespread resistance to the admission of refugees that made even emergency actions on behalf of Jewish refugeee children impossible during the late 1930s[16] has yielded to a new statutory scheme that recognizes that refugees are a special category of immigrant and authorizes their special admission.[17] Overall immigration numbers have risen, in some years approaching the peak levels of the first decades of the twentieth century. Yet the current "openness" toward aliens (which appears to be quickly eroding) is only relative: virtually every act of national generosity toward intending immigrants is firmly anchored in restrictive immigration law. Courts interpreting that law have sometimes questioned its procedural application.[18] They have seldom questioned the right of Congress[19] (or in recent years the executive branch[20]) to enact *substantive* restrictions on who may enter the United States. Thus, case law, including some of quite recent vintage, has validated *ex post facto* exclusionary legislation,[21] exclusionary legislation that bars aliens because of their "subversive" speech and associations,[22] legislative preference categories that discriminate against the fathers of illegitimate alien children,[23] statutes that exclude illegal entrants from the benefits of international refugee conventions signed by the United States and ratified by the Senate,[24] and special executive action directed at aliens originating in countries regarded as "hostile" to the United States.[25] The general principle emerging from this hodgepodge of cases is simple: The United States has the legal authority to determine its own national interests, and to exclude any alien or class of aliens that it deems threatening to those interests.[26]

Under this formulation, the liberality of the moment can at any time give way to more restriction. Nothing in the history of American immigration politics suggests that present admissions levels are sacrosanct, that today's exclusionary categories might not be made more general and discriminatory tomorrow, or that the special privileges now accorded to refugees might not be snatched away summarily. If such results are to be avoided, it will only be because politicans—and judges—incorporate moral ideas into their actions more openly, concretely, and consistently than they have ever done in the past and invest those ideas with a content that they have traditionally lacked under the security-based, Hobbesian conception of the political universe that has stood behind much of American immigration law and politics.

III

The obvious question raised by an immigration control system is the morality of *any* state limitations on the entry of aliens. Although every modern nation, including the United States, imposes some limits on immigration (or, except in extraordinary circumstances, bars it altogether), the moral justifications for this exercise of power are far from obvious. Thus, as Peter Schuck has noted:

[I]n a truly liberal polity, it would be difficult to justify a restrictive immigration law or perhaps any immigration law at all. National barriers to movement would be anomalous. Criteria of inclusion and exclusion based upon accidents of birth, criteria that label some individuals as insiders and others as outsiders, would be odious. Wealth, security, and freedom would not be allocated on such grounds, especially in a world in which the initial distribution of those goods is so unequal. Instead, individuals would remain free to come and go, to form attachments, and to make choices according to their own aspirations, consistent with the equal right of others to do likewise. No self-defining, self-limiting group could deny to nonmembers the individual freedom of action that liberalism distinctively celebrates.[27]

This argument is rendered even stronger if the characteristic marks of liberalism are regarded as a growing awareness (or acceptance) of the inherent and essential political equality of all human beings, and a commitment to rationality that in taking that equality into account, requires as an absolute precondition for moral discourse that self-interested preferences give way to universal principles that apply to everyone alike.[28] Rationality, in this sense, defines the moral point of view, for it "requires us to regard the world from the perspective of one person among many rather than from that of a particular self with particular interests, and to choose courses of action, policies, rules, and institutions on grounds that would be acceptable to any agent who was impartial among competing interests involved."[29] In a truly liberal polity, then, national borders would simply lack moral significance. Relying upon them to argue for immigration restriction would offend basic principles of justice.

However, traditional legal analysis, with its characteristic emphasis on "reasons of state" as the linchpin of the argument for a restrictive immigration policy, frequently manages to avoid addressing the question of justice at all. It does so by focusing on the narrow issue of sovereignty, which is based on a theory of power and the moral implications of its exercise by the state. Because sovereign power, at least in immigration cases, has usually been presented as the ultimate political value, the issue of unequal global allocation of resources, which necessarily raises more complex questions about morality and distributive justice, has usually been ignored. National borders, on this view, place a limit on the universalizability of moral principles.

The original (and still classic) American formulation of the sovereignty argument was rendered by Justice Field in 1889. Writing for a unanimous Supreme Court in the *Chinese Exclusion Case*,[30] which permitted the wholesale exclusion of all Chinese, Field stated:

That the government of the United States, through the actions of the legislative department, can exclude aliens from its territory is a proposition which we do not think open to controversy. Jurisdiction over its own territory to that extent is an incident of every independent nation.... If it could not exclude aliens it would be to that extent subject to the control of another power.[31]

Nearly a century later, the United States Court of Appeals for the Eleventh Circuit justified the refusal to grant "parole" (that is, release from detention and temporary, conditional entry) to Haitians in the custody of the U.S. government on these grounds: "A foreign leader eventually could compel us to grant physical admission via parole to any aliens he wished by the simple expedient of sending them here and then refusing to take them back."[32]

Implicit in the sovereignty argument used by both courts are four inchoate theses:

1. Political authority must be unitary (or, in the American context, hierarchical, with the federal government holding ultimate power);[33]
2. The United States exists within an international system that puts it into competition with other nations, with control over a particular territory, its resources, and its inhabitants ultimately at issue;
3. Immigration from another nation to the United States, at least under some circumstances, should be regarded as the functional equivalent of war, with incoming or intending migrants posing threats to the stability of the state—and hence to the existing government and power structure of the nation—which are similar to those posed by an invading army;
4. When this warlike state of affairs exists, the scope of the government's power to limit immigration should be essentially identical to its power to wage war and circumscribed by few (if any) constitutional restrictions.[34]

Clearly, there are circumstances where the military analogy is credible. Manipulation of human misery to the detriment of others has long been common, emerging for instance in the long conflict between Ethiopia and Somalia, with migrations forced by famine and warfare used by the former as a means of inflicting hardship on the latter. During the forty-year history of the cold war, the movement of "expellees," "escapees," and refugees across national borders has been exploited by both sides to secure economic, intelligence, and ideological advantages—and on occasion, to promote covert warfare.[35] The Cubans who entered southern Florida in 1980 were characterized, correctly, by one White House aide as "bullets aimed at the United States,"[36] since the boatlift that brought them was, to some extent at least, a premeditated action by Fidel Castro to discommode and embarrass the Carter administration.[37]

However, the uses of the military analogy in *Jean v. Nelson* and in the *Chinese Exclusion Case* were both misleading, at least on the literal level. Even at the height of their influx during the late 1970s and early 1980s, the number of Haitian migrants illegally entering the United States was only a tiny fraction of the total flow of undocumented aliens, and except in a few cities (including Miami), economically insignificant. Nor was there any evidence that the regime of Jean-Claude Duvalier was intentionally exporting its undersirables or in any way attempting to disrupt the political or social life of the United States. Judge Kravitch, in her *Jean* dissent,[38] was thus correct in characterizing the "scenario" of foreign aggression that the majority used to justify its opinion as "unnecessarily alarmist."[39] It is clear that Justice Field—and the "people of the coast" whose views he purported to represent—were similarly alarmist when they "saw, *or believed they saw*, in the facility of immigration and in the crowded millions of China . . . great danger that at no distant day [the Pacific Coast states] would be overrun by [Chinese] unless prompt action were taken to restrict their immigration" (emphasis added).[40]

In representing nineteenth-century Chinese immigration as "vast hordes of [China's] people crowding in upon us," equating that "crowding" with the decisions of the Chinese state "acting in its national character," and proclaiming that the "highest duty of every nation" is "to preserve its independence, and give security against foreign encroachment and aggression," Field, relying on popular sentiment, yielded to exaggeration.[41] Clearly, under the set of economic assumptions prevalent in the nineteenth century, Chinese immigration, like Irish immigration or immigration from other parts of Western Europe, did pose a threat to "native" jobs.[42] As significantly, it contributed to considerable "culture shock" in the Pacific Coast states, whose inhabitants for the first time were exposed to a large (and rapidly growing) population of settlers who were neither "white" nor Christian. There was no likelihood, however, of California and Oregon "going Chinese" virtually overnight.[43]

The most obvious lessons to be learned from the *Chinese Exclusion Case* and *Jean v. Nelson* are that military analogies and the appeal to national-security interests are perennial, and that courts frequently overstate the concrete dangers to the body politic posed by the unregulated immigration of particular groups of aliens. Yet even when the facts of a particular case do not support the view that immigration is tantamount to literal warfare, the tendency of the courts to assume the opposite must still be explained. The readiest explanation is the usual willingness of the judiciary—in common with most politicians (and, for that matter, most political theorists)—to presume the general validity of the Hobbesian conception of the political universe.

The fulcrum upon which Hobbes' theory turns is a pessimistic vision of human nature and hence of human possibilities. In the "state of nature," Hobbes argues, human beings are predisposed to struggle with one another for dominance, motivated by "a perpetual and restless desire of power after power, that ceaseth only in death."[44] Trapped in their respective self-regarding egos, and impelled by greed, fear, and vainglory, their natural inclination is to engage in indiscriminate violence: the "war of every man against every man."[45] In the absence of some higher authority, such warfare is not always violent; yet it always stands in the background as a possibility and a threat:

During the time that men live without a common power to keep them in awe, they are in that condition which is called war. . . . For WAR, consisteth not in battle only, or the act of fighting; but in a tract of time wherein the will to contend by battle is sufficiently known. . . . [A]s the nature of foul weather, lieth not in a shower or two of rain; but in an inclination thereto of many days together: so the nature of war, consisteth not in actual fighting, but in the known disposition thereto, during all the time there is no assurance to the contrary.[46]

The consequence of this predisposition to unregulated violence is a state of anarchy in which no industry, commerce, or culture can flourish, and in which, as a consequence, people are doomed to a life which is "solitary, poor, nasty, brutish, and short."[47] Therefore, the principal purpose of all social organization, Hobbes argues, *must* be the creation of some entity, that through the monopolization of force in its own hands, can assure its members that the individual predisposition toward unrestrained competition and violence is, if not eradicated, at least brought under effective communal control. LEVIATHAN, that is, the commonwealth or state, is the entity created by those threatened by violence to exercise that control. Surrendering their freedom to pursue their own ends ruthlessly and subordinating their individual wills to the authority of sovereigns and their laws are the prices they implicitly pay for security.

Much of Hobbes' political writing is devoted to the terms—and the logical

consequences—of this surrender. People, we are told, form states by contracting away all but their fundamental right to self-defense and the absolute
necessities of life, "the use of fire, water, free air, and place to live in":[48]

The only way [to obtain security] is to confer all their power and strength upon one
man, or upon one assembly of men, that may reduce all their wills, by plurality of
voices into one will . . . and therein to submit their wills, every one to his will, and
their judgments to his judgment. This is more than consent or concord; it is a real
unity of them all, in one and the same person, made by covenant of every man with
every man, in such manner, as if every man should say to every man, *I authorize
and give up my right of governing myself, to this man or this assembly of men, on
this condition, that thou give up thy right to him, and authorize all his actions in
like manner.*[49]

States, so created, are creatures of contract. Once created, however, their
subsistence depends on the relationship of three types of actor: the founders,
who having subordinated their individual power and wills to the State for
life, have no right to back out of the "contract"; the states themselves, which
having been granted a monopoly of power by their creators, do not willingly
relinquish it to the afterborn and to newcomers; and these "new" citizens,
who Hobbes suggests, are *obligated* to respect and, at least implicitly, renew
the original covenant.
    Nothing in Hobbes' formulation reveals what the maximum size of a state
can be—or, indeed, explains why a single, world commonwealth is impossible. Instead, an unsupported empirical observation gives rise to the view
that there are—and therefore, it seems, must be—a multitude of states,
unbeholden to any common authority, each with conflicting interests:

Convenants without the swords, are but words, and of no strength to secure a man
at all. . . . [I]n all places, where men have lived as small families, to rob and spoil
one another has been a trade. . . . And as small families did then; so now do cities
and kingdoms which are but greater families, for their own security, enlarge their
dominions, upon all pretenses of danger, and fear of invasion, or assistance that may
be given to invaders, and endeavour as much as they can, to subdue, or weaken
their neighbors, by open force and secret arts.[50]

In the presence of such competition, no invariable formula for ideal size can
be given: "the multitude sufficient to confide in for our security, is not
determined by any certain number, but by comparison with the enemy we
fear."[51] The idea of a single or even very large human *polis*, however, is
rejected out of hand as being fundamentally incompatible with Hobbes'
vision of human nature: "If we could suppose a great multitude of men to
consent in the observation of justice, and other laws of nature, without a
common power to keep them in all in awe; we might as well suppose all
mankind to do the same; and then there neither would be, nor need to be

any civil government, or commonwealth at all; because there would be peace without subjection."[52]

Thus, in the Hobbesian universe, states can provide some security to their inhabitants by depriving residents of the legitimate power to injure and exercise personal domination over one another, and by fostering the common enterprise necessary to fend off foreign aggression. Yet that security can never be absolute, since it is never certain that all the citizenry that has promised to abandon selfish ends will live up to its obligation (although the existence of coercive state power serves as a significant incentive to do so). Futhermore, since individual states are not subject to supernational power, they can always be presumed to have the "known disposition" toward aggression that Hobbes identifies with war.

This disposition toward aggression makes the international realm a "state of nature" directly analogous to that in which individuals find themselves before establishing a commonwealth. Thus, the international situation, as Hobbes describes it, is one in which "in all times, kings, and persons of sovereign authority, because of their independency, are in continual jealousies, and in the state and posture of gladiators; having their weapons pointing, and their eyes fixed on one another; that is, their forts, garrisons, guns upon the frontiers of their kingdom; and continual spies upon their neighbors, which is a posture of war."[53]

The moral implications of this situation are clear: Nations have no other duty than to act in their own best interests, since "in states, and commonwealths not dependent on one another, every commonwealth . . . has an absolute liberty, to do what it shall judge, that is to say, what that man or assembly that representeth it, shall judge most conducing to their benefit."[54]

This picture of international relations produces its own conception of rationality and, hence, morality. While interdependency, common interests, and a common authority combine to provide a rational basis for persons to act toward one another in morally acceptable ways, such is not the case among nations. In a world of independent states, each competes against the others for the power to ensure its survival, domestic tranquility, and economic prosperity. And without a common authority to adjudicate among these competing interests, it would be irrational for a nation to risk its interests by acting other than on behalf of those interests. On this conception of rationality, a nation fulfills its moral duties to the extent that it protects its interests.

In Hobbesian terms, immigration of aliens, particularly in large numbers, simultaneously poses internal and external threats to the stability of the receiving state. Both the external and the internal threat derive from Hobbes' identification of a "place to live" as one of the necessities of life that the individual cannot be obligated to relinquish in his or her "convenant" with the state. Hobbes appears to anticipate Thomas Malthus by more than a century in recognizing that increasing population threatens the wealth, well-

being, and governability of particular nations. To counteract the dangers of
overpopulation (and unemployment), he suggests that commonwealths promote nonaggressive *emigration*: "The multitude of poor, and yet strong
people still increasing, they are to be transplanted into Countries not sufficiently inhabited: where, nevertheless. they are not to exterminate those
they find there; but constrain them to inhabit closer together, and not to
range a great deal of ground, to snatch what they find; but to court each
little Plot with art and labour, to give them their sustenance in due season."[55]
Inevitably, however, at some point even peaceful migration will lose its
pacific character: "When all the world is overcharged with Inhabitants, then
the last remedy of all is Warre; which provideth for every man, by Victory,
or Death."[56]

According to the Hobbesian view, then, it is sometimes in the interests
of states to promote emigration; but even more fundamentally, it is also
within the range of the nonnegotiable interests of those states' inhabitants
to seek *lebensraum*. Whether pushed out by their governments or motivated
by their individual needs, these migrants always pose a threat to the established political order. When they enter regions that are already populated,
there is no guarantee that they can be integrated into, or even coexist with,
that order. Their presence can lead to a renewal of the ultimate Hobbesian
evil, anarchy. Indeed, it was the prospect of such anarchy that contributed
to Justice Field's decision in the *Chinese Exclusion Case*:

[The Chinese] were generally industrious and frugal. Not being accompanied by
families, except in rare instances, their expenses were small; and they were content
with the simplest fare, such as would not suffice for our laborers and artisans. The
competition between them and our people was for this reason altogether in their
favor, and the consequent irritation, proportionately deep and bitter, was followed,
in many cases, by open conflicts, to the great disturbance of the public peace.[57]

IV

The fear of civil disturbance that is central to Hobbes' theory of government cannot be deprived of its normative significance simply by pointing to
the many situations involving nations living at peace with one another,
engaging in cooperative ventures, or permitting more or less regular movement of visitors or intending immigrants across their borders. Hobbes' root
assumption, that humanity is naturally predisposed toward violence and can
be constrained only by membership in powerful but atomized political communities, each in a state of actual or potential hostility with one another,
reflects a depth of pessimism that is considerably greater than that of many
of the political theorists and sociologists who have followed him. Yet, none
of the attempts to substitute a "cooperative" for a "competitive" model of
international relations appear to deal effectively with Hobbes' root concerns.

To offer just one example, in a recent critique of the Hobbesian analogy of international politics to the "state of nature," Charles Beitz has argued that *none* of the things necessary to support it hold true in the contemporary world, since nation-states are highly (and apparently increasingly) dependent on one another, frequently establish quite stable associations and coalitions for addressing common problems, and in fact *do* establish "rules of cooperation" with "reliable expectations of reciprocal compliance" *despite* "the absence of a superior power capable of enforcing these rules."[58]

Arguments like these, when supplemented with a theory of "regimes" that elaborates on the origins and features of a nascent international "order," clearly are relevant when considering immigration law and policy.[59] The idea that states must mobilize to resist an "invasion" of unwanted immigrants and must therefore have the unfettered power to close their borders and vest their political branches of government with unlimited (and judically unreviewable) powers is undercut significantly if it can be demonstrated that migration problems, like problems involving tariffs or the disposal of nuclear waste, are in fact amenable (to some significant and predictable extent) to solutions generated by bilateral agreement or by the creation of a multilateral regime responsible for facilitating *and* regulating the international movement of migrants.[60] Examples of bi- and multinational approaches to migration problems are plentiful. Before World War II, for example, the United Kingdom, France, and several other European nations took mutual steps to protect German and Austrian refugees. Greater success was achieved after that war ended, when substantial refugee problems in occupied Europe after World War II were alleviated through the cooperative efforts of a number of nations that banded together to form the International Refugee Organization (IRO), the Office of the United Nations High Commissioner for Refugees (UNHCR), and the Intergovernmental Committee for European Migration (ICEM), channeled relief money to the refugees through these organizations and provided mutual assurances that they would each provide a significant number of resettlement places to those unable or unwilling to return to their original destinations.[61] Another example of international cooperation, based more clearly on mutuality of interests, is the "guest worker" programs the United States established with Mexico. During the 1940s and the early 1950s, the United States experienced an acute shortage of agricultural labor, while Mexico found it impossible to find enough jobs to satisfy its rapidly expanding population. The establishment by treaty of successive "bracero" programs permitting Mexicans to enter the United States as "guest workers" was mutually advantageous to both countries and permitted substantial "controlled" migration to the United States that was accompanied by virtually no "illegal" immigration.[62]

The difficulty with these examples is that they fall short, on both practical *and* theoretical terms, of dislodging the central Hobbesian premise, which is not that nations are always in a state of active hostility with one another, but instead, that their separate interests inevitably *predispose* them to take independent, contradictory, and—in the end—mutually antagonistic actions. Under such a premise, international relations can sometimes be regularized by cooperative agreements or arrangements between or among states—and probably *should* be so regularized wherever possible; yet cooperation will always be transitory and does not constitute the sort of underlying harmony that would permit the dismantling of national immigration policies based on the assertion of "sovereign" interests. The examples of international cooperation set forth above support this contention. Thus, the pre–World War II refugee conventions and agreements were signed by very few nations and afforded refugees very limited rights.[63] In the setting of the Great Depression, however, even the limited protection they did afford was quickly eroded, and signatory nations quickly began pushing destitute refugees back across their borders. The refugee regime established in the aftermath of World War II has fared better, and forty years later, is still in existence. Yet despite its many successes in spreading the burden of refugee care and resettlement—and perhaps in persuading some countries to define their interests less narrowly—it has always been limited by the finite willingness of its members to commit resources, immigration opportunities, or both to people who are not citizens.[64] National "generosity" appears to be correlated directly with the economic situation prevailing at any given moment and to have suffered a significant setback in the comparatively hard times of the 1980s. Further, the priorities of the regime have always been heavily influenced by the priorities of its richest and most powerful members, most notably the United States. Thus, even when sovereign interests have been amalgamated institutionally and labeled "common humanitarian concerns," the underlying political reality has frequently involved considerable tension among those participating in the regime, has led some countries to act independently of the regime,[65] and has sometimes deprived the regime of the ability to perform its protective or assistance functions in an even minimally competent way.[66]

Bilateral arrangements that have permitted the temporary migration of workers from less developed countries to more developed ones have been commonplace in the twentieth century. The U.S. "bracero" programs have been imitated (although not replicated) in "guest worker" programs that brought Turks to Germany, Yugoslavs to Sweden, Angolans to South Africa, and even Haitians to the Dominican Republic. Arguably, the existence of such arrangements reflects complex patterns of nonreciprocal economic and social interdependence that are grounded in history and *should* obligate those countries which have traditionally employed foreign workers from particular countries to continue doing so.[67] Yet if such an obligation can be said to exist—and we will argue below that under some circumstances it might—it is surely not based on Hobbes' exclusively prudential concept of political morality. Instead, it seems to run directly counter to that morality, since as Hobbes himself recognized, the importation of more laborers into a society where work is already scarce can pose a *direct* threat to the political stability of the state. Virtually every nation that has depended on guest workers has taken steps over the last decade to limit their entry, and many have also attempted to return such workers (and their families) to their countries of origin.[68] Therefore, while it is possible to argue that the development of a transnational pattern of labor migration may demonstrate that nation-states are more interdependent than they once were, it is not possible to argue that such interdependence has abolished (or even substantially diminished) the priority on national self-interest and the predominant concern for the situation of natives and citizens that has long been characteristic of such states.

In sum, then, it appears that Hobbesian arguments for an immigration policy based on a restrictive (and exclusively prudential) concern about the security of the nation-state are not contradicted by evidence of agreements or arrangements which have in the past led to ad hoc cooperative action among states or the creation of transnational regimes. Nor does it appear that the Hobbesian arguments can be refuted by *any other* evidence of cooperative action unless it can also be demonstrated that such cooperation will *necessarily* lead to a more stable world order, and to the realization of individual states that they and their citizens will benefit directly from that stability. Demonstrating either proposition convincingly appears to be impossible.

Therefore, Hobbesian arguments must be given some credence. If their effect is to be limited—and we argue below that they should be—the limitation must derive from some definition of "national self-interest" that is not reducible simply to the minimization of external and internal conflict.

V

The "Hobbesian fear" generated by the current state of international relations might seem to preclude the practical possibility of applying beyond one's borders principles of morality that embody notions of impartiality and equal consideration of interests. For a nation to commit itself to principles that, if acted upon, could lead to the destruction of its vital interests would be highly irrational. But to acknowledge that prudential considerations constrain the role that universal moral principles can play in foreign policy is not to imply that a nation's nondomestic policies ought to be unconstrained by moral considerations, much less that automatic credence is due every policy or judicial decision that presumes justification in terms of the national interest. For if a nation can truly be said to have interests, these must ultimately be determined by, dependent upon, or reducible to the interests of its citizens. Thus, if the concept of national interest has any normative

force in justifying a nation's policies, this force must somehow derive from
the normative content of the interests held by citizens.

We shall argue that those who invoke the national interest to justify restrictive immigration policies often ignore moral values that must be counted
among the various kinds of interests that U.S. citizens hold. This can blunt
the moral force that these interests could have in illuminating and controlling
conceptions of the national interest and thus in justifying policy decisions
and can in turn lead to policies that not only fail to serve but may in fact be
contrary to the national interest.

The term "national interest" is ordinarily used to refer in a very general
way to the physical security of a nation's population and territory, its economic well-being, and the preservation of its institutions and values. Since
the vast majority of citizens has an interest in these things, the concept has
wide popular appeal. This fact is not lost on policymakers who find it a
convenient device for disguising decisions that are actually designed to promote the most effectively deployed partisan or ideological interests. Such
abuse of the concept is no reason to doubt, of course, that it can be properly
employed to refer to a fairly clear range of legitimate considerations. But it
does point out how the ill-defined nature of the concept can lead to serious
distortions in both understanding and application.

Two features of the concept of national interest make it especially vulnerable to confusion and error, particularly in a pluralistic democracy such
as the United States. The first is the presumption it seems to carry that
sufficient unity exists among the interests of citizens to permit the concept
to be applied all-inclusively. As David Truman has noted, claims of a totally
inclusive interest within a nation have little descriptive content:

Many . . . assume explicitly or implicitly that there is an interest of the nation as a
whole, universally and invariably held and standing apart from and superior to those
of the various groups included within it. . . . Particularly in times of crisis . . . such
claims are a tremendously useful device by means of which a particular group or
league of groups tries to reduce or eliminate opposing interests. . . . Assertion of an
inclusive "national" or "public" interest is an effective device in many less critical
situations as well. In themselves these claims are part of the data of politics. However,
they do not describe any actual or possible political situation within a complex nation
state.[69]

One may safely assume, of course, that citizens have a common interest in
their physical and economic well-being, and in having certain basic rights
protected. One may not assume, however, that citizens share a moral or
ideological perspective that evaluates every action their government might
perform only in terms of how that action would affect their physical and
economic well-being.

The other suspect feature of the concept of national interest is its open-
ended "expansiveness." In this respect the concept of national interest is

like the narrower concept of national security. Daniel Yergin's characterization of the latter applies as well to the former:

[The concept of national security] postulates the interrelatedness of so many different political, economic, and military factors that developments halfway around the globe are seen to have automatic and direct impact on America's core interests. Virtually every development in the world is perceived to be potentially crucial. An adverse turn of events anywhere endangers the United States. Problems in foreign relations are viewed as urgent and immediate threats. Thus, desirable foreign policy goals are translated into issues of national survival, and the range of threats becomes limitless. The doctrine is characterized by expansiveness, a tendency to push the subjective boundaries of security outward to more and more areas, to encompass more and more geography and more and more problems. It demands that the country assume a posture of military preparedness; the nation must be permanently alert.[70]

When the world is viewed in this way, the concept of national interest is used primarily as a reflexive alarm to be sounded at the slightest real or imagined incursion on the privileges enjoyed by U.S. citizens.[71] Such a view not only presupposes that the interests of citizens can be homogenized into *the* national interest, but assumes that every response or reaction of the United States to any event in the world can be justified if it can be shown to be in the nation's prudential self-interest. National interest thus tends to become identified with a particular ideology and the maintenance of a high level of economic affluence.

This indiscriminate and paranoic use of "the national interest" is well illustrated in a recent article by Georges Fauriol.[72] In calling for a more restrictive U.S. immigration policy, Fauriol argues that current "laid-back" and "head-in-the-sand" attitudes threaten the domestic strength and international stability of the nation:

Without sovereign control over national borders, the United States can lose control over the size and nature of its labor force, population size, and linguistic and political unity. Furthermore, the size of the nation's population will determine the adequacy of natural resources and the extent to which damages to the environment can be mitigated. This in turn will influence the productivity of the economy and the ability of the United States to compete successfully internationally. Finally U.S. foreign policy may be greatly undermined by a continuation of the currently fluid nature of immigration policy; foreign powers will increasingly use the emigration threat to induce U.S. concessions or threaten retaliation should the United States move to strengthen its immigration statutes. . . . All things considered immigration policy must be related to broad economic, demographic, and foreign policy themes.[73]

Fauriol concludes his article by calling for a "redirection of U.S. immigration policy as guided by a rational calculation of the national interest."[74]

Fauriol does not describe what "a rational calculation of the national interest" would involve. But his list of various aspects of American life that he believes are threatened by current immigration policy indicates that he conceives the goal of such calculations to be a maximization of what policy analysts call "the welfare of society," which is ultimately to be understood in terms of maximum satisfaction of individual preferences. To speak of a person's interests, in this view, is to speak in a purely descriptive manner: a certain policy, or institution is "in a person's interest" if and only if it increases that person's opportunities to get what he or she wants. Policy decisions are based on analytic techniques that first quantify individual preferences and then factor them into some sort of cost-benefit algorithm that determines the policy that would promote most effectively the "aggregate welfare" of society. Although the ethical basis for this procedure is seldom questioned by the persons who employ it, those who defend it claim that it is the only fair way to make public policy in a pluralistic democracy. Herman Leonard and Richard Zeckhauser contend, for example, that "cost benefit analysis . . . would gain the hypothetical consent of the citizenry. We know of no other mechanism for making [policy] choices that has an ethical underpinning."[75] Their claim, apparently, is that if citizens were in a hypothetical situation in which they were ignorant of their individual interests, they would (if they were rational) agree on a cost-benefit mechanism that would maximize the satisfaction of their preferences, whatever these might turn out to be.

We do not know if rational citizens would in fact do this, but even if they did, this would not provide an ethical basis for cost-benefit analysis as a means of determining public policy. The reason is not that it fails to be "fair" in adjudicating among the competing individual interests of citizens, but that it systematically ignores the difference in normative content that makes some interests different *in kind* from other interests. Specifically it ignores the difference between interests based on moral values and those based on nonmoral values. Calculations of the national interest that regard both kinds of interests as mere preferences assume that they are commensurable—that trade offs can be made between them. It is absurd, however, to think of a moral value such as self-respect as simply one more thing we prefer to have, along with lower produce prices and cheaper gasoline. The difference between these two kinds of interests is not merely a function of the different degrees of displeasure a person would experience if one or the other interest were thwarted: moral values are not merely stronger preferences than nonmoral values. The difference lies in the meaning we attach to our lives. We do not conceive of ourselves as mere locations where preferences can be found, but as beings who find meaning in relationships, commitments, and activities that transcend mere satisfaction of wants.

Among the kinds of moral values that citizens possess, and utilitarian calculations of the aggregate national interest ignore, are the intersubjective values that citizens often ascribe to their nation as a whole. Consider, for example, the words of Ronald Reagan when he accepted the Republican nomination for President: "Can we doubt that only a Divine Providence placed this land, this island of freedom here as a refuge for all those people who yearn to breathe free? Jews and Christians enduring persecution behind the Iron Curtain; the boat people of Southeast Asia, Cuba, and of Haiti; the victims of drought and famine in Africa; the freedom fighters in Afghanistan."[76] These words cannot be meaningfully understood if they are taken to be merely an expression of Reagan's personal preferences, for presumably the moral concern they express was not based upon the personal advantage that he, or any other citizen, would gain from aiding refugees.[77] Nor can the words be understood merely as an expression of Reagan's personal moral values, since the subject to which the implicit moral concern was being attributed was not him, but the nation. The words can only be understood as an expression of what Reagan conceived to be the shared (intersubjective) values that embody what he thought a conscientious nation stands for and, consequently, what it must oblige itself to do.

The intersubjective values that citizens attribute to the nation qua nation cannot be reduced to or understood in terms of individual preferences. To do so would be to misunderstand seriously what it means to be a *citizen*, as opposed to a mere member of an aggregate. As Mark Sagoff points out, this difference is crucial in a democracy:

When individuals participate in the political process to determine the common values and purposes that hold them together as a community or as a nation, they regard themselves as judges of policy decisions, not merely as critics of their own welfare. Debates in which individuals or their representatives discuss and decide on public values need have no analogy, then, with markets where one determines and pursues one's own interests. In a democracy, the application of a cost-benefit formula cannot replace the public discussion of ideas; it is not just what the individual *wants* but what he *thinks* that counts.[78]

Conceptions of the national interest that take no account of what citizens *think* will lack the moral content that would invest it with the normative force necessary to justify policy decisions. Conversely, if the concept of national interest is to have any normative force in justifying policy, then it must reflect the intersubjective, public values in virtue of which citizens identify themselves as members of the political community.

Our view that any normatively meaningful concept of the national interest must reflect the intersubjective values of the nation's citizens presupposes that there *are* such values and that it makes sense to attribute them to the nation as a whole. This notion may seem suspect to those who see it as implying some sort of organic theory of the state or as an endorsement of the theory that a "general will" exists over and above the individual wills of citizens. But our view does not have these implications. That citizens acknowledge such values and discourse meaningfully about them is not a metaphysical presupposition, but an observable fact. It is not at all uncommon for a person to express shame *as an American,* for example, because the United States refused to let 20,000 Jewish children immigrate from Nazi Germany. The shame is not due to anything that individual has done personally, but from being a citizen of a nation that fell below *its* moral principles, in other words, principles in terms of which the citizen identifies with the nation.

The values that underlie these principles are revealed in the judgments that people make about the conduct of their nation, not necessarily in the actual conduct itself. We discover what people *think* by attending to the moral vocabulary they use when they express their expectations or complaints about national policy, or when they praise, blame, or excuse the actions of their government.[79] Furthermore, this moral language is used by the government itself in intelligible and persuasive ways, for example, when its officials feel obliged to promote or excuse policy decisions or justify a proposed piece of legislation. Using this shared vocabulary to influence and persuade generates a commitment on the part of citizens and governments alike to a structure of moral distinctions and arguments that places definite limits on what actions can be reasonably engaged in. It does so not by determining which decisions must be made—a morality is not in itself a decision procedure—but by constraining and influencing these decisions. Hence, to characterize a particular policy as "unjust" is not merely to condemn it (that is, express a preference) but to do so for particular reasons. It is to make a claim that requires appropriate kinds of evidence for its justification.

This process of justification marks the crucial distinction between intersubjective moral values and subjective preferences. For when citizens take positions about what *their nation* ought to do, they often wish to be respected for the *reason* they give, not for the private interests they may have at stake. (Indeed, locating a private interest behind the moral position impugns rather than enhances it.) Because the moral language that is used to express such reasons possesses a definite structure, such terms as "the national interest" are not infinitely elastic. They can be stretched only so far before breaking the bonds that give them their justificatory force.

VI

Theoretical moral arguments and general appeals to intersubjective values cannot alone determine the kind of immigration policy the United States should have. This determination depends on empirical data, much of which is controversial or lacking altogether. But moral arguments that are grounded in the kinds of intersubjective values that we have been discussing *can* help to analyze available data and to evaluate the institutions and procedures that make and implement policy. Americans have traditionally expressed great pride in their nation's openness and hospitality to immigrants and refugees. Even if this pride has often been evident more in rhetorical and symbolic modes of activity than in actual practice, it is nevertheless a powerful argument against Hobbesian-inspired xenophobia and isolationism. The force of the argument derives from the fact that Americans regard the values that underlie it to be stitched into the moral fabric of the nation. One of the most basic of these values, which is of particular pertinence to "political refugees," resides in the concept of human rights.

Human rights are a particularly important class of moral considerations for Americans, and they illustrate clearly the kind of moral constraints that intersubjective values place on the concept of the national interest. Concern about human rights in the United States has evolved out of a long and still ongoing process of political and moral deliberation about what a nation with its particular history and constitutional heritage ought to do about certain kinds of injustice. Domestically, this deliberation has resulted in a series of statutes and court decisions designed to end racial and sexual discrimination.[80] In the area of foreign policy, it has led to legislation that makes foreign aid contingent upon the recipient country's human rights policy.[81] It has brought U.S. law with respect to the immigration of refugees into conformity with international human rights standards.[82] To be sure, the moral principles that underlie these statutes maintain, at best, an uneasy state of coexistence with the ideological and partisan interests that more often than not dominate governmental decisionmaking. But an explicit human rights policy makes it more difficult in any particular case for such interests to predominate over moral concern. As Stanley Hoffman points out,

If a nation pursues a human rights policy, it means that the protection of those rights abroad is in its national interest. But there is a big difference between asserting that this is indeed the case—that the best way to enhance the nation's security, prosperity, and values abroad is to promote human rights in the world . . . and deciding that such promotion will be undertaken only in the specific cases when it directly and demonstrably contributes to the power and prestige of the nation in the world. The first interpretation entails precisely the coincidence of interest and morality, or, if you prefer, the lofty and nonselfish view of interest. . . . The second uses morality as a selective tool of selfish policy.[83]

Any policy couched in the language of human rights puts that policy into a context wherein a proffered justification in terms of the national interest can either be vindicated or exposed as hypocrisy. U.S. refugee policy provides one of the clearest illustrations.

The Refugee Act of 1980 removed the last statutory vestiges of discrimination from U.S. immigration law. By adopting the language of the United Nations Protocol Relating to the Status of Refugees, the United States formally renounced its previous ideologically based definition of "refugee" in favor of a human rights–based definition. Thus, a refugee was no longer defined as a person fleeing persecution from a Communist or Communist-dominated country, but rather as *any* person who flees his or her country because "of persecution or a well-rounded fear of persecution on account of race, religion, nationality, membership in a particular social group, or political opinion."[84] The motivation for the act was made clear by its original sponsor, Senator Edward M. Kennedy: "This Act gives statutory meaning to our national commitment to human rights and humanitarian concerns—which are not now reflected in our immigration law."[85] For a nation to acknowledge formally that there are universal human rights and to conform its laws to the standards implicit therewith, is not *merely* to bring about a set of legal prescriptions and prohibitions. It is to bring the law explicitly into a realm wherein moral considerations are paramount; it is to commit the nation to a moral vocabulary that severely restricts what can count as a justification for its actions.

The concept of a human right, for example, is ideologically and politically neutral: human rights accrue to persons no matter what country they live in and regardless of the historical and political conditions in that country. Political murder, torture, and imprisonment are violations of human rights whether they occur in countries "friendly" or "unfriendly" to the United States, whether they are ruled by leftist or rightist regimes. Since this neutrality is part of the very concept of a human right, and since U.S. refugee law is explicitly based on this concept, it follows that ideological selectivity on the part of the U.S. government in classifying refugees will lack an overriding normative justification, even if statutory loopholes might permit it a legal justification.

Yet ideology continues to dominate the U.S. government's refugee-classification and asylum-granting processes. Persons fleeing countries whose regimes are "friendly" to the United States (that is, regimes with which the U.S. government has identified significant foreign policy interests) are blatantly and systematically denied refugee status, despite the fact that they fulfill the legal definition of "refugee" at least as fully as those who, fleeing "unfriendly" countries, are permitted to enter the country. The most dramatic (though by no means the only) examples of such ideological discrimination have been the U.S. government's programs to detain, deport, or deny entry to virtually all Haitians and Salvadorans seeking refuge, while it has simultaneously welcomed with comparatively open arms the large numbers of Cubans, Cambodians, and Vietnamese fleeing Communist regimes. Since 1960, the United States has admitted over 1.5 million refugees from the latter countries under a variety of executive and statutory programs.[86] "Asylum" for those who seek to remain after entering illegally or overstaying their visas has always been harder to obtain. Yet cumulative statistics provided by the Immigration and Naturalization Service from June 1983 through September 1986 show that applicants from Romania, Afghanistan, Poland, Hungary, and the Soviet Union have been ten to twenty to fifty times more successful than applicants from El Salvador, Honduras, and Guatemala. In addition, a significant number of applicants from the favored list, although not granted formal asylum status, have been granted special relief from deportation—so-called "extended voluntary departure"—that has not been generally available for others seeking refuge.

The nondiscriminatory intent of the Refugee Act notwithstanding, doesn't the overwhelming number of potential asylum seekers demand that the United States be selective with respect to whom it lets in? And if it must be selective, is there anything morally objectionable about the executive branch's using whatever discretion Congress has afforded it to select, from among those qualified, only persons fleeing countries that are ideological enemies of the United States? Michael Walzer suggests not only that doing so would not be wrong, but that we might be morally obligated to adopt such a policy:

[We] can . . . be bound to help men and women persecuted or oppressed by someone else—if they are persecuted or oppressed because they are like us. Ideological as well as ethnic affinity can generate bonds across political lines, especially, for example, when we claim to embody certain principles in our communal life and encourage men and women elsewhere to defend those principles. The repression of political comrades, like the persecution of co-religionists, seems to generate an obligation to help, at least to provide a refuge for the most exposed and endangered people. Perhaps every victim of authoritarianism and bigotry is the moral comrade of a liberal citizen: that is an argument I would like to make. But that would press affinity too hard, and it is in any case unncessary. So long as the number of victims is small, [the principle of] mutual aid will generate similar practical results; and when the number increases, and we are forced to choose among the victims, we will look, rightfully, for some more direct connection with our own way of life. . . . [C]ommunities must have boundaries, and however these are determined with regard to territory and resources, they depend with regard to population on a sense of relatedness and mutuality. Refugees must appeal to that sense. One wishes them success; but in particular cases, with reference to a particular state, they have no right to be successful.[87]

Walzer, then, denies that every person who would definitionally qualify as a refugee (that is, "every victim of authoritarianism and bigotry") has an equal right to our moral concern. Rather, once the number of refugees becomes significant, the strength of our obligation to help is contingent upon the refugee's ideological or ethnic affinity with "our own way of life," or upon how successfully he or she is able to appeal to our "sense of relatedness and mutuality."

It is no argument against Walzer's principle of selection merely to point out that it is strongly at odds with the liberal principle of justice based on fundamental equality and human rights that provides the moral basis for the Refugee Act of 1980, for it seems to be part of his overall intent to argue against the theory of universal humans rights in favor of a view that rights are generated by certain communitarian relations among persons. Thus, for Walzer, "admission and exclusion are at the core of communal independence. They suggest the deepest meaning of self-determination. Without them, there could not be *communities of character*, historically stable, ongoing associations of men and women with some special commitment to one another and some special sense of their common life."[88]

Walzer's argument, however, relies on a strong notion of community that is largely a fiction—at least insofar as it is meant to describe the United States. Such phrases as "our own way of life" and "a sense of relatedness and mutuality" either lack clear referents on the national level, or, if they do refer, they denote a shared sense of history, tradition, and political heritage that speaks in favor of an ideologically neutral refugee policy based on universal human rights. The political loyalties and ideological beliefs of U.S. citizens are too diverse to support a notion of political community sufficiently unified to suit Walzer's purposes. (Is it true, for example, as Walzer seems to assume, that Americans feel a stronger affinity with Cuban or Vietnamese refugees than with Salvadoran or Haitian refugees?[89] The answer, of course, will depend on which Americans you ask.[90]) Nor can one assume that a communal will of the people is somehow embodied in the dominant social and political institutions that determine refugee admissions. The attitudes of citizens toward these institutions may, at any given time, range from strong loyalty or approval, to quiet acquiescence, to outright opposition.

We are not saying, of course, that U.S. citizens are devoid of a national self-identity. Indeed, as we argued earlier, it makes good sense to speak of intersubjective values that are attributable to the nation as a whole, and in terms of which persons identify themselves as citizens. But the unity that these values provide the nation cannot plausibly be considered to imply basic agreement about what ethnically or ideologically constitutes "our own way of life." On the contrary, it more likely reflects an implicit moral agreement about how the nation's social and political institutions ought to be governed, *given the fact that individuals disagree* fundamentally over what that way of life is or ought to be. The form of community—if it can be called such—that results from a liberal concept of justice does not come from close feelings of relatedness and mutuality; such a concept of justice would be unnecessary in that case, since the feelings of love and benevolence that are natural under such conditions would be sufficient to guarantee moral consideration of others, just as it usually is in families.[91] Precisely because the unity of the United States is not analogous to that of a family (or a tribe, or a neighborhood, or a club), then, moral consideration of others must be guaranteed by making justice an impersonal function of social and political institutions rather than feelings of relatedness and mutuality. The form of community—if it can be called such—that results from a liberal concept of justice does not arise naturally among persons but is *superimposed* on citizens; it provides individuals a common status, such as equality of certain rights before the law, *despite* the economic, religious, social, and ideological polarities that exist among them.[92] Thus, insofar as it makes sense to speak of the United States as a national community, the values that would bind it into one will necessarily be opposed to using ideology as a basis for selecting refugees.

An important part of Walzer's argument, however, has not yet been addressed, for he explicitly makes the moral permissibility of using an ethnic or ideological standard of refugee selection contingent upon the *number* of refugees seeking admission. As he puts it, "when the number increases, and we are forced to choose among the victims, we will look, rightfully, for some more direct connection with our own way of life." A similar argument seems implicit in the Reagan administration's refusal to grant "extended voluntary departure"—temporary safe haven—to Salvadorans, even though this status is routinely granted to Polish refugees. According to INS commissioner Alan C. Nelson, to provide such status to Salvadorans could "lead to an invasion of feet people magnifying the migration from that region, making what we already see as a stream become a torrent."[93]

Let us grant the empirical premise of Walzer's argument: it is prudentially impossible for the United States to grant asylum to every refugee who might want to immigrate. This is simply to acknowledge that there are Hobbesian limits on what the United States is obligated to do under the principles of justice to which it subscribes. Walzer's conclusion that the United States is morally permitted to select refugees on ideological or ethnic grounds, however, does not follow from this premise. To understand why it does not, consider a hypothetical domestic example. Suppose that the United States were unable to feed all its hungry citizens. This would not morally justify replacing principles of racial or political equality—principles that reflect essential intersubjective values of the nation—with principles that favored feeding one racial or political class of citizens over another. We must distinguish between the *scope* of a principle of justice and the *magnitude of the duties* the principle imposes on those who subscribe to it.[94] The scope of a principle determines the population upon whom the rights and duties fall, and is indefinite with respect to the number of persons who fall within it. The magnitude of the duties that the principle imposes, on the other hand, determines how much must be done by those on whom the duties fall.[95] The magnitude of one's duties will be at least partially determined by the contingencies of the world in which one must act. Since the scope and magnitude of a principle are logically independent variables, a change in one will not necessarily entail any change in the other.

To illustrate the distinction in terms of our hypothetical example, assume that the United States operated on a principle of distributive justice within whose scope all hungry citizens had the right to food and the nation had the duty to provide this food. Assume further that the nation allocated 1 percent of its budget to meet this obligation. No increase in the number of hungry citizens would morally justify replacing the given principle with one under which, for example, only hungry Catholics, or hungry Republicans, or hungry whites had the right to food. But neither would such an increase automatically impose a heavier duty on the nation. An increase in the number of hungry citizens might simply lead to a reallocation of the same 1 percent of the budget from less urgent to more urgent cases of hunger. (This would be the case, however, only if 1 percent of its budget were all the nation could reasonably be expected to allocate in fulfilling its duty. Otherwise, justice might require an increase in the magnitude of the duty, which would entail increasing the food budget at the expense of some morally less important expenditures.[96])

The distinction between the scope and magnitude of a principle of justice explains why Walzer is wrong in thinking that an overwhelmingly large number of refugees seeking admission would morally permit the United States to select among them on the basis of ideology or ethnic affinity. The principles on which the 1980 Refugee Act is based are universal in scope: they provide to *any person* who meets the definition of a refugee the moral right to remain in a country of refuge, and they impose on the United States (as well as other countries) the correlative duty to provide that refuge, as well as basic civil and economic rights. When the United States, through its democratic processes, translated those principles into law, it acknowledged these duties. This means that the nation not only is obligated generally on moral grounds to those refugees who reach its borders, but also has in a political and legal sense acknowledged that obligation. No increase in the number would justify admission decisions by the United States that are based on ideology or ethnic affinity.

Determining the scope of a principle, however, is easier than determining the magnitude of the duties it imposes, and the latter problem ultimately poses the greater moral and political challenge. It is one thing to argue, as we have, that the value the United States places on human rights morally prohibits it from discrimination in granting asylum; it is quite another to specify on the basis of this value the number of refugees that the nation is morally obligated to accept. The obvious—but hardly helpful—answer is that the nation is obligated to accept as many as it can without jeopardizing its vital interests. Since the interests at stake here are those of U.S. citizens, the question is: how much can reasonably be expected of citizens in meeting the needs of refugees? On the one hand, meeting the demands of justice clearly would likely result in *some* net reduction in the material well-being of U.S. citizens. Those who measure the national interest strictly in terms of this index will argue that *any* such reduction is too much to ask. We argued earlier that this conclusion relies on an overly constricted notion of the national interest.

On the other hand, it is also clear that there are Hobbesian limits on how much any principle of justice can reasonably demand of the nation. As Henry Shue notes, "It is a reasonable constraint upon what justice can require that some normal (non-saintly, non-heroic) persons could in fact be convinced to act accordingly."[97] These limits involve the extent to which U.S. citizens are willing to detach themselves from their personal projects and commitments in order to meet the impersonal demands that the national commitment to refugees makes upon them. It is not clear, then, in any given case what the upper limit to justice must be. Whatever it is, it will define the degree of priority a government must accord the private interests of citizens over those of refugees and itself will be defined by the Hobbesian constraints that the government must work within.[98]

The question of limits, then, is in large part a practical question, and the answer will be determined as much by the sociopolitical conditions that predominate as by the content of moral principles. How many refugees can the United States admit, for example, without stimulating its citizens to large-scale opposition, or even open rebellion? It is in answering empirical questions like this that moral arguments for increased admissions must take into account the reality of the Hobbesian world in which we live. To acknowledge this is not to relegate morality to an inferior status with respect to politics, much less to ignore the moral dimensions of the national interest. It is merely to point out that any moral argument for increasing refugee admissions must factor into account the moral costs of enforcing such a policy. If, for instance, the state could not meet the formal demands of justice without using a significant degree of coercion against the citizens on whom the refugee burden fell, then the practical limits of what justice can reasonably require would probably have been exceeded regardless of how selfish or otherwise morally unworthy were the motives of the opposing citizens.

But justice also has a lower limit. Just as practical considerations work to keep the demands of justice from exceeding maximum levels of sacrifice, moral considerations work to keep these demands from dropping below certain minimum levels of effectiveness. Hence, the government may run the risk of opposition or rebellion no less in maintaining an overly restrictive refugee policy than in yielding to any overly generous one, especially if that policy pays for the reduced number of admissions at the expense of the nation's most deeply rooted moral values.[99]

Acknowledging a Hobbesian-imposed upper limit to the number of refugees that the United States is obligated to admit does little to blunt the moral force of arguments for a more generous policy. (In fact, it may strengthen the practical effect of such arguments by eliminating the imaginary specter of endless hordes of invading refugees that so often makes people resistant to admitting *any* refugees.) Since those arguments rely on the shared sense of justice that U.S. citizens acknowledge as part of their national self-identity, the degree of sacrifice required by justice will be grounded in the same source of history and tradition that gives rise to that sense.

VII

In 1870, in the aftermath of the American Civil War and the Thirteenth, Fourteenth, and Fifteenth Amendments to the Constitution, Congress passed two major statutes that had as their immediate object the elimination of *de jure* discrimination. The first was a voting rights act. The second amended the naturalization statute, which had previously benefited only white aliens, to permit others "of African race or descent" to become citizens of the United States. In the Senate debate on the naturalization act, Charles Sumner, one of the nation's most impassioned abolitionists, argued that the new statute should remove *all* reference to "race" and that the Chinese as well as blacks should be given the opportunity to assimilate themselves to American society.

Quoting the Declaration of Independence, Sumner argued that the "great, self-evident, inalienable rights," which it proclaimed, "belong to 'all men.' It is 'all men,' and not a race or color that are placed under the protection of the Declaration. . . . [S]uch was the baptismal vow of this nation. According to this vow, *all* men are created equal and endowed with inalienable rights. . . . The word 'white,' wherever it occurs as a limitation of rights, must disappear."[100] But anti-Chinese sentiment was in full bloom, and Sumner's plea fell on deaf ears. Only eight senators voted with him. Slightly more than a decade later, the first of the Chinese exclusion acts was passed, and the United States initiated eight decades of overt racial and ethnic discrimination in its immigration laws.

That discrimination was not only established by statute, but countenanced by the courts on explicitly Hobbesian grounds. Thus, the *Chinese Exclusion Case*, decided in 1889, recognized an inherent sovereign authority, unencumbered by any nonprudential moral considerations, to exclude "foreigners of a different race in this country who will not assimilate with us" summarily on the grounds that their presence was "dangerous to [national] peace and security."[101] *Fong Yue Ting v. United States*, decided in 1893, employed the same reasoning to permit the summary deportation of Chinese who had long been resident in the United States.[102] In that case, the majority rejected two relevant dissenting arguments: that the power to deport on the basis of race opens up a Pandora's box of potential discrimination ("It is true that the statute is directed only against the obnoxious Chinese; but if the power exists, who shall say it will not be exercised tomorrow against other classes and other people?"[103]); and that deportable aliens, having become subject to our laws, are inherently entitled to equal justice under the law ("Arbitrary and despotic power can no more be exercised over them with reference to their persons and property, than over the persons and property of native-born citizens. They differ only from citizens in that they cannot vote or hold any public office. As men having our common humanity, they are protected by all the guarantees of the Constitution"[104]).

In 1952, eight years after the Supreme Court had found the internment of Japanese-Americans for the duration of World War II constitutional,[105] Justice Frankfurter insisted that "national self-interest" was a purely "political" matter, not subject to legitimate second-guessing by the courts:

> The conditions for entry of every alien, the particular classes of aliens that shall be denied entry altogether, the basis for determining such classification, the right to terminate hospitality to aliens, the grounds on which such determination shall be based, have been recognized as matters solely for the responsibility of Congress and wholly outside the power of this Court to control. . . .
>
> In their personal views, libertarians like Mr. Justice Holmes and Mr. Justice Brandeis doubtless disapproved of some of these policies, departures as they were from the best traditions of this country and based as they have been on discredited racial theories.
>
> . . . But whether immigration laws have been crude and cruel, whether they may have reflected xenophobia in general or anti-Semitism, or anti-Catholicism, the responsibility belongs to Congress. . . . [T]he underlying policies . . . are for Congress exclusively to determine even though such determination may be deemed to offend American traditions and may, as has been the case, jeopardize peace.[106]

Since 1952, the Supreme Court has continued to emphasize the "plenary" power of Congress to categorize aliens for the purpose of deportation or exclusion, and, while hinting that there might be some constitutional limits to the practice,[107] has rejected the opportunity to confront the issue head-on[108] and left intact past decisions that authorize such categorization on the basis of race or ethnic origin.[109]

The reluctance of the judiciary to act decisively and repudiate ancient precedent can be attributed to a variety of factors, including an institutional bias in favor of *stare decisis*, the Court's implicit "statist" values that endow the traditional "sovereignty" argument with exceptional longevity and strength, a real commitment by its current members to "separation of powers" principles, and perhaps, their concerns that the Court will lose "legitimacy" in the eyes of the public if it substitutes its "political" will for that of the Congress or the executive branch. Nowhere are assertions of the right to discriminate more firmly embedded, and perhaps more popularly based, than in American immigration law. A long colloquy between restrictionists, the Congress, and the courts shaped that law, which is at its root "discriminatory," since by definition, it establishes legal categories that permit some classes of aliens to enter or remain in the United States while it excludes or deports others. If the American experience with immigration is indicative, Michael Walzer is surely correct in believing that human societies, from the level of the neighborhood to the level of the State, seek "closure."[110] The closure that restrictionists traditionally sought in the United States (and eventually won) demanded the exclusion of Asians and blacks, southern and eastern Europeans, contract laborers, the illiterate, the poverty-stricken, the diseased, the criminal, the immoral, and the politically radical.

The problem, though, is that while these grounds of limitation may all be politically equivalent, they are not—as Charles Sumner recognized—morally equivalent. Walzer has attempted to ground the difference in immigration history:

To say that states have a right to act in certain areas is not to say that anything they do in these areas is right. One can argue about particular admission standards by appealing, for example, to the condition and character of the host country and to the shared understandings of those who are already members. Such claims have to be judged morally and politically as well as factually. The claim of American advocates of restricted immigration (in 1920, say) that they were defending a homogeneous white and Protestant country, can plausibly be called unjust as well as inaccurate: as if non-white and non-Protestant men and women were invisible men and women who didn't have to be counted in the national census! Earlier Americans, seeking the benefits of economic and geographic expansion, had created a pluralist society; and the moral realities of that society ought to have guided the legislators of the 1920's.[111]

In other words, by the 1920s it was already "too late" to be racist, or otherwise prejudiced against immigrants because of their ethnic background. "If we follow the logic of the club analogy, however, we have to say that the earlier decision might have been different, and the United States might have taken shape as an Anglo-Saxon nation-state (assuming what happened in any case: the virtual extermination of the Indians . . .)"[112]

But was it too late in 1870, when Charles Sumner spoke? Or even in 1882, when the first Chinese Exclusion Act was passed? Before 1854, the United States was populated almost entirely by whites from northern Europe and blacks who had entered as slaves. There were virtually no Asians resident in American territory. Beginning in 1854, limited Chinese immigration commenced.[113] In 1870, according to official census figures, of a total foreign-born population of 5.5 million, only 63,042 were Chinese. In 1880, according to those same figures, of a foreign-born population of 6.6 million, only 104,468 were Chinese.[114] In 1882, the year of peak Chinese immigration, 39,579 Chinese entered the United States, almost exactly 5 percent of the immigrant total for that year.[115] Only in California, which had a Chinese population of approximately 100,000 in 1882, was there any significant Chinese—or any Asian—presence.[116] At its peak, the Chinese population of the United States was considerably smaller than the largely extinguished American Indian population.[117]

There are simply no adequate consequentialist responses to the question.

When one strips away the Hobbesian "national security" argument (which would apply if the nation actually were inundated with migrants from *any* country, or were confronted with migrants from a country actually hostile to the United States, or even had to deal with a significant number of migrants in direct labor competition with U.S. citizens), one is left with the naked preferences of a majority which remains substantial long after the advent of the first Chinese or of any other national of an "unfamiliar" country.[118] (Indeed, the majority may grow as earlier immigrant groups are "assimilated" with "natives" in rejecting the newcomers. That certainly happened in California, when the Irish were among the most vociferous opponents of Chinese immigration.) Without intersubjective values that recognize the moral status of "equality" *before* any particular immigration event, even in a pluralistic society those who are different from the majority in *any* way can be rejected.

Our point, as we have indicated earlier, is that in a universe that takes morals seriously, only certain reasons count. Reasons that protect individual security (a fundamental right) without seriously compromising the other fundamental values are defensible; reasons that compromise those values without adding significantly to the security are not.[119] For instance, the Hobbesian argument that supports a nation's right to limit the number of refugees to whom it grants asylum, will *a fortiori* support that nation's right to limit the number of other immigrants. It will also permit excluding immigrants who come with "contagious diseases," criminal records, or an intent to wreak political violence. The principal ground for this right is neither a sacrosanct doctrine of national sovereignty nor an ever-expanding, all-inclusive concept of national interest. Rather, it is the practical argument that a state protect the individual rights of those persons within its territory by preserving domestic stability and maintaining essential resources. If admitting dangerous individuals or large numbers of immigrants—whatever their country of origin, and whether refugees, guest workers, or ordinary immigrants—significantly impedes the state's ability to provide this protection, then the state is justified in reducing that number.[120] There is a clear sense, then, in which "the national interest" justifies immigration control. The normative force of this justification, however, stems from the interests that citizens have in maintaining their basic rights and not from the aggregate sum of quantified citizen preferences, although the latter may provide enough justification when the prospective immigrant is not a refugee, but a person who has no special claim on our moral concern.

However, when racial or certain other forms of "ethnic" or "national origins" classification become the basis of immigration decisions, special claims on our moral concern do arise. Implicit in such decisions is an invidious denial of the essential equality of human beings that is central to any notion of universal human rights.[121] Thus, it might have been appropriate to exclude virtually all German nationals between 1917 and 1919, and again between 1941 and 1945, simply because we were at war with the German nation and had reason to be suspicious of most German travelers. But it was hardly defensible to exclude them (or their victims during the Nazi era) on the grounds that they were "inherently inferior" human beings. To the extent that Hobbesian arguments are used to mask invidious discrimination, they carry no weight at all.

The moral limitation on the right of the state to engage in invidious discrimination probably was implicit in the Declaration of Independence, as Charles Sumner argued. Yet explicit in antebellum society and law were many forms of overt discrimination, including the institution of slavery and a variety of laws restricting the rights of women. The Civil War lent new prominence to moral issues raised by discrimination, bur even the passage of three constitutional amendments and numerous civil rights statutes did not resolve them. Despite the fact that moral insights were incorporated into political argument, it took considerable time for that argument to develop more fully and to be more fully incorporated into the political landscape. Not until 1920, for instance, did women gain the vote. Not until 1954 did the Supreme Court rule that *de jure* racial segregation was illegal. Not until 1965 did Congress formally abolish the racially motivated national origins quota system. In every case, political success depended on a development of interest-group pressures, an effective union of arguments about what was "good" with arguments about what was "expedient."

Despite this history of gradualism, the Supreme Court has been especially slow in addressing the constitutionality of racial categories in immigration law. Thus, as the Court has noted, Congress when dealing with immigrants, "regularly makes rules that would be *unacceptable* if applied to citizens" (emphasis added).[122] "Unacceptable" to whom? To the members of the Court, of course, who in other contexts would have had no hesitation in striking down as unconstitutional many of the disabilities imposed on immigrants generally, or on particular classes of immigrants.[123] Peter Schuck characterized the situation:

Immigration has long been a maverick, a wild card, in our public law. Probably no other area of American law has been so radically insulated and divergent from those fundamental norms of constitutional right, administrative procedure, and judicial role that animate our legal system. In a legal firmament transformed by revolutions in due process and equal protection doctrine and by a new conception of the judicial role, immigration law remains the realm in which government authority is at its zenith, and individual entitlement is at the nadir.[124]

Faced with such atavism, it is natural to expect change. For as Louis Henkin has noted in an article in the *Harvard Law Review*:

The doctrine that the Constitution neither limits governmental control over aliens nor secures the right of admitted aliens to reside here emerged in the shadow of a racist, nativist mood a hundred years ago. It was reaffirmed during our fearful, cold war, McCarthy days. It has no foundation in principle. It is a constitutional fossil, a remnant of a prerights jurisprudence that we have proudly rejected in other respects. Nothing in our Constitution, its theory, or history warrants exempting any exercise of governmental power from constitutional restraint. . . .

As a blanket exemption of immigration laws from constitutional limitations, *Chinese Exclusion* is a "relic from a different era." That era was one . . . when orotund generalities about sovereignty and national security were a substitute for significant scrutiny of governmental action impinging on our individual rights; when the Bill of Rights had not yet become our national hallmark and the principal justification and preoccupation of judicial review. . . .

The power of Congress to control immigration and to regulate alienage and naturalization is plenary. But even plenary power is subject to constitutional restraints. I cannot believe that the Court would hold today that the Constitution permits either exclusion on racial or religious grounds or deportation of persons lawfully admitted who have resided peacefully here.[125]

Henkin well may be right; perhaps the dinosaur is about to be buried.[126] Yet the apparently deep-seated urge that nations, like more genuine communities of sympathy, have to define themselves by excluding those who are "different" on the grounds that their differences constitute "danger" makes us skeptical. The Hobbesian argument enunciated in the *Chinese Exclusion Case* has a continuing, fundamental appeal. Sketching its proper limits by defining the scope and interpersonal origins of the "national interest" is a difficult task for those who style themselves academics or philosophers. For judges, who always sit at the edge of public controversy, it may prove impossible.

NOTES

1. We do not deny, however, that utilitarian theories can have a basis in moral considerations. For example, in our discussion of the Hobbesian conception of the state, we assume that the avoidance of anarchy is a moral value. However, we argue that it is a value that does not contribute to—and indeed, conflicts with—the moral conceptions of distributive justice that are central to any sophisticated discussion of immigration policy and law.

2. "Modern state," as used here, includes only those nations that have the bureaucratic capacity to regulate substantially the movement of persons across their borders. Under this definition, countries like Zaire, which was the unwilling host to hundreds of thousands of refugees during the 1960s and 1970s, do not qualify. It is unclear whether Pakistan, which has admitted more than 4 million Afghan refugees over the last seven years, qualifies or not.

3. See, particularly, "The Intellectuals" and "The Modern Prince," in *Selections from the Prison Notebooks*, ed. Q. Hoare and G. N. Smith (New York: International Publishers, 1971), pp. 12–13, 169–170, 180–184, and 195–196.

4. Clifford Geertz, "Ideology as a Cultural System," in *Ideology and Discontent*, ed. David E. Apter (New York: Free Press, 1964), pp. 61–75.

5. For a discussion of that rhetorical tradition as it has manifested itself in the U.S. reception of refugees, see Gilburt Loescher and John A. Scanlan, *Calculated Kindness: Refugees and America's Half-Open Door, 1945–Present* (New York: Free Press, 1986), particularly pp. xiii and 209.

6. However, the ability to control borders may not be terribly significant if a nation, such as the United States, prefers to bear the costs of illegal migration in preference to the anticipated costs of labor shortages. In such a case, it may still be politically and socially useful for the nation to be able to claim that it has "control over its own borders," but that utility is likely to be essentially rhetorical. See John A. Scanlan, "Immigration Law and the Illusion of Numerical Control," *University of Miami Law Review* 36 (1982): 819.

7. For one example, involving the 1980 exodus from Cuba, see John Scanlan and Gilburt Loescher, "U.S. Foreign Policy, 1959–1980: Impact on Refugee Flow from Cuba," *Annals of the American Academy of Political and Social Science* 467 (May 1983): 132–135.

8. Thus, Bruce Ackerman argues that at some point, unlimited immigration can threaten the continuance of the ongoing "liberal conversation," which, he implies, is the hallmark of the modern democratic state and the basis of its claim to being an instrument of social justice. See *Social Justice in the Liberal State* (New Haven, Conn.: Yale University Press, 1980), pp. 313–314; 93–95.

9. It is impossible to quantify what the effects of an "open border" would be. It is at least significant that over the last decade, some million illegal entrants a year have been turned away at the U.S.–Mexican border.

10. Attempts at border control extended back to colonial times, and were enforced by individual states during the period from 1787 until 1875, when the first general federal immigration legislation was enacted. The most comprehensive legal account is Edward P. Hutchinson, *Legislative History of American Immigration Policy, 1798–1965* (Philadelphia: University of Pennsylvania Press, 1981). The best general social history of these controls is John Higham, *Strangers in the Land: Patterns of American Nativism* (New Brunswick, N.J.: Rutgers University Press, 1955).

11. Such limits do not, of course, guarantee that significant illegal immigration will not occur; see notes 6 and 9 above. The limits specified in the following paragraphs are set forth in various sections of the Immigration and Nationality Act (INA), which was enacted in 1952 and has since been amended many times. The provisions of the INA have been incorporated in title 8 of the United States Code (8 U.S.C.). See especially, INA §§ 201 and 203 (annual quota; distribution of quota slots among preference categories); INA § 1157 (annual refugee quota); and INA § 1182 (grounds for exclusion from the United States).

12. However, citizens who have not yet reached the age of twenty-one cannot petition for grant of an immigration visa for their parents. See 8 U.S.C. § 1151(b).

13. *Kleindienst v. Mandel*, 408 U.S. 753, 770 (1972).

14. *Knauff v. Shaughnessy*, 338 U.S. 537, 542–544 (1950).

15. *Jean v. Nelson*, 727 F.2d 957 (11th Cir.), *aff'd on other grounds*, 472 U.S. 486 (1985).

16. See David Wyman, *Paper Walls: America and the Refugee Crisis, 1938–41* (Amherst, Mass.: University of Massachusetts Press, 1968).

17. The framework for the new legal order was established by the Refugee Act

of 1980, 94 Stat. 102. For a good history of the legislation, see Deborah Anker, "The Forty Year Crisis: A Legislative History of the Refugee Act of 1980," *San Diego Law Review* 19 (1981): 9–98.

18. See, for example, *Woodby v. INS*, 385 U.S. 276 (1966) (government must employ a heightened evidentiary standard when determining if alien is deportable) and, in the exclusion context, *Landon v. Plasencia*, 459 U.S. 21 (1982) (certain aliens with "permanent resident" status are entitled to procedural due process if they leave the United States temporarily and the government attempts to bar their return).

19. See, for example, *Galvan v. Press*, 347 U.S. 522, 531 (1954): "policies pertaining to the entry of aliens [are] entrusted exclusively to Congress" (Justice Frankfurter, for the Court).

20. See, for example, *United States ex rel. Knauff v. Shaughnessy*, 338 U.S. 537 (1950); *Shaughnessy v. United States ex rel. Mezei*, 345 U.S. 206 (1953).

21. *Harisiades v. Shaughnessy*, 342 U.S. 580 (1952). *Galvan v. Press*, 347 U.S. 522 (1954).

22. *Harisiades v. Shaughnessy*, 342 U.S. 580 (1952).

23. *Fiallo v. Bell*, 430 U.S. 787 (1977). The *statute* that the Court interpreted in the *Fiallo* case has since been amended to remove the discrimination that the Court found constitutional. See 8 U.S.C. § 1101(b)(1)(D), as amended by the Immigration Reform and Control Act of 1986, 100 Stat. 3359.

24. See *Matter of Dunar*, 14 I&N Dec. 310 (1973); *INS v. Stevic*, 467 U.S. 407 (1984).

25. *Narenji v. Civiletti*, 617 F.2d 745 (D.C. Cir. 1979), *cert. denied* 446 U.S. 957 (1980) (permitting special action against Iranian students).

26. See *Harisiades v. Shaughnessy*, 342 U.S. 580, 596 (1952) (Justice Frankfurter, concurring): "Ever since national states have come into being, the right of people to enjoy the hospitality of a State of which they are not citizens has been a matter of political determination by each State. . . . Though as a matter of political outlook and economic need this country has traditionally welcomed aliens to come to its shores, it has done so exclusively as a matter of political outlook and national self-interest."

27. Peter Schuck, "The Transformation of Immigration Law," 84 *Columbia Law Review* 1 (1984): 85–86.

28. These principles are clearly the starting point for Ackerman's treatment of justice in *Social Justice in the Liberal State* (1980), and they account for his skepticism about the morality of immigration restrictions under any circumstance not involving a threat to the continuance of his paradigmatic "liberal conversation." See especially pp. 89–95.

29. Charles Beitz, *Political Theory and International Relations* (Princeton, N.J.: Princeton University Press, 1979), p. 58.

30. 130 U.S. 581 (1889).

31. Ibid., pp. 603–604.

32. *Jean v. Nelson*, 727 F.2d 957, 975 (11th Cir. 1984), *aff'd on other grounds*, 472 U.S. 846 (1985).

33. *The Passenger Cases*, 48 U.S. (7 How.) 283 (1849) invalidated *state* taxes on immigrants, apparently on "commerce clause" grounds. No general federal immigration legislation was passed until 1875, although federal naturalization statutes had existed since 1790, and special restrictions on the importation of Chinese laborers

dated from 1866. The *Head Money Cases*, 112 U.S. 580 (1884) upheld the *federal* power to tax and regulate immigration.

34. "The government, possessing the powers which are to be exercised for protection and security, is clothed with the authority to determine the occasion on which the powers shall be called forth. . . . If, therefore, the government of the United States . . . considers the presence of foreigners of a different race in this country who will not assimilate with us, to be dangerous to its peace and security, their exclusion is not to be stayed because at the time there are no actual hostilities with the nation of which the foreigners are subjects. The existence of war would render the necessity of the proceeding only more obvious and pressing. The same necessity, in a less pressing degree, may arise when war does not exist." The *Chinese Exclusion Case*, 130 U.S. 581, 606 (1889).

35. See note 7, above. Also see Loescher and Scanlan, *Calculated Kindness*, pp. 29–40, 52–53, 60–61, 68–78.

36. Mario Rivera, "Cuban and Haitian Influxes of 1980 and the American Response: Retrospect and Prospect," U.S. House of Representatives Committee on the Judiciary, *Oversight Hearings: Caribbean Migration* (Washington, D.C.: Government Printing Office, 1980), appendix 4, p. 292.

37. See note 7, above.

38. 727 F.2d, pp. 986–990.

39. Ibid., p. 988.

40. 130 U.S., p. 495.

41. Ibid., p. 606.

42. Even Friedrich Engels shared the view that more immigration meant more labor competition and inevitably lower wages. See *Conditions of the Working Class in England*, ed. W. O. Henderson and W. H. Chaloner (Stanford, Calif.: Stanford University Press, 1968), p. 107. In today's post-Keynesian era, there is no unanimity about what the long-term economic effects of immigration on domestic labor markets is likely to be.

43. There were, however, a substantial number of Chinese in California in the 1870s and 1880s, perhaps numbering over 100,000 when the first Chinese Exclusion Act was passed in 1882. See section VIII, below.

44. Thomas Hobbes, *Leviathan* (New York and London: E. P. Dutton, 1950) (Everyman's Library ed.), chapter 11, p. 79.

45. Ibid., chapter 13, p. 105; chapter 14, p. 107.

46. Ibid., chapter 13, p. 103.

47. Ibid., p. 104.

48. Thomas Hobbes, *The Elements of Law*, 2d ed., ed. Ferdinand Tonnies (New York: Barnes and Noble, 1969) (part 1, chapter 17, para. 2), p. 88, quoted in Walzer, *Spheres of Justice*, p. 43.

49. Hobbes, *Leviathan*, chap. 17, pp. 142–143.

50. Ibid., pp. 139–140.

51. Ibid., p. 140.

52. Ibid., p. 141. Hobbes emphasizes this point when he pointedly rejects any analogy between the social order of the ants and bees, which Aristotle had proposed as a model for human society.

53. Ibid., chapter 13, p. 105.

54. Ibid., chapter 21, p. 181.

55. Ibid., chapter 30, p. 299.

56. Ibid.

57. 130 U.S. 581, 595 (1889). Aleinikoff and Martin, who quote this portion of the opinion, comment that the Workingmen's party of California, incensed by continuing Chinese immigration during a period of economic depression, threatened armed insurrection if required to continue "to labor beside . . . Chinese slave[s]." *Immigration Practice and Policy*, p. 2. Also see A. Saxton, *The Indispensable Enemy: Labor and the Anti-Chinese Movement in California* (Berkeley, Calif.: University of California Press, 1971).

58. Charles Beitz, *Political Theory and International Relations* (Princeton, N.J.: Princeton University Press, 1979), p. 36, and generally, pp. 35–50. Beitz also argues that there is a fourth element that must be empirically demonstrable if the "state of nature" analogy is to hold true: that individual states "have relatively equal power," p. 36. He does not believe the requisite power equality exists.

59. See Robert O. Keohane and Joseph S. Nye, eds., *Transnational Relations and World Politics* (Cambridge, Mass.: Harvard University Press, 1972), and Robert O. Keohane, *After Hegemony: Cooperation and Discord in the World Political Economy* (Princeton, N.J.: Princeton University Press: 1984).

60. From the time that the *Chinese Exclusion Case*, 130 U.S. 581 (1889) and *Fong Yue Ting v. United States*, 149 U.S. 698 (1893) were decided, the Supreme Court has invoked "sovereignty" arguments to limit its jurisdiction to review the essentially "political" judgments of Congress and the executive branch of government. See, e.g., *Harisiades v. Shaughnessy*, 342 U.S. 580, 596–597 (1952) (Justice Frankfurter, concurring).

61. The establishment of cooperative arrangements after World War II established a pattern for dealing with refugees that has persisted. For example, the First World approached the Indochinese refugee crisis in 1979 and the early 1980s by using surviving international organizations and collectively raising funds for "pledging" conferences. Similar approaches have been taken to other refugee problems.

62. The relationship between officially countenanced and illegal immigration is dealt with in some detail in Julian Samora, *Los Mojados: The Wetback Story* (Notre Dame, Ind.: University of Notre Dame Press, 1971).

63. Louise Holborn, "The League of Nations and the Refugee Problem," *Annals of the American Academy of Political and Social Science* 203 (May 1939): 124–135.

64. For example, the United States was influential during the Indochinese refugee crisis in pressuring other nations to accept more refugees. See Loescher and Scanlan, *Calculated Kindness*, pp. 145–146.

65. Independent action can be either "pro" or "anti" refugee. The United States, Mexico, and Spain have historically accepted an unusual number of Cuban refugees. During the Chilean political crisis of 1973, for example, the United States established significant barriers to the entry of Chilean refugees at a time when many of the countries of Western Europe were responding with considerable generosity. Ibid., pp. 97–101. More recently, Canada has been unusually willing to accept Salvadoran and other Central American refugees.

66. For an example focusing on the difficulties that the Office of the United Nations High Commissioner for Refugees has had extending aid or protection to Central American refugees, see G. Loescher and J. Scanlan, "Human Rights, Power Politics, and the International Refugee Regime: The Case of U.S. Treatment of

Caribbean Basin Refugees," World Order Studies Program Occasional Paper No. 14 (Princeton, N.J.: Center of International Studies, Princeton University, 1985).

67. Such is the argument that Judith Lichtenberg makes in "Mexican Migration and U.S. Policy: A Guide for the Perplexed," in P. G. Brown and H. Shue, *The Border that Joins: Mexican Migrants and U.S. Responsibility* (Totowa, N.J.: Rowman and Allanheld, 1983).

68. Not all family members of guest workers have affective ties to the workers' countries of origin. Some, for example, are the Swedish spouses of Yugoslav laborers, or the German-born children of Turkish *gastenarbeiter*. In the United States, all children born on U.S. soil are invested immediately with at least nominal U.S. citizenship. For a critique that advocates changing the American law of *jus soli*, so that "consensual" criteria for "membership" in the American "political community" will replace "ascriptive" criteria, see, generally, Peter Schuck and Rogers Smith, *Citizenship without Consent: Illegal Aliens in the American Polity* (New Haven, Conn., and London: Yale University Press, 1985).

69. David Truman, *The Governmental Process* (New York: Alfred A. Knopf, 1963), pp. 50–51.

70. Daniel Yergin, *Shattered Peace: The Origins of the Cold War and the National Security State* (Boston: Houghton Mifflin Co., 1977), p. 176.

71. This point is discussed by Peter G. Brown, ". . . in the National Interest," in Peter G. Brown and Douglas MacLean, *Human Rights and U.S. Foreign Policy* (Lexington, Mass.: Lexington Books, 1979), p. 163.

72. Georges Fauriol, "U.S. Immigration Policy and the National Interest," *The Humanist* 44:5, reprinted in *The Problem of Immigration*, ed. Steven Anzovin (New York: H. W. Wilson Co., 1985), pp. 96–116. References are to the reprint.

73. Ibid., p. 99.

74. Ibid., p. 115.

75. Herman Leonard and Richard Zeckhauser, "Cost-Benefit Analysis Applied to Risks: Its Philosophy and Legitimacy," Working Paper (College Park: University of Maryland, Center for Philosophy and Public Policy, June 1983). Cited by Mark Sagoff, "Values and Preferences," *Ethics* 96:2 (January 1986): 306.

76. Ronald W. Reagan, "Acceptance Speech," Detroit, Michigan, July 17, 1980, reported in *New York Times*, July 18, 1980, p. 8.

77. In fact, they may not be expressing a personal preference at all, but only expressing a common—and politically helpful—value. Such an interpretation is supported by the minimal efforts that the Reagan administration actually made to encourage the migration of African drought victims, as well as its active opposition to the granting of political asylum to Haitians. See Loescher and Scanlan, *Calculated Kindness*, pp. 188–195.

78. Sagoff, "Values and Preferences," p. 302.

79. For a relevant discussion of the importance of moral language, see Michael Walzer, *Just and Unjust Wars* (New York: Basic Books, 1977), pp. 10–16; and Terry Nardin, *Law, Morality and the Relations of States* (Princeton, N.J.: Princeton University Press, 1983), pp. 245–247.

80. E.g., the Civil Rights Act of 1964, 78 Stat. 241, codified in 42 U.S.C. §§ 1975a et seq., and 2000a et seq., and the Voting Rights Act of 1965, 79 Stat 437, codified in 42 U.S.C. §§ 1973 et seq.

81. See, for instance, section 25 of the Foreign Assistance Act of 1974 (Pub. L.

No. 559, 94th Cong., 2d Sess., 1974), cutting off all military and most economic aid to Chile. This provision was the prototype of later general restrictions on aid to human rights violators in the annual foreign assistance appropriation process, as well as the short-lived specific provisions requiring "certification" of human rights progress in El Salvador as a condition for additional aid.

82. The Refugee Act of 1980, 94 Stat. 102, codified in various sections of title 8 of the United States Code.

83. Stanley Hoffman, *Duties Beyond Borders* (Syracuse, N.Y.: Syracuse University Press, 1981), pp. 113–114.

84. The Refugee Act of 1980, sec. 101(a)(42)(A), 8 U.S.C. § 1101(a)(42)(A).

85. U.S. Senate Committee on the Judiciary, *Review of U.S. Refugee Resettlement Programs and Policies* (Report), 96th Cong., 2d Sess., 1980, p. 80.

86. See, generally, Loescher and Scanlan, *Calculated Kindness.*

87. Michael Walzer, *Spheres of Justice: A Defense of Pluralism and Equality* (New York: Basic Books, 1983), pp. 49–50.

88. Ibid., p. 62.

89. Ibid., p. 49.

90. Walzer explicitly recognizes this diversity when he criticizes earlier American attempts to admit only racially and religiously "pure" immigrants: "The claim of American advocates of restricted immigration (in 1920, say) that they were defending a homogeneous white and Protestant country, can plausibly be called unjust as well as inaccurate: as if non-white and non-Protestant citizens were invisible men and women, who didn't have to be counted in the national census!" (ibid., p. 40). Curiously, however, Walzer does not see the same injustice in admissions standards based on ideological and ethnic affinity as he sees in those based on religion and race.

91. Walzer apparently thinks that the national sense of community is sufficiently analogous to that of the family to provide this moral basis: "Clearly, citizens often believe themselves morally bound to open the doors of their country—not to anyone who wants to come in, perhaps, but a particular group of outsiders, recognized as national or ethnic 'relatives.' In this sense, states are like families . . . , for it is a feature of families that their members are morally connected to people they have not chosen, who live outside the household" (ibid., p. 41).

92. See Gerald Doppelt, "Walzer's Theory of Morality in International Relations," *Philosophy and Public Affairs* 8:2 (Fall 1978): 19.

93. Quoted in Claudia Dreifus, "No Refugees Need Apply," *The Atlantic* 259:2 (February 1987): 32.

94. Henry Shue, "The Burdens of Justice," *The Journal of Philosophy*, 80:11 (November 1983): 602.

95. Ibid.

96. Ibid., p. 603.

97. Ibid., pp. 606–607.

98. Compare Charles Beitz, "Cosmopolitan Ideals and National Sentiment," *The Journal of Philosophy* 80:11 (November 1983): 598.

99. This is surely one of the more significant lessons provided by the U.S. sanctuary movement, which may be the most important source of civil disobedience since the civil rights movement of the 1960s. Having begun as a few individual churches whose members felt morally compelled to provide private asylum to those

fleeing persecution in Central America—but whom the United States refused to recognize as legitimate refugees—the movement now includes over 400 congregations, 22 cities, 3 states, and 12 colleges or universities, as well as thousands of individuals who have committed themselves to protecting the refugees from deportation.

100. *Congressional Globe* (July 4, 1870), p. 5155.

101. 130 U.S., p. 606.

102. 149 U.S. 698 (1893).

103. Ibid., p. 743 (Justice Brewer, dissenting).

104. Ibid., p. 754 (Justice Field, dissenting).

105. *Korematsu v. United States*, 323 U.S. 214 (1944).

106. *Harisiades v. Shaughnessy*, 342 U.S. 580, 597 (1952) (Justice Frankfurter, concurring).

107. See *Fiallo v. Bell*, 430 U.S. 787, 793 n. 5 (1977) ("Our cases reflect acceptance of a limited judicial responsibility even with respect to the power of Congress to regulate the admission and exclusion of aliens, and there is no occasion to consider in this case whether there may be actions of the Congress that are so essentially political in character as to be nonjusticiable.")

108. See *Jean v. Nelson*, 472 U.S. 846 (1985). The case involved a program that specially selected illegal Haitian entrants for detention pending deportation. It reached the Supreme Court after the 11th Circuit rejected the argument that the program constituted a violation of the "equal protection clause" of the Fourteenth Amendment, on the grounds that the government had "plenary power" to discriminate against excludable aliens. As Justice Marshall correctly noted in his special dissent, the Supreme Court avoided the constitutional issue presented by the 11th Circuit only by misreading—and thus limiting the scope of—the regulation that the government relied on to pursue its discriminatory detention program.

109. In 1975, for example, the Supreme Court refused to review a Court of Appeals decision that had upheld a "national origins" immigration classification discriminating against Mexican nationals. See *Dunn v. INS*, 499 F.2d 856 (9th Cir. 1974) *cert. denied* 419 U.S. 1106 (1975).

110. Walzer, *Spheres of Justice*, pp. 34–40.

111. Ibid., p. 40.

112. Ibid.

113. Thus, forty-seven Chinese entered the United States in 1853 (to that point an all-time high). But in 1854, according to official census figures, 13,100 entered. U.S. Department of Commerce, Bureau of the Census, *Historical Statistics of the United States: Colonial Times to 1970* (Washington, D.C.: Government Printing Office, 1975), vol. 1, p. 108 (Table C 89–119: "Immigrants, by Country, 1820–1870").

114. Ibid., p. 117 (Table C 228–295: "Foreign-Born Population, by Country of Birth, 1850–1870").

115. Ibid., pp. 106, 108 (Table C 89–119).

116. See Mary Roberts Coolidge, *Chinese Immigration* (New York: Henry Holt and Co., 1909; reprint ed. New York: Arno Books and The New York Times Co., 1969), p. 498.

117. See U.S. Department of Commerce, Bureau of the Census, *Historical Statistics*, p. 92 (Table C 15–24). According to the 1890 census, 117,386 "whites" and

208,083 "non-whites" were residing on Indian reservations. Clearly, the total American Indian population was considerably larger.

118. See Coolidge, *Chinese Immigration*, p. 345. Despite labor riots in 1866–1867 directed at the Chinese in California, "The Chinese were almost wholly engaged in occupations where there was the greatest scarcity of laborers."

119. The distinction between rights-based and preference-based components of the national interest is crucial if the United States is to develop a comprehensive immigration policy that reflects its deepest values. A simple example will help clarify the distinction. Consider the concern that U.S. citizens have, respectively, in protecting their physical security and in paying low prices for fruits and vegetables. A policy designed to protect or promote either of these goods could be said to be in *the* national interest if all that is meant is that the policy would satisfy the preferences of a significant number of citizens. There is a crucial difference, however, between the respective moral bases that underly these two kinds of interest. Hence there is a difference between the respective justifications of policies designed to protect or promote them. Policies that protect citizens' physical security are justified in terms of the basic right that persons have to be secure from physical assault. Policies designed to maintain low produce prices, on the other hand, cannot appeal to the basic right that persons have to low food prices because there simply is no such right.

To distinguish interests based on rights from those based on mere preferences is not to imply that the U.S. government is free to ignore the latter when determining national policy. The point is only that the distinction is morally relevant when the national interest is invoked to justify policy. Thus, an immigration policy that would put at significant risk the physical security of even a small number of U.S. citizens would probably be unjustifiable regardless of what other interests such a policy might favor, and regardless of how many persons favored that policy. But a policy that would lead to higher produce prices might well find justification in rights-based considerations that superceded the "national interest" in maintaining low prices, regardless of how many persons preferred them. (This would be the case, for example, if the low prices were the result of using slave labor.) In short, rights-based interests take priority over interests based on mere preferences. U.S. immigration policy cannot be automatically justified, therefore, by showing that it might enhance the aggregate well-being of Americans. At the very least a rationale for the policy would need to specify which interests were being served at what cost to which persons.

120. It is often assumed that both the number of migrants admitted *and* the terms of their admission ought to be determined by the same standard: U.S. economic interests. Admitting a large number of migrant workers can certainly be advantageous to the United States. Migrants can provide a supply of efficient labor for low-level and low-paying jobs, thus preserving threatened U.S. industries and the jobs of American workers in such industries, as well as holding down inflation and imports. On the safe assumption that a significant number of Americans would prefer these economic benefits, it would be in the national interest to adjust the flow of migrant workers according to whether or not the given number serves the aggregate of preferences. Furthermore, using U.S. economic interests to determine the number of migrant workers does not in itself violate moral principles that underlie the rights-based interests of Americans. Clearly, though, this conclusion is not the end of the

matter. For instance, an exclusionary policy might be directed only at guest workers with particular or racial characteristics, thus raising the issues addressed in this segment of the essay. Or certain racial or ethnic groups might be recruited for certain types of menial jobs on the theory that they are innately inferior to other migrants.

Obviously, such considerations *must* come into play when guest workers are discriminated against as a *class after entry.* The likelihood that they will be treated in such a manner must be taken into account in evaluating the morality of a particular immigration program.

121. "The individualistic premises of a liberal legal order, of course, did not lead ineluctably to a restrictive immigration policy and a conception of absolute sovereignty that utterly denied aliens' claims to legal protection. Liberalism, after all, does not merely confirm the primacy of individual consent as the bedrock of political and juridical relationships. *It also locates fundamental legal rights in individuals by reason of their universal humanity and without regard to contingencies of their status or condition"* (emphasis added). Schuck, "Transformation of Immigration Law," p. 7.

122. *Matthews v. Diaz,* 426 U.S. 67, 80 (1976).

123. For example, compare the Court's treatment of the rights of the fathers of "native" and "alien" illegitimate children in *Stanley v. Illinois,* 405 U.S. 645 (1972) and *Fiallo v. Bell,* 430 U.S. 787 (1977).

124. Schuck, "Transformation of Immigration Law," p. 1.

125. Louis Henkin, "The Constitution and United States Sovereignty: A Century of *Chinese Exclusion* and its Progeny," *Harvard Law Review* 100 (1987): 862–863.

126. Apparently Peter Schuck believes that *all* of American immigration law, including its racially discriminatory provisions, has embarked on a slow process of "transformation": "Social conditions and a changed legal consciousness have begun to undermine the foundations of classical immigration law. In its growing decrepitude, we can glimpse both the remnants of the individualistic legal order that once gave it life and legitimacy, and the outlines of the communitarian one that promises to transform it. The courts are busy razing the old structure and designing the new one, largely along the lines laid down by the contemporary administrative and constitutional orders. Immigration is gradually joining the mainstream of our public law" (Schuck, "Transformation of Immigration Law," p. 90).

We do not regard the evolution of American immigration law as something that can be adequately comprehended in the individualistic/communitarian dichotomy that Schuck elaborates. And we believe that if judges were construction workers, they would be fired for bringing the building project—assuming that one exists—to a virtual standstill. With these provisos, our response to Henkin is also a response to Schuck.

BIBLIOGRAPHY

Ackerman, Bruce. *Social Justice in the Liberal State.* New Haven, Conn.: Yale University Press, 1980.

Aleinikoff, T. Alexander, and David Martin. *Immigration: Process and Policy.* St. Paul, Minn.: West Publishing, 1985.

Anker, Deborah. "The Forty Year Crisis: A Legislative History of the Refugee Act of 1980." *San Diego Law Review* 19(1981): 9–89.

Beitz, Charles. "Cosmopolitan Ideals and National Sentiment." *The Journal of Philosophy* 80(1983).
———. *Political Theory and International Relations.* Princeton, N.J.: Princeton University Press, 1979.
Brown, Peter G. ". . . in the National Interest." In *Human Rights and U.S. Foreign Policy*, edited by Peter G. Brown and Douglas MacLean, pp. 161–171. Lexington, Mass.: Lexington Books, 1979.
Chinese Exclusion Case. 130 U.S. 581 (1889).
Coolidge, Mary Roberts. *Chinese Immigration.* New York: Henry Holt and Co., 1909. Reprint, New York: Arno Books and the New York Times Co., 1969.
Doppelt, Gerald. "Walzer's Theory of Morality in International Relations." *Philosophy and Public Affairs* 8(1978): 3–25.
Dunn v. INS. 499 F.2d 856 (9th Cir. 1974) *cert. denied* 419 U.S. 1106 (1975).
Fauriol, Georges. "U.S. Immigration Policy and the National Interest." In *The Problem of Immigration*, edited by Steven Anzovin, pp. 96–116. New York: H. W. Wilson Co., 1985.
Fiallo v. Bell. 430 U.S. 787 (1977).
Fong Yue Ting v. United States. 149 U.S. 698 (1893).
Galvan v. Press. 347 U.S. 522 (1954).
Geertz, Clifford. "Ideology as a Cultural System." In *Ideology and Discontent*, edited by David E. Apter, pp. 47–76. New York: Free Press, 1964.
Gramasci, Antonio. "The Intellectuals" and "The Modern Prince." In *Selections from the Prison Notebooks*, edited by Q. Hoare and G. N. Smith. New York: International Publishers, 1971.
Harisiades v. Shaughnessy. 342 U.S. 580 (1952).
The Head Money Cases. 112 U.S. 580 (1884).
Henderson, W. O., and W. H. Chaloner. *Conditions of the Working Class in England.* Stanford, Calif.: Stanford University Press, 1968.
Henkin, Louis. "The Constitution and United States Sovereignty: A Century of *Chinese Exclusion* and its Progeny." *Harvard Law Review* 100(1987): 853–856.
Higham, John. *Strangers in the Land: Patterns of American Nativism.* New Brunswick, N.J.: Rutgers University Press, 1955.
Hobbes, Thomas. *The Elements of Law*, 2d ed. Edited by Ferdinand Tonnies. New York: Frank Cass and Company, Ltd., 1969.
———. *Leviathan.* New York: E. P. Dutton, 1950.
Hoffman, Stanley. *Duties beyond Borders.* Syracuse, N.Y.: Syracuse University Press, 1981.
Holborn, Louise. "The League of Nations and the Refugee Problem." *The Annals of the American Academy of Political and Social Science* 203 (May 1939): 124–135.
Hutchinson, Edward P. *Legislative History of American Immigration Policy, 1798–1965.* Philadelphia: University of Pennsylvania Press, 1981.
INS v. Stevic. 467 U.S. 407 (1984).
Jean v. Nelson. 727 F.2d 957 (11th Cir.), *aff'd on other grounds*, 472 U.S. 486 (1985).
Keohane, Robert O. *After Hegemony: Cooperation and Discord in the World Political Economy.* Princeton, N.J.: Princeton University Press, 1984.

————, and Joseph Nye, eds. *Transnational Relations and World Politics*. Cambridge, Mass.: Harvard University Press, 1972.

Kleindiest v. Mandel. 408 U.S. 753 (1972).

Knauff v. Shaugnessy. 338 U.S. 537 (1950).

Korematsu v. United States. 323 U.S. 214 (1944).

Landon v. Plasencia. 459 U.S. 21 (1982).

Leonard, Herman, and Richard Zeckhauser. "Cost-Benefit Analysis Applied to Risks: Its Philosophy and Legitimacy." Working Paper. College Park: University of Maryland, Center for Philosophy and Public Policy, June 1983.

Lichtenberg, Judith. "Mexican Immigration and U.S. Policy: A Guide for the Perplexed." In *The Border That Joins: Mexican Migrants and U.S. Responsibility*, edited by Peter Brown and Henry Shue, pp. 13–30. Totowa, N.J.: Rowman and Littlefield, 1983.

Loescher, Gilburt, and John Scanlan. *Calculated Kindness: Refugees and America's Half-Open Door, 1945–Present*. New York: Free Press, 1986.

————. "Human Rights, Power Politics, and the International Refugee Regime: The Case of U.S. Treatment of Caribbean Basin Refugees," World Order Studies Program Occasional Paper No. 14. Princeton, N.J.: Center of International Studies, Princeton University, 1985.

Matter of Dunar. 14 I&N Dec. 310 (1973).

Mathews v. Diaz. 426 U.S. 67 (1976).

Nardin, Terry. *Law, Morality, and the Relations of States*. Princeton, N.J.: Princeton University Press, 1983.

Narenji v. Civiletti. 617 F.2d 745 (D.C. Cir. 1979).

The Passenger Cases. 48 U.S. (7 How.) 283 (1849).

Reagan, Ronald. "Acceptance Speech." Detroit, Michigan, July 17, 1980, reported in the *New York Times*, July 18, 1980, p. 8.

Rivera, Mario. "Cuban and Haitian Influxes of 1980 and the American Response: Retrospect and Prospect." U.S. Congress, House, *Oversight Hearing: Caribbean Migration*, Appendix 4. Washington, D.C.: Government Printing Office, 1980.

Samora, Julian. *Los Mojados: The Wetback Story*. Notre Dame, Ind.: University of Notre Dame Press, 1971.

Saxton, Alexander. *The Indispensable Enemy: Labor and the Anti-Chinese Movement in California*. Berkeley: University of California Press, 1971.

Scanlan, John. "Immigration Law and the Illusion of Numerical Control." *University of Miami Law Review* 36(1982): 819–864.

————, and Gilburt Loescher. "U.S. Foreign Policy, 1959–1980: Impact on Refugee Flow from Cuba." In *The Annals of the American Academy of Political Science*, pp. 116–137. Gilburt Loescher and John Scanlan, special eds. Beverly Hills, Calif.: Sage, 1983.

Schuck, Peter. "The Transformation of Immigration Law." *Columbia Law Review* 84(1984): 1–90.

————, and Rogers Smith. *Citizenship Without Consent: Illegal Aliens in the American Polity*. New Haven, Conn.: Yale University Press, 1985.

Shaughnessy v. Mezei. 345 U.S. 206 (1953).

Shue, Henry. "The Burdens of Justice." *The Journal of Philosophy* 80(1983).

Stanley v. Illinois. 405 U.S. 645 (1972).

Truman, David. *The Governmental Process*. New York: Alfred A. Knopf, 1963.

U.S. Congress, Senate, *Review of U.S. Refugee Resettlement Programs and Policies* 96th Cong., 2nd Sess., 1980.

U.S. Department of Commerce, Bureau of the Census. *Historical Statistics of the United States: Colonial Times to 1970*. Washington, D.C.: Government Printing Office, 1975.

Walzer, Michael. *Just and Unjust Wars*. New York: Basic Books, 1977.

———. *Spheres of Justice: A Defense of Pluralism and Equality*. New York: Basic Books, 1983.

Woody v. INS. 385 U.S. 276 (1966).

Wyman, David. *Paper Walls: America and the Refugee Crisis, 1938–41*. Amherst: University of Massachusetts Press, 1968.

Yergin, Daniel. *Shattered Peace: The Origins of the Cold War and the National Security State*. Boston: Hougton Mifflin Co., 1977.

PART II

REFUGEE ADMISSION

4

The Ethics of Refugee Policy

Peter and Renata Singer

THE SHELTER

It is February 1998 and the world is taking stock of the damage done by the brief nuclear exchange between the United States and the Soviet Union at the close of the previous year. Although a belated outbreak of sanity on both sides stopped hostilities before more than a few warheads had been detonated, the level of radioactivity now and for about eight years to come is so high that only those living in fallout shelters can be confident of surviving in reasonable health. For the rest, who must breathe unfiltered air and consume food and water with high levels of radiation, the prospects are grim. Probably 10 percent will die of radiation sickness within the next two months; another 30 percent are expected to develop fatal forms of cancer within five years; and the remainder will have rates of cancer ten times higher than normal, while the risk that their children will be malformed is fifty times greater than before the war.

The fortunate ones, of course, are those who were far-sighted enough to buy shares in the fallout shelters built by real estate speculators in the early 1990s. Most of these shelters were designed as underground villages, each with enough accommodation and supplies to provide for the needs of 10,000 people for twenty years. The villages are self-governing, with democratic constitutions that were agreed to in advance. They also have sophisticated security systems, which enable them to admit to the shelter whoever they decide to admit and keep out all others.

The news that it will not be necessary to stay in the shelters for much more than eight years has naturally been greeted with joy by the members of an underground community called Fairhaven. But it has also led to the first serious friction among them. For above the shaft that leads down to Fairhaven, there are thousands of people who are not investors in a shelter. These people can be seen, and heard, through television cameras installed at the entrance. They are pleading to be admitted. They know that if they can get into a shelter quickly, they will escape most of the consequences of exposure to radiation. Yet at first, before it was known how long it would be until it was safe to return to the outside, these pleas had virtually no support from within the shelter. Now, however, the case for admitting at least some of them has become much stronger. Since the supplies need last only eight years—or even if we are conservative, certainly no more than ten—they will stretch to three or four times the number of people presently in the shelters. Accommodation presents only slightly greater problems: Fairhaven was designed to function as a luxury retreat when not needed for a real emergency, and it is equipped with tennis courts, swimming pools, and a large gymnasium. If everyone were to consent to keep fit by doing aerobics in their own living rooms, it would be possible to provide primitive but adequate sleeping space for all those whom the supplies can stretch to feed.

So those outside now do not lack advocates on the inside. The most extreme, labeled "bleeding hearts" by their opponents, propose that the shelter should admit an additional 10,000 people, as many as it can reasonably expect to feed and house until it is safe to return to the outside. This will mean giving up all luxury in food and facilities, but the bleeding hearts point out that the fate for those who remain on the outside will be far worse.

The bleeding hearts are opposed by some who urge that these outsiders generally are inferior people, for they were either not sufficiently far-sighted or not sufficiently wealthy to invest in a shelter; hence, it is said, they will cause social problems in the shelter, placing an additional strain on health, welfare, and educational services, and contributing to an increase in crime and juvenile delinquency. The opposition to admitting outsiders is also supported by a small group of philosophically trained members of the community who say that it would be an injustice to those who have paid for their share of the shelter if others who have not paid their share benefit by it. These opponents of admitting others are articulate, but few; their numbers are bolstered considerably, however, by many who say only that they really enjoy tennis and swimming and don't want to give them up.

Between the bleeding hearts and those who oppose admitting any outsiders stands a middle group: those who think that, as an exceptional act of benevolence and charity, some outsiders should be admitted, but not so many as to make a significant difference to the quality of life within the shelter. They propose converting one of the five tennis courts to sleeping accommodations and giving up a small public open space which has attracted little use anyway. By these means, an extra 500 people could be accommodated, which the self-styled "moderates" think would be a sensible figure, sufficient to show that Fairhaven is not insensitive to the plight of those less fortunate than its own members.

A referendum is held. There are three proposals: to admit 10,000 outsiders; to admit 500 outsiders; and to admit no outsiders. For which would you vote?

THE REAL WORLD

The United Nations High Commission for Refugees (UNHCR) estimates that there are at least 10 million refugees in the world today.[1] The great majority of these refugees are receiving refuge, at least temporarily, in the poorer and less developed countries of the world. For instance, in 1988 Pakistan and Iran together host nearly 5 million Afghan refugees. More than half the nations of Africa harbor refugees, the greatest number being of Ethiopian origin and concentrated in the Horn (Djibouti, Ethiopia, and Somalia) and Sudan. There are also refugees from Uganda, South Africa, Chad, Mozambique (over 200,000 in recent months and increasing) and from Zaire. In Central America there are thought to be 2 million refugees, though only about 120,000 benefit from UNHCR assistance. The refugees include Guatemalans, Nicaraguans, and Salvadorans and are mostly in Mexico, Honduras, and Costa Rica.

What is the effect on a country like Pakistan of receiving a sudden influx of 2.8 million Afghan refugees, mainly in the North West Frontier province? Pakistan does get some outside assistance: the World Food Program provided 370,000 tons of food for refugees in Pakistan during 1986. Nevertheless, the effects on Pakistan of bearing the burden of the world's largest refugee population for the last seven years can be seen in the deterioration of the area surrounding refugee villages. Whole hillsides are being denuded of trees as a result of the collection of wood for fuel for the refugees.

The claim of refugees to protection is enshrined in the 1948 United Nations Declaration of Human Rights. Article 14 of the declaration states that "everyone has the right to seek and to enjoy in other countries asylum from persecution." The United Nations High Commission for Refugees was established in 1950 and the Commissioner entrusted with the protection of "any person who is outside the country of his nationality because of a well founded fear of persecution by reason of his race, religion, nationality or political opinion, and is unwilling or unable to avail himself of the protection of his own government."

This definition was originally designed to meet the dislocation caused by World War II in Europe. It is a narrow one, demanding that claims to refugee status be investigated case by case. It has failed to cover the large-scale movements of people in times of war, famine, or civil disturbance that have occurred since. So there are two categories of refugees: those strictly defined on a case-by-case basis who come under the U.N. definition, and the other, large groups of people who flee from their country of origin. Only the former are conceded the right of asylum.

Governments are generally reluctant to recognize large groups of people as refugees because they will then come under pressure to accept them for resettlement or to find places for them elsewhere. But governments are also reluctant to define certain groups of people as refugees for more directly political reasons. The same international disorder that makes people refugees also prevents their recognition as refugees, for the statement that people face persecution in their own country implies criticism of that country, and most countries are slow to criticize allies, particularly when their own support of those allies has contributed to the suffering of the refugees. So, for example, it will be difficult for the United States to grant refugee status to large numbers of people from El Salvador when it is committed to supporting the government there.

The less generous response to refugees in recent years, at a time when some Western economies have moved into recession, is usually justified by blaming the victim. Thus it has become common to distinguish "genuine refugees" from "economic refugees" and to claim that the latter should receive no assistance. This distinction is dubious, for most refugees leave their countries at great risk and peril to their lives, crossing seas in leaky boats under attack from pirates, or making long journeys over armed borders, to arrive penniless in refugee camps. To distinguish, in meeting the need for protection, refuge, food, and resettlement, between someone fleeing from political persecution and someone who flees from a land made unin- habitable by prolonged drought is difficult to justify, although the latter person would not be classified as a refugee under the U.N. definition.

What are the possible durable solutions for refugees in the world today? The main options are: voluntary repatriation, local integration in the country to which they first flee, and resettlement.

Probably the best and most humane solution for refugees would be to return home. Unfortunately for the majority voluntary repatriation is not possible, because the conditions that caused them to flee have not changed sufficiently. As wars last longer and longer, voluntary repatriation is a realistic alternative for only a few refugees. Recently refugees have returned to Uruguay and Argentina and to Uganda with changes of government in these countries. But elsewhere, for instance for Palestinians, the hope of voluntary repatriation—the option probably most desired by the world's refugees—is coming no closer to being realized.

Local settlement, where refugees can remain and rebuild their lives in neighboring countries, is too often impossible because of the inability of poor, economically struggling—and politically unstable—countries to absorb a new population when their indigenous people face a daily struggle for survival. This option works best where ethnic and tribal links cross national frontiers.

The difficulty of achieving either voluntary repatriation or local settlement leaves resettlement in a more remote country as the only remaining option. The number of refugees in need of resettlement has reached dimensions that have never before been experienced. The main response of the industrialized countries has been to institute deterrent policies and close their doors as tightly as they can. Admittedly, resettlement can never solve the problems that make refugees leave their homes, nor can it solve the world refugee problem. Only about 2 percent of the world's refugees are permanently resettled. Resettlement nevertheless provides markedly better lives for a significant number of individuals, and it affects the policies of those countries to which refugees first flee. If such countries have no hope that refugees will be resettled, they know that their burden will grow with every refugee who enters their country. As we have seen, most of the countries of first refuge are among those least able to support additional people.

When the resettlement option tightens, the countries to which refugees first go, like Thailand, adopt policies to try to discourage potential refugees from leaving their country. This policy will include turning people back at the border, making camps as unattractive as possible, and screening the refugees as they cross the border. In Thailand Cambodian refugees who make their way across the border are classified as illegal aliens. They are put in border camps where they cannot be interviewed by foreign delegations, and the camps are closed with limited services and little future for their children. (Such closed camps also exist in Hong Kong, where they are administered by the Correctional Services Department and built like prisons, holding up to 200 people in each cell block, including women and children.) So some refugees flee from one "concentration" camp to another. They leave their countries because conditions are intolerable but in such large numbers that the international community is not prepared to resettle them. Because resettlement is not an option, most of the countries to which they come treat them in such a way as to discourage others from coming.

Resettlement is the only solution for those who cannot return to their own countries in the foreseeable future and are only welcome temporarily in the country to which they have fled; in other words for those who have nowhere to go. There are millions who would choose this option if there were countries who would take them. For these refugees, resettlement may mean the difference between life and death. It certainly is their only hope for a decent existence.

The "Ex Gratia" Approach

In 1980 the United States Congress passed the Refugee Act, which has set the legal framework for United States government action on refugees since then. The act requires the president to stipulate in advance the number of refugees to be admitted in a year and to divide this number among different geographical regions. But these figures are ceilings, not goals. As the Office of the U.S. Coordinator for Refugee Affairs has put it, "the underlying principle is that refugee admissions is an exceptional *ex gratia* act provided by the United States in furthering foreign and humanitarian policies."[2]

In keeping with this principle, the U.S. administration has frequently admitted many fewer refugees than the total authorized by Congress. For example, in 1982, the Reagan administration was authorized to admit 140,000 refugees, but actually accepted only 99,200. For 1983, the administration submitted a reduced ceiling of 98,000, but actually took only 73,651.

The Coordinator's statement undoubtedly expresses a widely held attitude to refugees. The attitude is that as a nation we are under no moral or legal obligation to accept any refugees at all, and if we do accept some, it is an indication of our generous and humanitarian character. Popular as this view may be, however, it is not self-evidently morally sound. Indeed, it appears to conflict with other attitudes that are, if we can judge from what people say, at least as widely held. This is the belief in the equality of all human beings and the rejection of principles that discriminate on the basis of race or national origin. For whereas all developed nations safeguard the welfare of their residents in many ways—protecting their legal rights, educating their children, and providing social security payments and access to medical care, either universally or for those who fall below a defined level of poverty—refugees receive none of these benefits unless they are accepted into the country. Since the overwhelming majority of them are not accepted, the overwhelming majority will not receive these benefits on the grounds that they are not residents of the countries that provide them to residents. But is this distinction in the way in which we treat residents and nonresidents compatible with our professed belief in the equality of all human beings?

Of course not only refugees suffer from the way we draw our moral boundaries around our national residents. Our moral attitude to foreign aid for humanitarian purposes is in many ways parallel to our attitude to accepting refugees. Though people may be starving to death in Cambodia or Ethiopia, we persist in thinking of foreign aid as a "charity," which means that we do well if we give it, but we are not subject to blame or reproach if we do not.

We see ourselves as under no obligation to save the starving of Africa or Asia, even if doing so would entail no real sacrifices at all.[3]

Some writers on topics in ethics avoid the need to justify our very different treatment of residents and nonresidents by the simple expedient of ignoring the problem. They frame their discussion in terms of how members of a community should treat each other, and overlook the fact that the majority of our fellow human beings are not members of our community. The most notable example is John Rawls, whose book, A Theory of Justice, has been the most widely discussed account of justice since its publication in 1971.[4] Among the set of principles of justice that Rawls proposes is what is known as "the difference principle." This states that inequalities in basic goods such as income are justified only if they are gained under conditions of equal opportunity, and only if they work out to the advantage of the least well-off group. Thus, it would be justifiable to pay doctors more than typists only if everyone has an equal opportunity to become a doctor, and if paying doctors more is beneficial to the worst-off group, perhaps because in this way better people are attracted to medicine, and the worst-off get better medical care than they would if there were no salary differential.

Just how much change it would take to apply Rawls' principles of justice *within* a society like the United States is open to debate; Rawls' account has been seen by some as a defense of a capitalist system, with an emphasis on equal opportunity and a justification of differences of income on the ground that they are to the advantage of all. But there can be no debate at all about the fact that to apply Rawls' principles of justice *across* different societies would require the most radical changes in the world order. The "worst-off group" would then be the poor and destitute of the Third World, including most of the 10 million refugees. All of these people are deliberately excluded by the immigration laws of the developed countries from competing under conditions of equal opportunity for a place among the better off, that is, the residents of the developed countries. Indeed, the immigration laws of developed countries effectively confer on their residents the benefits of membership in the better-off group, without giving the worst-off group any opportunity at all—never mind *equal* opportunity—to be among the better-off.

In sharp contrast to Rawls, who can write a 500-page treatise on justice without seeing the need to justify his restriction of scope to a single community, Michael Walzer opens his Spheres of Justice with a chapter entitled "The Distribution of Membership" in which—before he even begins to discuss principles of justice in the distribution of goods—he asks how we constitute the community within which distribution takes place. In the course of this chapter Walzer seeks to justify something close to the present situation with regard to refugee policy. His arguments are perhaps the most sophisticated recent attempt to defend current immigration policy on ethical grounds and therefore merit detailed examination.[5]

The first question Walzer addresses is: Do countries have the right to close their borders to potential immigrants? His answer is based on the claim that without such closure, at least the power to close borders if desired, distinct communities cannot exist:

The distinctiveness of cultures and groups depends upon closure and cannot be conceived as a stable feature of human life without it. If this distinctiveness is a value, as most people (though some of them are global pluralists and others only local loyalists) seem to believe—more strongly, if individuals have a right to form distinct and stable communities—then closure must be permitted somewhere. At some level of political organization something like the sovereign state must take shape and claim the authority to make its own admissions policy, to control and sometimes to restrain the flow of immigrants.[6]

Given that the decision to close borders can rightfully be made on this basis, Walzer then goes on to consider how it should be exercised. He compares the political community with a club and a family. Clubs are examples of the *ex gratia* approach: "Individuals may be able to give good reason why they should be selected, but no one on the outside has a right to be inside."[7] Walzer therefore considers the possibility that the states are like clubs with sovereign power over the selection of their members. But he considers the analogy imperfect: "Clearly, citizens often believe themselves morally bound to open the doors of their country—not to anyone who wants to come in, perhaps, but to a particular group of outsiders, recognized as national or ethnic 'relatives.' In this sense, states are like families rather than clubs, for it is a feature of families that their members are morally connected to people they have not chosen, who live outside the household."[8]

Walzer uses the analogy of a family to justify the principle of family reunion as a basis for immigration policy, and he also argues that where a community represents a particular national or ethnic group, outsiders of the same national group have a legitimate expectation of being taken in when they are persecuted in the land where they live. Thus after World War II, both East and West Germany had special obligations to take in German refugees expelled from Poland and Czechoslovakia; and Greeks in Turkey, and Turks in Greece, had a claim to be accepted by the country of their nationality when they were unable to stay where they were.

Then Walzer asks the crucial question: Can a political community exclude destitute and hungry, persecuted and stateless—in a word, necessitous—men and women simply because they are foreigners? Walzer makes the assumption that there is no formal obligation to accept outsiders. So in his view the community is bound by nothing stronger than the principle of mutual aid; he rightly notes, however, that this principle may have wider effects when applied to a community than when applied to an individual, because so many benevolent actions are open to a community which will only marginally affect its members. To take a stranger into one's family is something that we might consider goes beyond the requirement of mutual aid; but to take a stranger, or even many strangers, into the community is far less burdensome.

In Walzer's view, a nation with vast unoccupied lands—he takes Australia as his example, though by assumption rather than by any examination of the relevant facts—may indeed have an obligation in mutual aid to take in people from densely populated, famine-stricken lands of Southeast Asia. The choice for the Australian community would then be to give up whatever homogeneity their society possessed, or to retreat to a small portion of the land they occupied, yielding the remainder to those who needed it.[9]

Walzer treats political refugees as a special case, arguing that our obligations depend on political affinity, a kind of analogue of ethnic affinity. So in the context of the Cold War, Britain and the United States (and presumably Australia, too) had a particular obligation to take in Vietnamese refugees, since they had helped to create the situation that gave them a need for refuge. But in the absence of any sense of political affinity to which refugees can appeal, Walzer says, "they may well have no right to be successful."[10]

Walzer is ready to admit that his argument does not "suggest any way of dealing with the vast numbers of refugees generated by twentieth century politics."[11] Instead of exploring this problem further, however, he switches the discussion to the separate topic of asylum, saying:

The cruelty of this dilemma is mitigated to some degree by the principle of asylum. Any refugee who has actually made his escape, who is not seeking but has found (at least a temporary) refuge can claim asylum . . . and then he cannot be deported so long as the only available country to which he might be sent "is one to which he is unwilling to go owing to well-founded fear of being persecuted for reasons of race, religion, nationality . . . or political opinion."[12]

Ethiopian refugees living in the Sudan would no doubt find little mitigation of the cruelty of this situation in this principle; and they would surely wonder why if, by some miracle, they could set foot on the shores of a country like the United States, they would be entitled to jump the queue over their compatriots who had been patiently waiting for years for the chance of a place. Walzer is aware of the puzzle here, but can only say; "We seem bound to grant asylum for two reasons: because its denial would require us to use force against helpless and desperate people, and because the numbers likely to be involved, except in unusual cases, are small and the people easily absorbed (so we would be using force for "things superflous"). But if we offered a refuge to everyone in the world who could plausibly say that he needed it, we might be overwhelmed."[13]

Neither of these grounds is satisfactory. The first appeals to a dubious distinction between using force in the form of forcibly expelling someone from one's territory, and passively leaving them in a situation where they are in danger of persecution when one could grant them permission to come to one's territory. The distinction appears to be a variant of the act/omission distinction, much discussed—and much criticized—in other contexts, especially medical ethics. In our view the critics have demonstrated that the distinction between acts and omissions has no intrinsic significance.[14] When countries like the United States denied permits to Jews in Nazi Germany, they were just as surely consigning them to persecution—and as it turned out, often to death—as they would have been if they had deported a German Jew who had reached America and sought asylum. If there is any difference at all in the two cases, it lies in the symbolic significance of using force against an identifiable, harmless individual. We may rightly react strongly against the kind of callousness, which can force people to go back to situations of great danger, but we should also react strongly against the kind of callousness which can leave people in such situations. If we take satisfaction in being too humane to deport someone seeking asylum while we continue to reject all applications from those in similar situations who have not made it to our shores, we are being hypocritical.

The second reason offered for preferring the claims of those seeking asylum to the claims of refugees is equally spurious. Walzer contrasts the relatively small numbers likely to be seeking asylum with the enormous numbers of refugees, but why is this the relevant contrast? Why should it be assumed that if we are to say that there is an obligation to take some refugees, we must say that there is an obligation to take all of them? Walzer's argument implies that if we are prepared to take, say, 10,000 people in need of a place to live, we should take *all* those seeking asylum—let us assume there are 5,000 of them—and only then take refugees to fill the remaining places? Why not just take the 10,000 neediest people? This does not, of course, answer the question of how many people in need a country *should* take. That certainly is the real issue, and though it cannot be given a precise answer in the absence of detailed information about the needs of the refugees and the capacities of a given country, we shall try to say something about it in the remainder of this essay. One thing we can say in advance of that discussion, however, is that there is nothing to be gained by dividing the total group of people in need into two groups—those who have reached our shores and those who have not—and then assuming that with each group it is an all-or-nothing matter: either we have an obligation to take all of them, or we have no obligation to take any of them.

The fallacy involved in this argument is illuminating, because people are prone to make it in many fields. For example, when approached to contribute to an appeal for famine relief, some people say (and even more think) that there is no point in contributing, because the problem is so vast that anything they can give will be "drops in the ocean." What they forget is that, wonderful as it would be to save *all* the victims of famine, famine is not an all-or-nothing thing. The victims of famine are individual human beings, and it is better to help one than none, better to help 10,001 than 10,000, and 1,000,001 than 1,000,000. Because this erroneous manner of reasoning is so often implicit in the refugee debate, and we shall have occasion to discuss it again, we shall call it "the all-or-nothing fallacy."

When we look over Walzer's conclusions as a whole, we find a striking match between what he recommends and what moderately liberal governments, prepared to heed at least some humanitarian sentiments, actually do. For Walzer, as for the United States government, communities have a right to decide whom they will admit; the claims of family reunion come first, and those of outsiders from the national ethnic group—should the state have an ethnic identity—next. The admission of those in need is an *ex gratia* act. The right of asylum can be respected, because the numbers are relatively small anyway, and are considered on a case-by-case basis. Refugees, unless they can appeal to some special sense of political affinity, have no real claim to be accepted and have to throw themselves on the charity of the receiving country. All this is in general agreement with immigration policy in the United States, Australia, and many other Western democracies. As far as refugees are concerned, the *ex gratia* approach is the current orthodoxy.

The current orthodoxy, as Walzer's defense of it indicates, is based on a view of rights in which the primary right is the right of the community to determine its own membership. A different view of rights, in which priority is given to the equal right of all people to the basic necessities of life, could lead to a radically different view of our obligations to refugees.[15] But we do not intend to pursue the possible theories of rights that could be deployed for or against the *ex gratia* approach. The appeal to rights generally turns out to be little more than an appeal to the moral intuitions of the author, dressed up in the language of rights so as to carry more weight. The arguments we have been considering provide another illustration of this generalization, already often noted in other contexts.[16] Walzer offers no underlying theory for his assertion that the right of a community to determine its membership takes priority over the rights of refugees. The view is a bare assertion, advanced with the assurance of one who finds it sitting happily with what he (and, he confidently believes, his readers) will take to be right. It is no coincidence that those who argue in this manner rarely reach conclusions which depart radically from the current orthodoxy.

The Obligation to Accept Refugees

In contrast to the rights-based arguments discussed so far, we hold that immigration policy in general, and refugee intake in particular, should be based on the interests of all those affected, either directly or indirectly, whether as an immediate result of the policy, or in the long run. Where the interests of different parties conflict, we would attempt to give equal consideration to all interests, which would mean that more pressing or more fundamental interests take precedence over those less pressing or fundamental.

There is nothing novel about approaching a social issue in this way. Nearly a hundred years ago, the great Victorian utilitarian Henry Sidgwick wrote in *The Elements of Politics*, "I shall take the happiness of the persons affected as the ultimate end and standard of right and wrong in determining the functions and constitution of government."[17] The important point, for our purposes, is that Sidgwick thought that the happiness *of the persons affected* should be the standard. He explicitly noted that his statement included both the happiness of persons who are not actually living now, but will live in the future, and he also accepted that "there are cases in which it is the duty of the members of one political society to make sacrifices for the good or welfare of other sections of the human race."[18]

The principle of equal consideration of interests is basic to classical utilitarianism, which recognizes only one interest, the interest in experiencing pleasure and the avoidance of pain. In keeping with modern versions of utilitarianism, we shall leave the meaning of "interests" unrestricted. It can be argued that the principle of equal consideration of interests is derivable from the principle of universalizability—"putting yourself in the shoes of the others affected by your decision"—and that no judgment can count as ethical unless it is universalizable.[19] But there is no need for us to enter into these questions here. The principle of equal consideration of interests is in any case a plausible basic moral principle and the most fundamental form of the principle of equality. That is grounds enough for seeing what follows from it in the field of refugee policy.

Familiar as the principle of equal consideration of interests is, its application to the situation of refugees involves a striking contrast to the current orthodoxy, which in effect gives the interests of present residents priority over those of refugees and other outsiders. (We have said "in effect" because it is not clear that the current orthodoxy is based on a consideration of interests at all. As already noted, it is more naturally defended on the basis of rights. But *if* one were to attempt to defend it on the basis of interests, it could only be by giving the interests of residents a strong, indeed virtually absolute, priority.)

The first step in applying the principle of equal consideration of interests is to identify those whose interests are affected. The first and most obvious group is the refugees themselves. Their most pressing and fundamental interests are clearly at stake. Life in a refugee camp offers little prospect of anything more than a bare subsistence, and sometimes hardly even that. Here is one observer's impression of a camp on the Thai-Cambodian border which is home for 144,000 people:

The visit of a foreigner causes a ripple of excitement. People gather round and ask earnestly about the progress of their case for resettlement, or share their great despair at continual rejection by the selection bodies for the various countries which will accept refugees. . . . People wept as they spoke, most had an air of quiet desperation. . . . On rice distribution day, thousands of girls and women mill in the distribution area, receiving the weekly rations for their family. From the bamboo observation tower the ground below was just a swirling sea of black hair and bags of rice hoisted onto heads for the walk home. A proud, largely farming people, forced to become dependent on UN rations of water, tinned fish and broken rice, just to survive.

Thousands upon thousands of people are living in the world today in such circumstances of dependency and uncertainty. Each day blurring into the next—same place, same faces, same absence of work, same rations. Yes, people do survive, but that is all.

Most of these people could hope for no significant change in their lives for many years to come. Yet I, along with the others from outside, could get into a car and drive out of the camp, return to Taphraya or Aran, drink iced water, eat rice or noodles at the roadside restaurant at the corner, and observe life passing by. Those simplest parts of life were invested with a freedom I'd never valued so highly.[20]

On the other hand, refugees accepted into another country have a good chance of establishing themselves and leading a life as satisfactory and fulfilling as most of us. In some cases, then, the interests of the refugees in being accepted are as basic as the interest in life itself. In other cases the situation may not be one of life or death, but it will still profoundly affect the whole course of a person's life.

The next most directly affected group is the residents of the recipient nation. How much they will be affected will vary according to how many refugees are taken, how well they will fit into the community, the current state of the national economy, and so on. Moreover, some residents will be more affected than others: some will find themselves competing with the refugees for jobs, and others will not; some will find themselves in a neighborhood with a high population of refugees, and others will not; and this list could be continued indefinitely, too. Of course, we should not assume that residents of the recipient nation will be affected for the worse: the economy may receive a boost from a substantial intake of refugees, and many residents may find business opportunities in providing for their needs. Others may enjoy the more cosmopolitan atmosphere created by new arrivals from other countries: the exotic food shops and restaurants that spring up, and in the long run, the benefits of different ideas and ways of living.

There is little or no information on the specific economic effects of taking in refugees, but there is information on the effects of immigration in general. A recent Australian study found that immigrants improve the job prospects of unemployed Australians and increase economic growth rates. It found no evidence that immigrants take jobs from Australian workers.[21] The Australian government clearly believes that more people are good for the economy as it has shown by announcing in December 1986 that it will increase the 1986–

1987 total immigration intake from the originally planned 95,000 to 115,000, with further increases in the intake planned in 1987–1988.

We cannot, of course, assume that findings about the economic effects of immigration in general will apply to refugees in particular. Yet one could argue that in many ways refugees make the best immigrants. They have nowhere else to go and must commit themselves totally to their new country, unlike immigrants who can go home when or if they please. The fact that they have survived and escaped from circumstances that most people have never been taxed with might suggest stamina, initiative, and resources that would be of great benefit to any receiving country. Certainly some refugee groups, for instance the Indochinese, have displayed great entrepreneurial vigor when resettled in countries like Australia or the United States.

In considering the effects of a large intake of refugees on the receiving nation, we must not neglect environmental effects. Walzer's reference to "the great empty spaces" of Australia would provoke an instant hostile response from Australians concerned about the preservation of the wilderness. These spaces are not "empty"; they are the sole remaining habitat of countless plants and animals, many of them found nowhere outside the Australian continent. To describe them as empty is to refuse to allow independent value to anything nonhuman, and we do not believe that such a refusal is defensible. In terms of equal consideration of interests, the pressure of increased population on the natural environment may affect the interests of the present population, who will have reduced opportunities for wilderness experience and for recreation in uncrowded areas. It may affect the interests of future generations, who could inherit an environment that is irreversibly damaged by the collapse of fragile ecosystems. Most directly, it will affect all those animals who are not human, but still have interests, and will probably starve to death if bulldozers destroy their habitat so that humans can make use of it.[22]

We believe that this covers the major categories of those directly afffected by refugee policy; but there are also some other *possible* and more diffuse consequences, which we at least need to think about. For example, it has been argued that to take large numbers of refugees from poor countries into affluent ones will simply encourage the flow of refugees in the future. Moreover, if poor and overpopulated countries can get rid of their surplus people to other countries, they will have a reduced incentive to do something about the root causes of the poverty of their people, and to slow population growth. Using a metaphor applied by Garrett Hardin to the issue of overseas aid, but perhaps also applicable to the refugee issue, one could say that the affluent nations are like lifeboats adrift in a sea of drowning people: if they try to pick them all up, the lifeboats will be swamped and everyone will drown. "Lifeboat ethics," Hardin would say, requires us to preserve our own margin of safety and beat off the hordes clamoring for room in our boat.

(In considering what happens to refugees at sea, lifeboat ethics becomes more than a metaphor.)

Consequences also arise from *not* taking significant numbers of refugees. Economic stability and world peace depend on international cooperation based on some measure of respect and trust; but the resource-rich and not overpopulated countries of the world cannot expect to win the respect or trust of the poorest and most crowded countries if they leave them to cope with most of the refugee problem as best they can. The effects of this can most clearly be seen on a regional basis. The United States has placed restrictions on acceptance of Central and South American refugees, leading to a deterioration in relations with other countries in the region. Similarly in Southeast Asia, Australia's strategically and economically important relations with Thailand and Malaysia have been strained by Australia's reluctance to accept large numbers of refugees from camps in those countries.

So we have a complex mix of interests—some definite, some highly speculative—to be considered. Equal interests are to be given equal weight, but which way does the balance lie? It may seem that the interests are so diverse that it is virtually impossible to reach a well-grounded decision. We will now show that this is not the case.

Consider a reasonably affluent nation that is not desperately overcrowded. Australia, Canada, New Zealand, and the United States could all serve as examples, and they are not the only ones. We shall take Australia as our example, simply because it is the country we know best. In 1986–1987 Australia will take at most 12,000 refugees. At the end of that year there will still be about 10 million refugees in refugee camps, of whom several million will have no hope of returning to their previous country and will be seeking resettlement in a country like Australia. Now let us imagine that Australia had accepted twice as many refugees during 1985–1986. What can we say are the definite consequences of such a decision, and what are the possible consequences?

The first definite consequence would be that 12,000 more refugees would have been out of the refugee camps and settled in Australia, where they could expect, after a few years of struggle, to share in the material comforts, civil rights, and political security of that country. So 12,000 people would have been *very* much better off.

The second definite consequence would have been that Australia would have had 12,000 more immigrants and that these additional immigrants would have been selected, not on the basis of possessing skills needed in the Australian economy, nor on the basis of having family ties with people in Australia, or in some other way being readily assimilable into the Australian community. They would therefore place an additional demand on welfare services. Some long-term residents of Australia may be disconcerted by the changes that take place in their neighborhood as significant numbers

of people from a very different culture move in. More refugees would make
some impact on initial post-arrival services such as the provision of English
language classes, housing in the first few months, job replacement, and
retraining. But the differences would be very minor; after all, Australia
accepted approximately 22,000 refugees in both 1980–1981 and 1981–1982.
There were no marked adverse effects from this larger intake.

At this point, if we are considering the *definite* consequences of a doubled
refugee intake, in terms of having a significant impact on the interests of
others, we come to a halt. We may wonder if the increased numbers will
lead to a revival of racist feeling in the community. We could debate the
impact on the Australian environment. We might guess that a larger intake
of refugees will encourage others in the country from which the refugees
came to become refugees themselves in order to better their economic
condition. Or we could refer hopefully to the contribution toward international goodwill that may flow from a country like Australia easing the burden
of less well-off nations in supporting refugees. But all of these consequences
are highly speculative.

Consider the environmental impact of an extra 12,000 refugees. Certainly,
more people will put some additional pressure on the environment. This
means that the increased number of refugees accepted will be just one item
in a long list of factors that includes the natural rate of reproduction; the
government's desire to increase exports by encouraging an industry based
on converting virgin forests to wood chips; the subdivision of rural land in
scenic areas for holiday houses; the spurt in popularity of vehicles suitable
for off-road use; the development of ski resorts in sensitive alpine areas; the
use of no-deposit bottles and other containers that increase litter . . . and the
list could be prolonged indefinitely. If as a community we allow these other
factors to have their impact on the environment, while appealing to the need
to protect our environment as a reason for restricting our intake of refugees
to its present level, we are implicitly giving less weight to the interests of
refugees in coming to Australia than we give to the interests of Australian
residents in having holiday houses, roaring around the bush in four-wheel-
drive vehicles, going skiing, and throwing away their drink containers without bothering to return them for recycling. There is no way such a weighting
can be defended within a framework of equal consideration of interests. It
is obvious enough that such a judgment can arise only from applying a very
heavy discount rate to the interests of those outside the Australian community.

The other arguments are even more problematical. No one can really say
whether doubling Australia's intake of refugees would have any effect at all
on the numbers who might consider fleeing their own homes; nor is it
possible to predict the consequences in terms of international relations. In
a situation in which the definite consequences of the proposed increase are

positive, it would be wrong to decide against the increase on such speculative grounds, especially since the speculative factors point in different directions.

So there is a strong case for Australia to double its refugee intake. And since there was nothing in this argument unique to the Australian situation, the same can be said about many other countries, including, but not limited to, Canada, New Zealand, and the United States. But there was also nothing in the argument that relied on the specific level of refugees now being taken by Australia. If our argument goes through, Australia should be taking not an extra 12,000 refugees, but an extra 20,000 refugees. The argument can then be reapplied to this new level: Should Australia be taking 40,000 refugees? How about 80,000? We can double and redouble the intakes of all the major nations of the developed world, and the refugee camps around the world will still not be empty. Indeed, the number of refugees who would seek resettlement in the developed countries is not fixed, and probably there is some truth in the claim that if all those now in refugee camps were to be accepted, more refugees would arrive to take their places. Since the interests of the refugees in resettlement in a more prosperous country will always be greater than the conflicting interests of the residents of those countries, it would seem that the principle of equal consideration of interests points to a world in which all countries continue to accept refugees until they are reduced to the same standard of poverty and overcrowding as the Third World countries from which the refugees are seeking to flee.

This is an attempted *reductio ad absurdum*: the claim is that if we follow through on the original argument it leads to consequences that we cannot possibly accept; and therefore there must be a flaw in the argument that has led us to such an absurd conclusion. In considering attempted refutations of this kind, one needs to ask two questions: Does the original argument really lead to the consequences that are regarded as unacceptable? And are the consequences really unacceptable?

In the present case the argument we put forward for doubling Australia's refugee intake does not really imply that the doubled intake should be redoubled, and redoubled again, *ad infinitum*. At some point in this process—perhaps when the refugee intake was four times what it now is or perhaps when it was sixty-four times its present level—the adverse consequences that are now only speculative possibilities would become probabilities or virtual certainties. There would come a point at which, for instance, the resident community had eliminated all luxuries that imperiled the environment, and yet the basic needs of the expanding population were putting such pressure on fragile ecological systems that a further expansion would do irreparable harm. Or there might come a point at which tolerance in a multicultural society was breaking down because of resentment among the resident community, who believed that their children were unable to get jobs because of competition from the hard-working new arrivals; and this loss of tolerance might reach the point at which it was a serious danger to the peace and security of all previously accepted refugees and other immigrants from different cultures. When any such point had been reached, the balance of interests discussed in the preceding pages would have swung against a further increase in the intake of refugees.

We readily admit that the present refugee intake might increase quite dramatically before any such consequences were reached, and some may take this as a sufficiently unacceptable consequence to support the rejection of the line of argument we have been advancing. Certainly anyone starting from the assumption that the *status quo* must be roughly right will be likely to take that view. But we regard the *status quo* as the outcome of a system of national selfishness and political expediency, not as the result of a considered attempt to work out the moral obligations of the developed nations in a world with 10 million refugees. We noted earlier how different the principle of equal consideration of interests is to the usually accepted "ex gratia" approach to the refugee issue. So we are not at all surprised that an attempt to reach an impartial assessment of the moral obligations of the developed nations should arrive at a very different conclusion.

It would not be difficult for the nations of the developed world to move closer to fulfilling their moral obligations to refugees. There is no objective evidence to show that doubling their refugee intake would cause them any harm whatsoever. Much present evidence, as well as past experience, points the other way, suggesting that they and their present population would probably benefit. But, the leaders will cry, what is moral is not what is politically acceptable! This we find a spurious excuse for inaction. In many policy areas, presidents and prime ministers are quite happy to try and convince the electorate of what is right—of the need to tighten belts in order to balance budgets, or to desist from drinking and driving. We feel that these leaders and the populations of potential refugee settlement countries should, on the basis of the principle of equal consideration of interests, gradually increase their refugee intakes. They should monitor the effects of the increase through careful research. In this way they would fulfill their moral and geopolitical obligations and would still benefit their own communities.

SHELTERS AND REFUGEES

How would you have voted in the referendum conducted in Fairhaven in 1998? We hope that you would have been prepared to sacrifice not just one, but all your tennis courts to the greater need of those outside. But if you would have voted with the "bleeding hearts" in that situation, it is difficult to see how you can disagree with our conclusion that affluent nations should be taking far, far more refugees than they are taking today. For the situation of refugees is scarcely better than that of the outsiders in peril from nuclear radiation, and the luxuries which we would have to sacrifice are surely no greater.

NOTES

1. These figures are as of January 1, 1986; see *Refugees* (a publication of the United Nations High Commission for Refugees (UNHCR), Geneva, Switzerland), no. 36 (December 1986), p. 22. The true figure is extremely difficult to establish. Part of the difficulty is that the term "refugee" is sometimes only used to refer to people who have been given official refugee status by UNHCR or a receiving country. For example, the approximately 250,000 Cambodians in refugee camps on the Thai-Cambodian border are not officially refugees but "displaced persons."

2. U.S. Department of State, Office of the U.S. Coordinator for Refugee Affairs, *Proposed Refugee Admissions and Allocations for Fiscal Year 1983* (Washington, D.C.: 1983), p. 14, quoted in Vernon Briggs, *Immigration Policy and the American Labor Force* (Baltimore: Johns Hopkins University Press, 1984), p. 201.

3. See Peter Singer, "Famine, Affluence and Morality," *Philosophy and Public Affairs*, 1 (1972): 229–243.

4. John Rawls, *A Theory of Justice* (Cambridge, Mass.: Harvard University Press, 1971).

5. Michael Walzer, *Spheres of Justice* (New York: Basic Books, 1983).

6. Ibid., pp. 9–10.

7. Ibid., p. 11.

8. Ibid., p. 12.

9. Ibid., p. 18.

10. Ibid., p. 21.

11. Ibid.

12. Ibid., p. 22. The internal quote is from E.C.S. Wade and G. Godfrey Phillips, *Constitutional and Administrative Law*, 9th ed., revised by A. W. Bradley (London: Longman, 1977), p. 424.

13. Ibid., pp. 22–23.

14. See, for example, Jonathan Glover, *Causing Death and Saving Lives* (Harmondsworth, Middlesex, England: Penguin, 1977) chapter 7; and James Rachels, "Active and Passive Euthanasia," *New England Journal of Medicine* 229 (1975): 78–80.

15. See, for example, Henry Shue, *Basic Rights: Subsistence, Affluence and U.S. Foreign Policy* (Princeton, N.J.: Princeton University Press, 1980).

16. See the remarks by R. M. Hare, in the context of the abortion debate, in his "Abortion and the Golden Rule," *Philosophy and Public Affairs* 4 (1975): 201–222.

17. Henry Sidgwick, *The Elements of Politics*, 2d ed. (London: Macmillan and Company, 1897), p. 38.

18. Ibid., p. 39.

19. See R. M. Hare, *Freedom and Reason* (Oxford: Clarendon Press, 1963) and *Moral Thinking* (New York: Oxford University Press, 1981); for a summary account see Peter Singer, *Practical Ethics* (Cambridge: Cambridge University Press, 1979), chapter 1.

20. Rossi van der Borch, "Impressions of a Refugee Camp," quoted in *Asian Bureau Australia Newsletter*, No. 85 (October-December 1986).

21. Committee for Economic Development of Australia, *The Economic Effects of Immigration in Australia* (Canberra: CEDA, 1985).

22. On the ethical obligation to consider the interests of nonhuman animals, see Peter Singer, *Animal Liberation* (New York: Avon, 1977). For discussion on the likely impact of a substantially increased population on Australia's environment, see Robert Birrell and Douglas Hill, "Population Policy and the Natural Environment" and George Seddon, "Population and the Environment," both in Robert Birrell, Leon Glezer, Colin Hay, and Michael Liffman, *Refugees, Resources, Reunion: Australia's Immigration Dilemmas* (Melbourne: VCTA Publishing, 1979). There are further questions too, discussion of which would take us too far afield: What of the possible extinction of some rare species? Is the destruction of wilderness not a loss in itself, apart from the loss to the animals who live in it?

BIBLIOGRAPHY

Birrell, Robert, and Douglas Hill. "Population Policy and the Natural Environment." In *Refugees, Resources, Reunion: Australia's Immigration Dilemmas*, edited by Robert Birrell, Leon Glezer, Colin Hay, and Michael Liffman. Melbourne: VCTA Publishing, 1979.

Briggs, Vernon. *Immigration Policy and the American Labor Force*. Baltimore: Johns Hopkins University Press, 1984.

Committee for Economic Development. *The Economic Effects of Immigration in Australia*. Canberra: CEDA, 1985.

Glover, Jonathan. *Causing Death and Saving Lives*. Middlesex, England: Penguin, 1977.

Hare, R. M. "Abortion and the Golden Rule." *Philosophy and Public Affairs* 4 (1975): 201–222.

———. *Freedom and Reason*. Oxford: Clarendon Press, 1963.

———. *Moral Thinking*. New York: Oxford University Press, 1981.

Rachels, James. "Active and Passive Euthanasia." *New England Journal of Medicine* 229 (1975): 78–80.

Rawls, John. *A Theory of Justice*. Cambridge, Mass.: Harvard University Press, 1971.

Seddon, George. "Population and the Environment." In *Refugees, Resources, Reunion: Australia's Immigration Dilemmas*, edited by Robert Birrell, Leon Glazer, Colin Hay, and Michael Liffman. Melbourne: VCTA Publishing, 1979.

Shue, Henry. *Basic Rights: Subsistence, Affluence and U.S. Foreign Policy*. Princeton, N.J.: Princeton University Press, 1980.

Sidgwick, Henry. *The Elements of Politics*, 2d ed. London: Macmillan and Company, 1897.

Singer, Peter. *Animal Liberation*. New York: Avon, 1977.

———. "Famine, Affluence and Morality." *Philosophy and Public Affairs* 1 (1972): 229–243.

———. *Practical Ethics*. Cambridge: Cambridge University Press, 1979.

Wade, E.C.S., and G. Godfrey Phillips, *Constitutional and Administrative Law*, 9th ed. revised by A. W. Bradley. London: Longman, 1977.

Walzer, Michael. *Spheres of Justice*. New York: Basic Books, 1983.

5

American Duties to Refugees

THEIR SCOPE AND LIMITS

Andrew E. Shacknove

Few forms of human misery are equal to being refugees, who by definition face a challenge to life or liberty that threatens their very survival.[1] But refugees are not alone in their suffering. Their wanderings can also jeopardize the elemental welfare and security of their neighbors. Imperiled by mere geographic proximity, citizens of asylum states may confront an odious choice between the extremes of heroic personal sacrifice and the expulsion of refugees to life-threatening circumstances.[2] Refugee migrations can even erode the security of entire regions, as the Lebanese tragedy attests. Thus preventing, containing, and managing refugee outflows is crucial not only to secure the basic survival of the refugee, but to insure the integrity of the national political community and the preservation of a minimum world order.

Before host states can formulate a response to such refugee emergencies, they must develop standards, both moral and political, by which policy can be evaluated. Clarity of purpose and direction in the conduct of refugee affairs is predicated on the establishment of first principles for the evaluation of current procedures and institutions and the crafting of preferred alternatives. Such principles derive directly from the just entitlements of both refugees and their American host communities. Lacking such principles or fundamental objectives, the United States will simply stagger from one disaster to another, divided internally by its inability to consolidate a domestic consensus and at odds internationally through any attempt to pass on the burden of assisting refugees to other states. From the Mariel debacle to the interdiction of Haitians on the high seas, from the rubble of El Salvador to the sanctuaries of Texas, recent history furnishes evidence of the need for first principles for the ordering of our refugee policy. When the government of the United States omits all consideration of just entitlements or the limits of obligation, when it turns away the destitute while aiding the celebrated, when it embitters its own citizens by requiring heroic sacrifices or disgraces them by perpetrating mean acts, the policy itself collapses under the weight of its own illegitimacy.

This essay addresses exclusively the issue of entitlements within the context of the United States as a country of first asylum: What are the scope and limits of our obligations to those refugees who quit societies in the neighboring regions of Central America and the Caribbean and come to us directly seeking safe haven or material relief?

American refugee policy should be guided by four principles: avoid depriving others of their basic needs, assume responsibility for our own actions, treat persons whose lives are threatened as equal before the law, and distribute the burden of assisting refugees within and between nations in accordance with the duty of mutual aid. These principles are deeply rooted in American conceptions of fairness, are adaptable to an evolving international system, and dramatically narrow the range of procedures and institutions that are morally acceptable and politically sound for the conduct of American refugee affairs. They reflect the valid moral claims and political objectives of both refugee and host. To the extent that American refugee policy fails to implement them, at least one party capable of frustrating the efforts of all others will experience unacceptable deprivation. Such deprivation is a measure of the failure of the refugee policy and is inimical to the integrity of the national community and to the preservation of world order. The challenge that refugees pose is not the expansion of moral categories and the imposition of cosmopolitan duties upon reluctant populations, but the formulation of procedures and institutions or the implementation of ancient and widely endorsed norms.

Regrettably, neither domestic nor international law offers adequate guidelines for evaluating and ordering American refugee policy. Indeed, few corners of the law diverge so markedly from common morality and the imperatives of contemporary politics as the domestic statutes and international conventions pertaining to refugees and other immigrants.[3] The principles offered here seek to establish a morally solid and politically sound foundation, independent of positive law, for the formulation of an American refugee policy. They identify what Americans owe, at a minimum, to the refugee and to themselves, what standards of legal process and protection apply to the hearing of applications for asylum and refugee status, and what constitutes an equitable distribution of burdens within the nation's communities and among the community of nations. Although first principles can only be approximated in practice, they can direct refugee policy away from the eyeless wanderings of the past generation and toward a more orderly regime for the management of refugee emergencies.

American refugee policy and the principles that guide it must be sufficiently flexible to accommodate an evolving international system. The traditional characterization of world politics as a state of nature is in crucial respects empirically inaccurate, and thus the brutish principles it prescribes for the conduct of foreign affairs are invalidated.[4] But the conception of international politics as an independent community in which the exercise of state power is severely bounded is also flawed, and thus the cosmopolitan principles of obligation and distribution for which it serves as the factual basis are called into doubt.[5] The power of states is an enduring quality of international politics, and interdependence is uneven. Neither the relations among states nor those among individuals are sufficiently interdependent to validate the claim that rights and obligations should be distributed equally among all actors. Some important universal entitlements and duties do exist, but they are few in number. Most moral relations are contextual, stemming from specific bonds between individuals and states.[6] Attempting to impose moral obligations where no empirical bond exists will engender bitterness and political backlash. Much of the complexity of contemporary refugee affairs stems from the varying power, penetration, and dependence of states and hence their varying responsibilities for the severely deprived. American refugee policy must oblige an international system that continues to be dominated by states and is characterized less by an equality among actors or a ubiquity of social and economic bonds than by a multitude of discrete moral and political relations.

COUNTRIES OF ORIGIN AND THEIR RESPONSIBILITIES

Our humanitarian sentiments and global role should not allow us to obscure the fact that it is usually the refugee's home state that shoulders the preponderance of all duties for these destitute people. Foreign challenges, notably in the form of invasion or support for an oppressive regime, foster their share of refugees, but most refugees are engendered by domestic persecution, insurrection, and governmental indifference to the local poor.

Refugees are citizens whose home country has failed to provide for their basic needs. The refugees' flight does not absolve that country of its threefold duties to avoid depriving its citizens of their basic needs, to protect them against such deprivation, and to aid those who are so deprived.[7] Such duties are morally (if not in fact) the responsibility of each home state. They are required if the basic needs of the citizens are to be met, and the satisfaction of these needs constitutes the normal, minimal rationale for joining in common. In the absence of such minimum obligations, the act of union becomes senseless and the meaning of political community unintelligible, leaving no moral or prudential rationale for the support of the commonwealth by the citizen. If it were a matter of choice, no sane person would consent to a social compact unless protection and aid were forthcoming from compatriots in times of destitution.

In addition to its duties to secure the basic needs of its own citizens, each state has an obligation to all other states not to create refugees. Writing in 1939, the international jurist R. Y. Jennings asserted that source countries are liable for the repercussions that a refugee exodus has on the material interests of third states. In his view, conduct resulting in "the flooding of other States with refugee populations" was illegal "*a fortiori* where the refugees are compelled to enter the country of refuge in a destitute condition. Domestic rights must be subject to the principle *sic utere tuo ut alienum non laedas* [act so as not to infringe the rights of others]. And for a state to employ these rights with the avowed purpose of saddling other states with unwanted sections of its population is as clear an abuse of right as can be imagined."[8] Thus when acts or omissions by the country of origin regarding the basic needs of its own population result in burdening other states with refugees, a violation of host state sovereignty has been perpetrated.

Furthermore, source countries now owe the international community the duty to accord their nationals a certain minimum standard of treatment in terms of human rights and fundamental freedoms.[9] They are obligated to exercise care in their domestic affairs in the light of other states' interests and to cooperate in the solution of refugee problems. Such cooperation includes facilitating both the voluntary return of nationals abroad and, in agreement with other states, the processes of orderly departure and family reunion.[10] It is evident that in order to secure the basic needs of refugees and to assure the rights and community integrity of asylum and resettlement states, the United States and all other countries that offer assistance to refugees must pursue an aggressive human rights policy. Each refugee we assist overseas or admit to our community is proof that we neglect human rights at our own peril.

THE DUTIES OF HOST STATES TO THEMSELVES

The burden of assisting refugees should be distributed among states and among citizens within states, so that the demands on each are modest. When persons or associations can improve the condition of the destitute at little cost to themselves, they bear a heavy moral obligation to do so. By the same token, as the burden increases, the obligation to assist the destitute diminishes. These are the dictates of good samaritanism, known more formally as the principle of "mutual aid."[11] Few moral precepts are at once so ancient and universally held, yet so consistently and unjustifiably disparaged. Mutual aid is a powerful principle that lends much to the ordering of refugee affairs.

For most states the issue is not whether to assist refugees, but how to do so without incurring unacceptably high risks to the welfare and security of their own citizens. Among the burdens and risks that states seek to avoid are unilateral provision of material relief for mass asylees; the extreme domestic economic deprivation resulting from a large-scale influx; disintegration of the domestic political structure because of changing ethnic, religious, or linguistic cleavages; erosion of the nation's ability to determine through the political process who should or should not be included within the national community; disruption of foreign relations, especially with the source country; the likelihood that temporary grants of asylum will lead, faits accomplis, to permanent resettlement; and loss of public confidence in the ruling regime as a result of the pervasive violation of national borders and community integrity. The desire to avoid such burdens and risks is both politically compelling and morally defensible.

The political and moral poverty of the current international procedures for managing refugee outflows stems as much from the heroic burdens they arbitrarily impose on geographically proximate host states as from the misery they fail to address among refugees. The more heroic the sacrifices demanded of asylum and resettlement states, the more dubious the refugee regime. When some are asked to sacrifice so much while others contribute so little, it is small wonder that the doors upon which refugees knock are opened with such reluctance.

Except for the (frequent) instances in which specific states bear special responsibility for a refugee's condition, the duty of mutual aid falls on the international community as a whole. However, such duties do not fall evenly on all states. Countries with a low population density, high per capita income, and a sophisticated managerial infrastructure clearly can assist refugees more easily than can countries lacking such assets. The central challenge of refugee affairs is to transform the current ad hoc arrangement requiring episodic and arbitrary acts of unilateral state heroism to a procedural and institutional regime that widely distributes the burden of aiding refugees in accordance with the principle of mutual aid, such domestic considerations as ethnic, religious, and linguistic compatability, and such international factors as the foreign policy interests of individual states. Host states are more likely to assist refugees if they can do so in a routine manner requiring modest and roughly similar contributions from year to year. Recent history has emphatically demonstrated that even countries as powerful and ethnically diverse as the United States cannot manage their refugee affairs unilaterally. Accommodating the many state interests and moral duties that arise in the refugee context requires the development of transnational procedures and institutions. Such a regime holds the prospect of diminishing the risks for each host state when lending assistance, thereby rendering the duty of mutual aid morally obligatory and improving the likelihood that aid will in fact be offered.

The principle of mutual aid applies in a similar fashion to the domestic conduct of refugee affairs. The burden of assisting refugees often falls arbitrarily on those regions that are geographically near the source country and inequitably on the local poor. However, the duty of mutual aid applies to the nation as a whole. Often, those who make refugee policy or favor increased admission are not those who bear the burden of providing assistance. When, as in the American Southwest, the local poor are forced to compete with refugees for federally subsidized housing or, as in Florida, a region is disproportionately taxed to provide social services for asylees, then the principle of mutual aid has been violated. Such violations immediately complicate the political process as interest groups and local officials challenge congressional immigration legislation and oppose federal officials including the president who fail to redistribute the burden of assisting refugees. As with states, so too with citizens: a failure to distribute burdens equitably is politically dangerous and immoral.

AMERICAN DUTIES TO REFUGEES

The consuming objective of the refugee is immediate, raw survival. By definition, the refugee inhabits a wilderness of acute deprivation where life is jeopardized by an extreme threat to minimum security or subsistence. Such threats are posed primarily by the refugees' compatriots, but there are many other challenges to their elemental welfare. Too often, the refugees' flights seem to involve movement from one ring of hell to the next. State predation of chaotic social collapse are merely exchanged for piracy, *refoulement*, or squalid incarceration in the detention camps of a reluctant host state.[12] The fact that such actions perpetuate rather than initiate a situation that threatens the security or subsistence of the refugee often renders them neither less lethal nor less immoral.

Our first duty to refugees is to avoid depriving them of their basic security, subsistence, and liberty unless some actual, proximate, and compelling interest of state is implicated. This is the principle of nondeprivation, whose ancient moral foundation is deeply rooted in the American ethic.[13] It is particularly relevant in the now frequent instances in which refugees arrive directly at our borders and shores seeking asylum.

In the refugee context, the principle of nondeprivation means that there is a strong presumption against:

1. depriving others of their basic needs;
2. protecting persons who deprive others of their basic needs;
3. assisting persons who deprive others of their basic needs; and
4. perpetuating the deprivation of basic needs.

The duty to avoid depriving persons, including foreigners, of life and liberty, unless some compelling state interest justifies doing so, stems from our equal moral worth as human beings. The moral equality of persons is an indispensable premise of communal life in the United States. From our lofty ideals to our routine chores, from access to the courts and protection by the police to the impatient wait in the post office queue, we presume an equality of human worth. Moreover, the principle of equal human worth is the primary moral given of those states and international agencies central to the management of refugee affairs. The crucial financial donors to the United States High Commission for Refugees (UNHCR) and the private relief agencies, the major countries of overseas resettlement, and many, if not all, asylum states consider moral equality to be the cornerstone of their social relations. It is precisely when moral equality is altogether denied by the persecution of one political or religious group by another, the invasion of one state by another, or gross disparities of wealth that refugees are fostered.

Moral equality entails, at the least, a recognition of the elemental integrity of each human life. Recall that, as an empirical matter, life requires the satisfaction of minimum security and subsistence. The absence of security or subsistence is fatal; hence, such needs are basic. Therefore, all persons whose moral calculus rests upon the principle of equal human worth must avoid depriving others of their basic needs, avoid protecting or assisting those who do, or demonstrate some compelling reason why such deprivation is justified. These duties constitute the principle of nondeprivation. In the absence of some solid justification, to ignore this principle is to violate the moral minimum.

Equal moral worth is not equal merit. We may judge persons according to their talents, skills, or character, but their worth is not subject to evaluation. "In this respect it differs from every kind of merit, including moral merit, in respect to which there are vast inequalities among persons."[14] In societies that accept the primacy of moral equality, all persons, including the infant, the feeble-minded, and the criminal, are entitled to an irreducible minimum of respect.

While moral equality is an assumption that cannot be logically proven or empirically confirmed, it can be defended on several grounds. First, refuting the principle convincingly and offering a preferred alternative are formidable tasks. Doing so requires demonstrating that certain persons are entitled to preferential treatment because they possess some special quality which distinguishes them from others. But which quality might this be? Plato argued for virtue, Friedrich Nietzsche for the will to power, Adolph Hitler for the Aryan race. Yet all such theses suffer from logical and empirical difficulties at least as severe as the principle of moral equality. Moreover, "it can be argued that equal human worth leads to a more just world, a way of organizing society for which we would all opt if we were designing our institutions afresh in ignorance of the roles we might one day have to play in them."[15]

We endorse the principle of equal moral worth because history has discredited all alternatives and because it offers at least the prospect of a well-ordered society.

The duty to avoid depriving others of life and liberty, like all other moral principles, is not absolute. Actions of state routinely involve moral conflict, and such conflict is often conspicuous in the refugee context. But when the government of the United States deprives a person, whether citizen or foreigner, of life or liberty, it bears the heavy burden of proving clearly that some crucial interest of state or of some group is at stake and that all less extreme actions are insufficient to meet that compelling interest. Triage situations, in which one person's basic needs must be sacrificed so that others may survive, or the collective equivalent of triage situations in which the preservation of a minority or of the nation as a whole is genuinely threatened are instances in which the deprivation of security or subsistence may be justified. Although states regularly allege that their institutional survival or the subsistence of their population is threatened so severely that *refoulement* is justified, their claims are often doubtful. In recent refugee emergencies burdening the Sudan, Somalia, and southern Africa, where the magnitude of the migrations was huge and the resources of the host states were meager, hospitality was the rule and *refoulement* the exception, casting doubt on the professed concerns of other, more affluent and stable host societies. The United States government's Haitian Interdiction and Detention Program is precisely the type of policy that perpetuates the deprivation of life and liberty and cannot be justified as meeting a compelling state interest. The United States is obligated to explore and exhaust other unilateral and regional policies before relying on such extreme measures.

There may be other justifications for depriving persons of life and liberty in the refugee context, but fear that the admission of a foreign minority might eventually threaten the cultural identity, political stability, or economic welfare of American citizens is not among them. Such fears lack both historical and moral bases. Historically, many groups once thought to be undemocratic, culturally backward, or genetically inferior have been fully assimilated into the American political, economic, and cultural mainstream. Today, Southeast Asians, Eastern Europeans, and Latin Americans are continuing the tradition of refugees who excel in American society. Morally, the fear of being overwhelmed by one or another legally sanctioned immigrant group is contrary to the conception of the United States as a pluralistic society where citizens with widely different ethnicity, ideology, and life plans are united by their acceptance of American laws and institutions. The United States is an experiment that domestic tranquillity can coexist with cultural, ethnic, and religious heterogeneity. Restricting legal immigration to the United States on the grounds that newcomers will rend the fabric of our society is an admission that the American experiment has failed.

Moreover, the permanent admission of all persons who seek asylum in the United States and are adjudged to be genuine refugees is not the only policy alternative to perpetuating a situation that deprives them of their basic needs. In the Central American and Caribbean region, where we face a situation of direct migration, the United States can pursue a host of regional political and economic strategies that have the potential to meet the basic needs of the refugees without always granting them permanent resettlement. The United States has not sufficiently explored policy alternatives that occupy a middle ground between the extremes of domestic resettlement for all asylees with valid claims and returning refugees to life-threatening circumstances.

When refugees from the regions to our south seek direct relief, we are confronted with a situation in which we cannot avoid action. Our limited alternatives are to:

1. grant asylum;
2. locate another state willing to grant asylum;
3. allow the refugees in question to repatriate voluntarily when the conditions which threaten their life or liberty improve; or
4. immediately expel (*refoule*) the refugees to their country of origin.[16]

Expulsion violates the principle of nondeprivation because it merely perpetuates jeopardy to the refugee's life or liberty. A compelling state interest would need to be implicated in order to justify expulsion, and no one has demonstrated that such an interest is threatened for the United States in the Caribbean or Central American context, or that all the less extreme alternatives have been exhausted. This leaves the United States with only three morally acceptable alternatives: to provide asylum, to locate another state willing to provide asylum, or to repatriate refugees when conditions no longer threaten their security or subsistence. Thus granting asylum is one of only three alternatives that satisfy the moral minimum. Given the brutality of expulsion and the fact that first asylum states are neither obligated nor able to manage mass refugee migrations unilaterally, it should be clear that the only alternatives that are both politically viable and morally satisfactory involve (1) a coordinated regional effort to provide temporary asylum for refugees who cannot be returned without placing their lives in jeopardy; (2) the provision of material relief for "subsistence" refugees who are victims of governmental or agrarian collapse rather than of state predation; and (3) the sustained use of diplomatic and economic power to encourage governments and elites in the countries of origin to address the conditions that foster refugee migrations. Often these undesired duties are imposed on host countries by pernicious regimes that deprive their own citizens of security, subsistence, or liberty. Yet the United States cannot, without dishonoring its first principles, order a leaky boat to tack toward tyranny or forcemarch the meek into an armed conflict.

Our second duty to refugees is to assume responsibility for our own actions that directly deprive others of their basic needs. Clearly, if all persons respected the basic needs of others, the issues of providing protection from deprivation and aiding the deprived would be moot. Regrettably, this prospect is unlikely. Lacking protection and assistance, people will continue to suffer extreme deprivation. Although it is generally agreed that states owe their own citizens the duties to protect and to aid, the question of whether these duties are universal remains controversial.

We have already established that the duty of nondeprivation is universal, because, barring a compelling state interest, it is impossible to deprive people of basic needs without simultaneously denying their equal moral worth. Thus, the controversy involves only the duties to protect from deprivation and to assist once deprived. Yet, even within this realm of controversy, certain crucial obligations to protect and to aid exist with certainty.

Because people are responsible for their own deeds and for the deeds of associations that act in their name, their hand in the deprivation of the security or subsistence of others, in the absence of a compelling state need, entails responsibilities for the restoration of these basic needs.[17] This obligation necessarily includes protection and assistance. As before, these duties are indifferent to borders. For, lacking a solid rationale, one cannot deny with impunity the basic needs of others, including foreigners, without thereby violating the principle of equal moral worth.

An account of obligations well tempered to the contemporary conditions of international politics must abandon the quantum distinction implicit in the terms "citizen" and "foreigner," adopting instead a conception of a causal chain leading to the deprivation of basic needs. When a person's security or subsistence is violated, responsibility for its restoration rests with those who are closest in the chain of causality. Because causal and geographic proximity frequently correlate, those responsible for the deprivation of basic needs are usually the victim's fellow citizens. But this is only a general rule. Frequently, foreign actors heavily influence the events that lead to an assault upon basic needs, especially in the case of those military and industrial powers, including the United States, whose strategic and economic penetration of smaller states is extensive. Nor is one person's influence upon the basic needs of another exercised exclusively through governments. Economic enterprises, churches, and a host of other transnational associations affect the basic needs of persons irrespective of nationality. To the extent that these associations act in our name as shareholders, managers, or parishioners, we are responsible for their deeds, including those that deprive others of security and subsistence. Moreover, when these associations indifferently tolerate acts of deprivation perpetrated by others over whom they enjoy influence, they become partners in the obligation to provide restitution.

It is not possible to derive a universal obligation to protect and to aid from the principle of equal human worth. Such duties derive from exceptional circumstances and specific relations. The exceptional circumstances in which one person is duty-bound to protect and to aid all others are those involving the principle of mutual aid, where a highly salutory improvement in the victim's condition can be effected at little cost to the benefactor. The special relations that obligate one person to protect or aid some, but not all, others are of many sorts, including the duty owed by parents to their minor children and by adult children to their aged parents. Most important for the refugee, when the actions of one person, association, or state deprive another of security, subsistence, or liberty, the perpetrator incurs a duty to restore the victim's basic needs. The same is true when the perpetrator acts with indifference. By the same token, where no special or contextual relation exists, no duty to protect or to aid is incurred. Acting may be laudable, but it is not morally mandatory. Thus, whereas the United States was obligated to assist refugees from Vietnam, Norway and Nigeria were not. Because the vast majority of all rights and duties stem from a specific context or relationship, an empirical characterization of the bond uniting one person to another is crucial for a determination of their moral relations.

In some instances, such as that of America's involvement in the Indochinese War or its support for the shah of Iran, the causal relationship between state policy and the existence of refugees is clear. In other instances the causal link is more ambiguous and the task of assessing responsibility more problematic. The task is often formidable because generalizations from one relation to another regarding the extent of the duties to protect and to aid are impossible. The impossibility of generalizing about duties to protect and to aid may run counter to our predilections for simplicity and order, but it is a necessary conclusion if our refugee policy is to be honest. Given the heterogeneity of relations in contemporary international politics and the fact that, even today, most persons and associations have little, if any, contact with each other, universal duties to aid and protect would be surprising indeed.

As a great power, assuming responsibility for American actions means that the possibility of fostering, and eventually having to care for, refugees should be an integral consideration in the formulation of foreign policy. A calculation of our interests in Haiti, El Salvador, Chile, South Korea, South Africa, or elsewhere is incomplete unless we consider the possibility that we may be saddled with major moral and political commitments to protect and aid future refugee populations.

Our third duty is to treat all persons whose lives are in jeopardy as equal before the law. A petition for asylum or refugee status deserves to be heard in accordance with the same standards of legal process and protection that apply to the adjudication of any domestic claim in which the life of a citizen is implicated. When such petitions are judged by standards altogether inferior to those governing domestic claims, the United States has failed in its basic duties both to the foreign applicant and to its own citizens. In cases in which a dual standard obtains, the government cannot determine with routine certainty which persons have, or lack, a justified claim to asylum or refugee status. In its ignorance, the United States will inevitably and regularly expel bona fide refugees to conditions that threaten life, thereby violating the principle of nondeprivation. Moreover, where a dual standard prevails, the government cannot assure its own citizens with confidence or regularity that material relief, asylum, or eligibility for citizenship is being offered only to persons with worthy claims to such preferential treatment.

In the United States, our fundamental principles of justice entitle persons whose lives are at stake to receive prior notice of hearing, to be apprised of their rights, and to enjoy sufficient time for preparation of an argument. Persons are further entitled to a formal, independent, and objective hearing where charges are brought, evidence presented, and the parties in dispute are represented by counsel. The American judiciary rightly considers due process a flexible concept. The courts determine how much process is due in a given instance by balancing the private interest at stake, the governmental interest involved, and an assessment of the gain to accurate determinations if the sought-after procedures are mandated.[18] Although the issue of what procedures are best suited for the determination of asylum and refugee status is crucial and complex, it is not the issue at hand. My contention here is that the process due such petitioners, whatever that might be, deserves to be determined in accordance with the same criteria that apply to similarly situated citizens. In addition to such due process guarantees, traditional principles of American jurisprudence require judicial review of administrative hearings, freedom from unnecessary or prolonged detention pending resolution of a case, and the separation of those who enforce the law from those who adjudicate the claim. If these principles apply to domestic proceedings in which life and liberty are implicated, then they should also apply to proceedings involving foreigners.

Equality before the law has in no way characterized the American legal system's treatment of petitioners for asylum and refugee status during the past generation. The doctrine that the fundamental principles of justice governing all other areas of American law should not apply to immigration and refugee matters received judicial endorsement in the 1950 case of *Knauff v. Shaughnessy*.[19] There the Supreme Court asserted that judicial scrutiny of congressional actions regarding immigration matters was illegitimate. It "is not within the province of any court, unless expressly authorized by law, to review the determination of the political branch of Government to exclude a given alien."[20] Further, in *Knauff* the Court refused to consider for itself what David Martin calls "due process writ large—systematic challenges to the basic structure of the notice and hearing provided by statute and regulation."[21] The majority in *Knauff* held, "Whatever the procedure authorized by Congress is, it is due process as far as the alien denied entry is concerned."[22] According to this logic, an alien whose life is threatened simply is not entitled to the same guarantees as citizens when petitioning the government or seeking redress. Despite the Supreme Court's contrary holding in the landmark case of *Yick Wo v. Hopkins* that the equal protection and due process clauses of the Constitution "are universal in their application, to all persons within the territorial jurisdiction, without regard to any difference of race, of color, or of nationality," a double standard for citizens and foreigners remains the surviving wisdom of a generation.[23] Such a double standard is incompatible with fundamental American moral and higher law traditions.

Exempting petitions for asylum and refugee status from the traditional standards of American justice, as well as the customary practice of positive law outside the field of immigration, is morally unacceptable because doing so will inevitably lead to the frequent violation of the principle of nondeprivation. Nondeprivation requires persons to avoid perpetuating situations which threaten security, subsistence, or liberty, unless some compelling interest is jeopardized and all less extreme alternatives have been explored and exhausted. Expelling bona fide refugees to a state where their lives are likely to be jeopardized transgresses this principle. Determining whether petitioners are, or are not, refugees requires a demanding factual inquiry.[24] An erroneous judgment may result in personal catastrophe. Because of such considerations, claims to asylum deserve to be adjudicated in accordance with the same criteria of legal process and protection that apply to cases involving the lives of citizens. In cases in which such protection is not afforded, judgments frequently will be in error, inevitably resulting in the expulsion of bona fide refugees and the violation of our moral duty of nondeprivation.

Martin has argued that aliens, including refugees and applicants for asylum, should not be considered equal before the law.[25] He sees three disturbing consequences resulting from an adherence to this principle: (1) Huge numbers of persons could easily present themselves at our borders and severely strain the legal process; (2) such strains could lead to renewed congressional and judicial support for drastically limited procedural guarantees for aliens; and (3) due process is an ever expanding concept that is difficult to cabin.

In an effort to address these troubling conditions in a principled manner, Martin proposes an alternative thesis that occupies a middle ground between the legal equality of persons endorsed by the Court in *Yick Wo* and the unlimited congressional authority granted in *Knauff* to determine what process is due excludable aliens. He seeks to avoid both the "paralyzing procedural exaggeration imposed by the courts" and a complete "abdication of constitutional protections."[26] His thesis is that "established community ties, which exist to varying degrees with respect to different categories of aliens, ought to count in deciding what process is due. We *owe more* procedural guarantees to citizens and permanent resident aliens than we do to aliens at the threshold of entry into our national community."[27]

This argument is not in conformity with the traditional American principle of equal moral worth. The thesis that citizens are due more process in all circumstances than similarly situated aliens must demonstrate that the protection of the laws is always, in Hart's words, "a special right" rooted in community membership rather than a "general right" enjoyed by all by virtue of their shared humanity. Martin believes that the protection of the law is always just such a special right arising from citizens' "mutual participation in a joint enterprise."[28] To the contrary, the equality of persons before the law is often a matter of general right. Indeed, with regard to applicants for asylum and refugee status, where life and liberty are at issue, legal equality is without exception a matter of general right.

Central to Hart's argument is the assertion that any adult human being capable of choice has the right to forbearance on the part of all others from the use of coercion save to hinder coercion.[29] The equal protection of the law is essential for deterring others, including governments, from arbitrary acts of coercion. This is the very purpose of law in a liberal society. Clearly, what would be coercion for citizens would be coercion for aliens as well. When a fundamental interest in life or liberty is in question, as it is in the case of applicants for asylum and refugee status, and when arbitrary coercion can result from an absence of full legal protection, then aliens are entitled, as a matter of their equal moral worth as human beings, to the same legal consideration as citizens.

Martin's argument that citizens are entitled to more legal protection than foreigners is also burdened with an empirical problem. According to his argument, citizens are entitled to greater protection as a result of their "mutual participation in a joint enterprise." Yet how can we say that a criminal or revolutionary who is also a citizen participates in a joint enterprise in a way that an industrious, law-abiding refugee does not? The fact that we do not question the right of the criminal or revolutionary to the full protection of the law indicates that their entitlements to legal protection rest on something other than allegiance to the community. Those entitlements, like those of the refugee, derive from each person's equal moral worth.

Adherence to the principle of equal moral worth does not obligate the United States to treat citizens and foreigners identically. By accepting persons as full members of our community, we have also accepted special obligations to assist them in their aspirations in ways we do not promise to assist foreigners. When a person's life is not threatened by coercion, community membership entails a wide range of substantive and procedural entitlements to social services and legal protection that are unavailable to foreigners. However, regarding the general right to be free from arbitrary coercion, we are all, citizens and foreigners alike, equal before the law.

Where a refugee's life is at stake and the equal protection of the laws is absent, we stand an excellent chance of violating our duty to avoid depriving others of life or liberty.

I share Martin's concern about the troubling policy consequences stemming from the principle of legal equality when life is at issue. However, I believe the challenge is better met by the development of procedures and institutions that can address these political problems than by the revision of our first principles.

In the refugee context, the legal equality of persons whose lives are threatened is usually viewed as a duty owed by the host government to the foreigner. But legal equality is also required by virtue of what a host society owes its own citizens, for a political community cannot define or preserve itself, nor defend the integrity of citizenship, when the persons actually admitted, if only temporarily, bear scant resemblance to those granted preference by citizens through the legislative process. The *Knauff* decision is a failure of means, not ends. The preservation of community that it sought is a worthy objective. Lacking a sense of kith and kin, our moral universe of blood relations, friends, and neighbors would be impoverished. But an equality before the law in the asylum context is necessary if we are to know whom we are taking in among us.[30] When the United States adopts inferior standards for the adjudication of refugee-related claims, it will frequently grant material relief, safe haven, and eligibility for citizenship to persons lacking just entitlements.

CONCLUSION

These are the principles by which the United States should order and evaluate refugee affairs. They establish at a minimum what is owed to refugees and to their American hosts. Americans may have other transnational obligations to protect and to aid, but they surely also have an obligation to avoid depriving others of their basic needs, to provide assistance when deprivation results from their own actions, and to treat all persons whose lives are threatened as equal before the law. A comprehensive theory of international obligation is unnecessary for the conduct of American refugee policy. The efficacy of the policy does not require the extension of moral norms, but compliance with traditional ones. The principles enumerated here serve to narrow dramatically the range of acceptable procedures, institutions, and policies for the conduct of American refugee affairs.

NOTES

1. By international law a refugee is a person who, "owing to a well-founded fear of being persecuted for reasons of race, religion, nationality, membership in a particular social group or political opinion, is outside the country of his nationality and

is unable or, owing to such a fear, is unwilling to avail himself of the protection of that country." United Nations Convention relating to the Status of Refugees, done July 28, 1951 (189 UNTS 137), art. 1A(2). The governing statute in the United States is currently the Refugee Act of 1980 (Pub. L. No. 96–212, 94 Stat. 102), which defines "refugee" in near conformity with the U.N. convention. For a critique of this definition and an alternative conception of "refugee," see Andrew Shacknove, "Who Is a Refugee?" *Ethics* 95: 2 (January 1985): 274–284.

2. The most dramatic instance in recent years of a reluctant host state's being forced by mere geographic proximity to make the extreme choice between domestic dislocation and the expulsion of refugees is the Malaysian treatment of Vietnamese boat people in 1979–1980. The Malaysian government saw the influx of ethnic Chinese as a threat to the delicate political balance within its society and banished the refugee boats to the high seas in a highly publicized and successful effort to obtain assistance from other states.

3. See Peter H. Schuck, "The Transformation of Immigration Law," *Columbia Law Review* 84 (1) (1984): 1–90. Schuck (p. 1) characterizes immigration law as "a maverick, a wild card, in our public law. Probably no other area of American law has been so radically insulated and divergent from those notions of constitutional right, administrative procedure, and judicial role that animate the rest of our legal system. In a legal firmament transformed by revolutions in due process and equal protection doctrine and by a new conception of judicial role, immigration law remains the realm in which government authority is at the zenith, and individual entitlement is at the nadir."

Although contemporary law offers little guidance, the treatises of early international jurists, especially Grotius and Vattel, are instructive. See Hugo Grotius, *De jure belli ac pacis*, trans. F. W. Lelsey (Oxford: Carnegie Endowment for International Peace, 1925), bk. II, chapter 21; Emer de Vattel, *Le Droit des gens ou principes de la loi naturelle; appliqués a la conduite et aux affaires des nations et des souverains* (Washington, D.C.: Carnegie Endowment for International Peace, 1916), vol. 3, secs. 23–33.

4. Charles R. Beitz has identified four propositions that must be true for the Hobbesian state of nature to be an accurate analogy to international relations:

1. the actors in international relations are states;

2. states have relatively equal power;

3. states can order their internal affairs independently of the internal policies of other states; and

4. there are no reliable expectations of reciprocal compliance by the states with rules of cooperation in the absence of a superior power capable of enforcing these rules.

Because all of these propositions are, to one degree or another, false, the empirical basis of so-called international political realism is weak (Beitz, *Political Theory and International Relations* [Princeton, N.J.: Princeton University Press, 1979], pp. 35–50).

5. For the classical statement of cosmopolitan justice see Immanuel Kant, *The Metaphysical Elements of Justice* [1797]. Part 1 of *The Metaphysics of Morals*, trans. John Ladd (Indianapolis: Bobbs-Merrill, 1965); and Kant, *Perpetual Peace* [1795] in *Kant's Political Writings*, ed. Hans Reis and trans. H. B. Nisbet (Cambridge: Cambridge University Press, 1971), pp. 93–130.

6. For a discussion of general rights held by all and of special, or contextual, rights stemming from discrete and particular relations see H. L. A. Hart, "Are There Any Natural Rights?" *The Philosophical Review* 64: 2 (1955): 175–191.

7. For an illuminating discussion of the threefold duties to avoid deprivation, protect from deprivation, and assist the deprived, see Henry Shue, *Basic Rights: Subsistence, Affluence, and American Foreign Policy* (Princeton, N.J.: Princeton University Press, 1980), pp. 35–64.

8. R. Y. Jennings, "Some International Law Aspects of the Refugee Question," *British Yearbook of International Law* 20: 98 (1939): 112–115; quoted in Guy S. Goodwin-Gill, *The Refugee in International Law* (Oxford: Clarendon Press, 1983), p. 227.

9. Goodwin-Gill, *Refugee*, p. 227.

10. Ibid., p. 228.

11. In its classic form, the principle of mutual aid envisions a passer-by who encounters a drowning child. If the passer-by can easily save the child, she is morally obligated to do so, even if the child is a complete stranger. Failure to save the child under such conditions would be universally condemned as callousness. If, to the contrary, the passer-by could hope to rescue the child only at great personal risk, no one would chastise her for not acting. The passer-by is not expected to sacrifice life or limb because of a chance encounter with a stranger. Doing so is heroic, but heroism by its nature is voluntary; it exceeds the limits of obligation. The analogy to the relation between refugee and host is readily apparent. For a discussion of the principle of mutual aid see John Rawls, *A Theory of Justice* (Cambridge, Mass.: Harvard University Press, 1971), pp. 114, 338, 406; James Fishkin, *The Limits of Obligation* (New Haven, Conn.: Yale University Press, 1982); Michael Walzer, *Spheres of Justice* (New York: Basic Books, 1983), pp. 33, 45–46, 65.

12. *Refoulement* is the expulsion or return of "a refugee in any manner whatsoever to the frontiers of territories where his life or freedom may be threatened." United Nations Convention Relating to the Status of Refugees, UNTS 189/137 (1951) art. 33, par. 1.

13. Myres McDougal, Harold Lasswell, and Lung-chu Chen, *Human Rights and World Public Order* (New Haven, Conn.: Yale University Press, 1980), pp. 3–6.

14. Gregory Vlastos, "Justice and Equality," in *Social Justice*, ed. Richard B. Brandt (Englewood Cliffs, N.J.: Prentice-Hall, 1962), pp. 31–72; quoted by Joel Feinberg, *Social Philosophy* (Englewood Cliffs, N.J.: Prentice-Hall, 1973), p. 89.

15. Feinberg, *Social Philosophy*, p. 94.

16. Although our language includes both male and female refugees, the feminine pronoun in the refugee context can be used because most refugees are women.

17. It is generally agreed that the only persons who are not fully responsible for their actions are children and the feeble-minded. Clearly, people are responsible for the actions of associations that they voluntarily join. The case of involuntary membership, such as citizenship in a state that denies emigration, or church affiliation in a society that lacks religious toleration, is more problematic. In such cases it is possible to speak of control but not of mutual rights and responsibilities, except among the dominant group. This group is obligated to restore the basic needs deprived by the association.

18. *Mathews v. Eldridge*, 424 U.S. 319, 334–335 (1976).

19. 338 U.S. 537 (1950).

20. Ibid., p. 543.

21. David A. Martin, "Due Process and the Treatment of Aliens," *University of Pittsburgh Law Review* 44: 2 (1983): 166.

22. 338 U.S. 537, p. 544.

23. 118 U.S. 356, 369 (1886). Justice Field, dissenting in the 1893 case of *Fong Yue Ting v. United States* (149 U.S. 698, 754), expanded on this theme: "The moment any human being from a country at peace with us comes within the jurisdiction of the United States . . . he becomes subject to all their laws, is amenable to their punishment and entitled to their protection. Arbitrary and despotic power can no more be exercised over them with reference to their persons and property, than over the persons and property of native-born citizens. They differ from citizens only in that they cannot vote or hold any public office. As men having our common humanity, they are protected by all the guaranties of the Constitution."

24. "It should be recalled that an applicant for refugee status is normally in a particularly vulnerable situation. He finds himself in an alien environment and may experience serious difficulties, technical and psychological, in submitting his case to the authorities of a foreign country, often in a language not his own" (UNHCR, *Handbook on Procedures and Criteria for Determining Refugee Status* [Geneva, 1979], p. 45.) The psychological difficulties of an applicant for refugee status may include a suspicion or fear of immigration authorities because in the refugee's home country such officials are often agents of a predatory state.

"The factual inquiry," in Martin's words, "is difficult in ways not found in most other adjudications known to our administrative law. Not only does the crucial determination require prediction—prediction based on political, not scientific, judgments—but also the basic factual materials on which to base such a prediction are notably elusive. The decision maker must learn of events in a distant country, as to which few witnesses are likely to be available here, other than the applicant himself" ("Due Process," p. 184).

25. Martin, "Due Process," p. 191.

26. Ibid., p. 234.

27. Ibid., p. 192.

28. Ibid., p. 193.

29. Hart, "Natural Rights," pp. 175–191.

30. Of course, factual determinations also are required when the relatives of citizens or an exceptionally skilled immigrant is being considered for admission. However, such determinations differ from those in asylum and refugee cases in that the latter are more factually ambiguous and potentially consequential for the elemental welfare of the petitioner.

BIBLIOGRAPHY

Beitz, Charles R. *Political Theory and International Relations*. Princeton, N.J.: Princeton University Press, 1979.

Feiberg, Joel. *Social Philosophy*. Englewood Cliffs, N.J.: Prentice-Hall, 1973.

Fishkin, James. *The Limits of Obligation*. New Haven, Conn.: Yale University Press, 1982.

Fong Yue Ting v. United States, 149 U.S. 698 (1893).

Goodwin-Gill, Guy S. *The Refugee in International Law*. Oxford: Clarendon Press, 1983.

Grotius, Hugo. *De jure belli ac pacis*, translated by F. F. Lelsey. Oxford: Carnegie Endowment for International Peace, 1925.

Hart, H. L. A. "Are There Any Natural Rights?" *The Philosophical Review* 64; 2 (1955): 175–191.

Jennings, R. Y. "Some International Law Aspects of the Refugee Question," *British Yearbook of International Law* 20: 98 (1939): 112–115.

Kant, Immanuel. *The Metaphysics of Morals*, translated by John Ladd. Indianapolis: Bobbs-Merrill, 1965.

Knauff v. Shaughnessy, 338 U.S. 537 (1950).

McDougal, Myres, Harold Lasswell, and Lung-chu Chen. *Human Rights and World Public Order*. New Haven, Conn.: Yale University Press, 1980.

Martin, David A. "Due Process and the Treatment of Aliens," *University of Pittsburgh Law Review* 44: 2 (1983).

Mathews v. Eldridge 424 U.S. 319 (1976).

Rawls, John. *A Theory of Justice*. Cambridge, Mass.: Harvard University Press, 1971.

Reis, Hans, ed. *Kant's Political Writings*, translated by H. B. Nisbet. Cambridge: Cambridge University Press, 1971.

Schuck, Peter H. "The Transformation of Immigration Law," *Columbia Law Review* 84: 1 (1984): 1–90.

Shacknove, Andrew E. "Who Is a Refugee?" *Ethics* 95: 2 (January 1985): 274–284.

Shue, Henry. *Basic Rights: Subsistence, Affluence, and American Foreign Policy*. Princeton, N.J.: Princeton University Press, 1980.

United Nations Convention relating to the Status of Refugees, done July 28, 1951 (189 UNTS 137).

United Nations High Commission for Refugees. *Handbook on Procedures and Criteria for Determining Refugee Status*. Geneva, 1979.

Vattel, Emer de. *Le Droit des gens ou principes de la loi naturelle: appliqués a la conduite et aux affaires des nations et des souverains*. Washington, D.C.: Carnegie Endowment for International Peace, 1916.

Vlastos, Gregory. "Justice and Equality," in *Social Justice*, edited by Richard B. Brandt. Englewood Cliffs, N.J.: Prentice-Hall, 1962.

Walzer, Michael. *Spheres of Justice: A Defense of Pluralism and Equality*. New York: Basic Books, 1983.

Yick Wo v. Hopkins, 118 U.S. 356 (1886).

6

Human Rights and U.S. Refugee Policy

Mark Gibney
and
Michael Stohl

The 1980 Refugee Act was passed with a modicum of promise that the East/West conflict would no longer dominate U.S. refugee admissions.[1] The act removed the ideological restrictions that had limited refugee admissions to those from the Middle East or from Communist countries.[2] The House Report clearly pointed to the direction that U.S. refugee policy was to take: "The Committee intends to emphasize that the plight of the refugees themselves, as opposed to national origins or political considerations, should be paramount in determining which refugees are to be admitted to the United States."[3]

Despite the passage of the 1980 Refugee Act, or, more accurately, because of it, critics of U.S. refugee policy have charged that foreign policy concerns, rather than the plight of the individual, continue to dominate refugee/asylum determinations.[4] Critics point to the granting of asylum to someone like Martina Navratilova, who defected from Czechoslovakia, while the United States has granted refugee status to only ninety-six individuals from El Salvador and Guatemala *combined* (all from El Salvador) since 1980. In addition, only 569 of the 21,892 applications for asylum from those two countries were successful. The rationale for questioning such policy outcomes, simply stated, is that the human rights situation in countries like Guatemala and El Salvador appears to be considerably worse than that in Czechoslovakia.

This essay explores the relationship between human rights violations and asylum practice. The first part explains why one would expect such a relationship to occur. The second attempts to break the deadlocked debate between critics and proponents of U.S. practice. There we offer a different kind of analysis than has heretofore been given. The analysis is an empirical one, using a data set that we developed on human rights conditions in other countries. The findings offer a unique view of U.S. practice, one that is at times (even at the same time) both hopeful and discouraging.

HUMAN RIGHTS AND REFUGEE POLICY

On an intuitive level, human rights violations and the notion of granting refugee status would go hand in hand. The commonly accepted definition of a refugee is one who has a "well-founded fear of persecution for reasons of race, religion, nationality, membership of a particular social group or political opinion."[5] It would seem to stand to reason that those nations that do terrible things to their citizens would, at the same time, be creating large numbers of refugees who would be in dire need of international assistance.[6] Consider this hypothetical situation. Without knowing anything about two individuals except their nationality—someone from Iran and someone from Japan—one would undoubtedly feel quite comfortable in concluding that if one of these individuals had a well-founded fear of persecution, it would be the person from Iran. The intuitive rationale that no doubt would be employed would be that Japan has an excellent human rights record while Iran does not. On a macro level, one would expect there to be more refugees from Iran in a given year than there would be from Japan.

The other side to this, explored in more detail later, involves nations receiving refugees. Our intuitions here would hold that a humanitarian nation concerned with the plight of others would be admitting a greater proportion of individuals as refugees from nations that have records of gross violations of human rights, rather than granting refugee status to sizable numbers from nations that have a relatively good human rights record. To stay with the present example, one would be puzzled if a country like Sweden admitted far larger numbers of "refugees" from Japan than from Iran.

Despite the fact that our intuitions dictate a positive relationship between human rights violations and refugees, it is not at all clear that international law and state practice conform to these conclusions. The current most politically charged example of the gap between intuitions and state practice, at least in terms of United States policy, is U.S. refugee policy with regard to Salvadorans. Some time will be spent on this example.

The Example of El Salvador

Setting aside, for the moment, the question of whether human rights conditions in El Salvador have improved since 1980, there is little dissent to the conclusion that in the early years of this decade human rights conditions in El Salvador were among the worst in the world. The following are excerpts from the State Department Country Report on Human Rights Practices for 1981 and the Amnesty International Report for that same year. First the State Department:

Throughout 1981 the human rights situation in El Salvador remained troubled. The civil strife and endemic violence which has convulsed the country for years continued. Human rights violations were frequent, but there was a downward trend in political violence. Extreme leftist terrorists and guerrillas, right-wing death squads and some members of the government's internal security forces all had a hand in violence.

Statistics on numbers of people killed as a result of El Salvador's current political violence are difficult to obtain and are unreliable. Available figures are useful principally to set trend lines. . . . The United States Embassy in San Salvador maintains its own count of deaths attributable to political violence, gleaned primarily from press reports. According to the embassy's count, there were 6,116 violent deaths during the twelve-month period ending January 1, 1982. The embassy's figures also show a decline in average monthly totals from around 800 per month in late 1980 and in the beginning of 1981 to 200–400 per month at the end of the year. Some church sources claim that perhaps twice as many non-combatants have been killed.[7]

The report goes on to say: "Disappearances in El Salvador are frequent and are attested by frequent petitions for information in the local press. Paramilitary or security forces personnel probably bear responsibility in a number of these cases. . . . The large number of corpses, often mutilated, discovered throughout El Salvador dictates quick, on-the-spot burial. It is often impossible to identify a corpse before it must be interred."[8]

Amnesty International provides an even more gruesome picture:

Amnesty International continued to receive reports of arbitrary arrests, abductions, and subsequent "disappearances", torture, and extra-legal executions. . . . Eye-witness reports received by Amnesty International consistently implicated the paramilitary unit ORDEN in human rights abuses. . . . In a context of widespread civil conflict the rural population in areas contested by military forces suffered indiscriminate violence in reported attempts to clear such zones of all potential support for the opposition. People trying to flee from such military operations were also killed.[9]

Despite these depictions of human rights abuses in El Salvador in 1981, during that fiscal year the United States did not admit any refugees from El Salvador and granted asylum to only two Salvadorans.[10] This policy is clearly contrary to what our intuitions would dictate. The figures for the entire period are consistent with this counterintuitive finding. Since 1980 the United States has granted refugee status to only ninety-six Salvadorans, and the acceptance rates for asylum claims has consistently been in the range of 2 to 3 percent.[11]

The continuing position of the United States government is that the overwhelming majority of the 600,000 or so Salvadorans in the United States illegally are here simply for economic betterment. To establish its position, the executive branch relies on several arguments. The first claim is that in order to reach the United States, Salvadorans have had to pass through several other countries that have granted temporary refuge to at least some of their fellow citizens. Since these other countries have shown a willingness to provide a safe haven to some Salvadorans, the fact that Salvadorans in the United States have not pursued this option (and it is presumed that this option has not been pursued, and that it is a viable option) indicates that something beside fear of persecution has prompted the migration to the United States and that "something else" is economic betterment. Another related argument in support of the claim of the United States government that illegal Salvadorans in this country are economic migrants is the extended history of Salvadoran migration to the United States for such purposes. A final argument in support of this position is that substantial sums of money are sent back home by Salvadorans who are in the United States illegally.[12]

It is interesting to note that the United States does not seem to challenge the notion that there are bona fide refugees fleeing El Salvador. For example, the documentation for the administration's proposed refugee admissions for fiscal year 1987 speaks of the need for temporary asylum of hundreds of thousands of individuals in Central America. "War and related economic hardships in Central America have generated substantial flows of economic migrants, displaced persons, and refugees. The long-standing tradition in the region of granting refuge to political exiles and refugees continues. Within Central America, about 232,500 persons have found temporary asylum in neighboring countries."[13]

Patricia Weiss Fagen has pointed out that in addition to its normal contributions to the United Nations Commission for Refugees, the United States also earmarks several million dollars in aid for Latin America, and some of this is further earmarked for Salvadorans.[14] What is inconsistent about U.S. policy (aside from the question of whether Salvadorans in the United States illegally are in fact economic migrants) is that although it recognizes that there are bona fide refugees fleeing from El Salvador, there is no apparent effort to share some of the burden of housing these individuals.[15] For example, although the United States government recognizes that there are well over 200,000 refugees in Central America, its proposed refugee admissions for fiscal year 1987 for that entire region is only 4,000.[16] That number, however, is quite misleading. For example, the proposed refugee admissions for Central America in fiscal year 1986 was 3,000, but ultimately the United States only admitted 150 refugees.[17]

In sum, although the United States recognizes the legitimate claims of some Salvadorans as refugees, it makes no real effort to discern which Salvadorans are bona fide refugees, and which ones are not, nor does it make a serious attempt to provide refuge to those who are viewed as bona fide refugees.[18] Instead, it has left this burdensome task to other nations in Central America.

A final argument on which the executive branch relies to defend its Salvadoran refugee policy—and it should be understood that this list of arguments is not meant to be exhaustive—is that those who have been returned to El Salvador have not in fact met persecution. The empirical evidence both in support of and against this position is generally weak because no systematic attempt has been made to monitor the problem. What is more certain is that the level of human rights abuses in El Salvador is among the highest in the world.[19]

The Reagan administration does not attempt to portray El Salvador as a safe place to live, although it has at times hinted in that direction.[20] Obviously it would be very difficult to argue this in the face of the 50,000 *civilian* deaths in that country since 1980.[21] The executive branch does, however, continually stress what it perceives as advances made in the human rights conditions in El Salvador.[22] The executive branch also concludes that while El Salvador might be unsafe for some, it is not unsafe for all. Finally, in terms of the human rights situation in the country generally and the relation of that situation to the full panoply of relief sought—refugee admissions, asylum, suspension of deportation, and extended voluntary departure status—the position is that there is no necessary connection at all. Stephen Palmer, deputy assistant secretary of state for human rights and humanitarian affairs, describes the nonrelationship this way: "Determination of a particular asylum claim . . . is not a general referendum on human rights in the home country. . . . Instead, we must apply a narrow and clearly focused standard established by treaty and by U.S. statutes."[23]

With a few notable exceptions, the judicial branch has generally acceded to the conclusions of the executive branch in terms of the widespread denial of Salvadoran claims for asylum in this country.[24] No attempt will be made to catalogue these cases; however, a few interesting trends do emerge. Despite its extraordinary brevity, *Martinez-Romero v. INS* is quite typical of how Salvadoran claims have been handled. The entire text reads:

The orders of the Immigration and Naturalization Service before us for review are affirmed.

If we were to agree with the petitioner's contention that no person should be returned to El Salvador because of the reported anarchy present there now, it would permit the whole population, if they could enter this country some way, to stay here indefinitely. There must be some special circumstances present before relief can be granted.[25]

The judicial search in these "asylum" cases, then, is for the presence or absence of these "special circumstances" that will differentiate the claim of one Salvadoran from all other Salvadorans.[26] In terms of the level of human rights abuses in El Salvador, most courts[27] seem to generally recognize such conditions,[28] but there is a concerted effort not to have this background prove decisive in a particular case.[29] In response, critics charge that in blocking out the level of human rights violations in El Salvador, the courts are missing the proverbial forest for the trees.[30] Such efforts, they contend, maintain the counterintuitive U.S. government policy of essentially denying any relief for Salvadorans.

The congressional response has certainly been more varied.[31] Most congressional efforts have centered around whether Salvadorans in the United States should be granted Extended Voluntary Departure (EVD) status.[32] Sponsors of this legislation have simply pointed to the level of human rights violations in El Salvador. Congressman Joe Moakley describes the need for EVD this way. "The primary conditions for granting E.V.D. or a temporary suspension of deportation . . . appear to be based on dangerous, unstable conditions in the aliens' homeland. At least, in the past these criteria have always been cited as the reason for approval of E.V.D. . . . Clearly the conditions in El Salvador, as documented by nearly every major human rights organizations [sic] in the world, are extremely dangerous."[33] Thus far congressional efforts to provide temporary refuge for Salvadorans have failed.[34]

There have been a number of noteworthy responses to the position of the United States government with regard to the claims of Salvadorans. The United Nations High Commissioner for Refugees (UNHCR) has been quite critical of the way the U.S. government has handled Salvadoran asylum claims.[35] Moreover, the UNHCR has stated that those leaving El Salvador bear a presumption that they are bona fide refugees.[36] As already noted, a number of other nations, such as Belize and Mexico, have been generous in terms of granting a temporary refuge to some Salvadorans. Finally, the United States government has been faced with the burgeoning sanctuary movement in this country, which offers a direct challenge to U.S. refugee policy.[37]

The sanctuary response embodies the intuitive position outlined earlier: Given the terrible human rights violations in El Salvador—whether it be the large-scale death squad activities in years past or the more recent aerial bombings of villages—how could one honestly conclude, particulary if you are the nation that is providing substantial amounts of military aid and advice on how to conduct this brutal civil war, that any of those leaving El Salvador are not refugees?[38]

The sanctuary-government impasse represents two completely differing views of the applicability of human rights violations to the determination of refugee status. To those in the sanctuary movement, these violations offer substantial proof that those coming to the United States are bona fide refugees, and that the U.S. government ought not to be sending these people back, given this country's legal and moral duties. The position of the United States government, while not negating the existence of these violations, at the same time maintains that the violations, by themselves, have no bearing (and should have no bearing) on a particular applicant's claim. The U.S. government correctly maintains that under international law the applicant for asylum has the burden of meeting the statutory standard of having a well-founded fear of persecution. What adds more than a certain degree of irony to the government's position, however, is that the burden of proof shouldered by Salvadorans (or other groups in this hemisphere, such as Haitians) is not necessarily carried by all who seek refuge here. In a 1982 study conducted by the Immigration and Naturalization Service, the service itself pointed out that some asylum applicants—specifically Salvadorans—had a much higher level of proof than nationals of other countries such as Poles.[39] Moreover, this same report conceded that those who were outside of the U.S. seeking refugee status often had a much lower burden of proof than did asylum applicants who were in the United States, despite the fact that the statutory standards are exactly the same.[40]

International Law and Practice

This rather extended discussion of the policy of the United States government with regard to the asylum claims of Salvadorans has been used to show the differing views of the applicability of human rights conditions in other countries in the refugee determination. The intuitive position posits a correlation between the two. U.S. policy—at least in terms of El Salvador—does not show this correlation. United States policy has been singled out, but the question raised about the connection between human rights violations and refugee policy need not be restricted to the policies of this country. The first place to explore the general relationship between refugee determinations and human rights violations is in the refugee standard itself. There are two particular questions that will be examined. One relates to what constitutes persecution. The other relates to the narrowed scope of persecution in the refugee standard. The latter point will be addressed first.

As noted earlier, the refugee definition speaks of a well-founded fear of persecution based on five specific criteria: race, religion, nationality, membership in a particular social group, or political opinion. By singling out certain grounds for persecution, the refugee definition (at least a narrow reading of it) might well exclude persecution on other grounds, or persecution for no apparent reason at all. This century has certainly known instances where a ruthless leader has turned the army loose against the general population. However, it is by no means apparent that individuals attempting to flee such slaughter would be "refugees." In this respect, then, persecution is a necessary but not sufficient condition for meeting the refugee standard. Another instance of a nonrelationship between human rights abuses and the notion of being considered a "refugee" is that civilians fleeing war situations have similarly been viewed as not falling within the convention protocol, despite the grave dangers they might be facing.[41] What tempers this cruel and counterintuitive result, to a degree, is the international norm of providing temporary refuge to those fleeing slaughter in their home country. Deborah Perluss and Joan Hartman contrast the norm of temporary refuge with the refugee standard this way:

Temporary refuge adopts a purely situational approach premised upon a de facto lack of national protection due to occurrences within the country of nationality. The applicability of the norm does not, therefore, depend upon the presence of a subjective and individualized fear or upon an objective membership in a particular social group. Thus, as a norm of customary humanitarian law, temporary refuge is far better equipped than current codified law to deal with situations of mass influx. Indeed, current codified refugee law is incapable of accommodating situations of mass influx for practical as well as juridicial reasons. As a practical matter, individualized determinations of refugee status based on claims of persecution are not logistically feasible when masses of people are involved. Moreover, sufficient factual evidence of persecution in the conventional sense may be unavailable.[42]

Implicit in the argument presented by Perluss and Hartman is the idea that the norm of temporary refuge is more commendable or at least more humanitarian than following a strict interpretation of the refugee definition. That is, rather than taking an overly legalistic approach, as the refugee definition does, the norm of temporary refuge dispenses not only with legal niceties, but also legal roadblocks. To its credit, the UNHCR has not confined itself to a strict reading of "refugee" and now devotes most of its resources to mass influxes.[43] Despite this commendable humanitarian practice, the legal distinctions remain.[44]

A second point to consider is the relationship between the notion of "persecution" and human rights violations. On one level the two would seem synonymous. That is, instances of "persecution" will also be instances of human rights violations. One problem with this view, however, is that seldom is persecution defined. The United Nations High Commissioner for Refugees can do no better than this: "There is no universally accepted definition of 'persecution' and various attempts to formulate such a definition have met with little success. From Article 33 of the 1951 Convention, it may be inferred that a threat to life or freedom on account of race, religion, nationality, political opinion or membership of a particular social group is always persecution. Other serious violations of human rights—for the same reasons—would also constitute persecution.[45]

One of the leading scholars in this area, Guy Goodwin-Gill, offers this description of "persecution."

Persecution within the Convention thus comprehends measures taken on the basis of one or more of the stated grounds, which threaten: deprivation of life or liberty; torture or cruel, inhuman, or degrading treatment; subjection to slavery or servitude; non-recognition as a person (particularly where the consequences of such non-recognition impinge directly on an individual's life, liberty, livelihood, security, or integrity); and oppression, discrimination, or harassment of a person in his or her private, home, or family life.[46]

Atle Grahl-Madsen describes both a "liberal" and a "restrictive" definition of persecution.[47] The restrictive definition purports to limit the scope of activities to deprivations of life or physical freedom, although the definition is loosened considerably by also including the loss of one's livelihood for a protracted period of time. The restrictive view excludes attacks on a person's integrity unless such attacks "may lead to the victim's death or implies loss of physical freedom."[48] The liberal interpretation of persecution, as its name suggests, labels less extensive state practices as "persecution," although it is not clear how far this definition would go. Which if any of the following constitute persecution: a two year stay at a reeducation camp? the burning of one's place of worship? the interference in the pursuit of a person's career because of a person's religious beliefs?[49]

Drawing the line on what is or is not persecution has been extremely difficult and politically charged.[50] The position taken here is that different levels of persecution (and human rights violations) are practiced in the world, and such levels ought to be recognized in making refugee admission determinations. Consider two situations. A person who is imprisoned for her political beliefs for seven years would suffer persecution; that much seems clear. Another individual who is imprisoned for the same length of time and who is repeatedly tortured would also be persecuted. Although both individuals are subject to "persecution" under the refugee definition, we would argue that the person who is tortured suffers more "serious" persecution than the person who is not.[51] Moreover, in terms of international assistance or refugee admissions, the person who has been tortured has a stronger claim for assistance.[52] This does not mean that the person who has not been tortured has not been persecuted or is not a refugee, or is somehow not deserving of our attention. However, being imprisoned and being tortured is worse than "merely" being imprisoned. Simply stated, it represents a more serious human rights violation.

It is interesting to note that under current refugee processing guidelines, the U.S. government recognizes in principle this notion of degrees of per-

secution. Part of the first admission priority of "compelling concern" is designed to meet the needs of individuals who are in immediate danger of loss
of life and for whom there appears to be no alternative to resettlement in
the United States. In theory this priority embodies the principle argued for
here: those with the most "serious" need have the stronger claim for assistance. In practice, U.S. policy falls far short of this standard. Few individuals are admitted under this first priority category. Instead, most refugees
are admitted under other categories—former U.S. government employees;
family reunification of close relatives; individuals with employment or educational ties with U.S. foundations, voluntary agencies, or business firms;
or family reunification for more distant relatives. A twofold charge has been
made against the present priority system. One is that the cart has come
before the horse in that the priority system often drives the original refugee
determination. The other is that the compelling concern category has been
systematically ignored, so that those with less compelling claims have been
taken to the head of the line.[53]

THE EMPIRICAL EVIDENCE

Simply looking at the gross numbers, the refugee policy of the United
States has been generous. Since 1975, the United States has admitted over
1 million refugees.[54] Nonetheless, as noted earlier, U.S. refugee policy has
had its critics. The most commonly expressed charge is that foreign policy
concerns determine who is a refugee and which refugees will be admitted
to this country.[55] Before 1980, U.S. refugee admissions were limited to those
from the Middle East or Communist countries. The 1980 Refugee Act removed these ideological restrictions and purportedly made the plight of the
individual paramount. One can therefore test whether the change in the law
also changed practices. The data indicate that the ideological bias is as strong
as ever.[56] Table 1 shows asylum adjudication rates and refugee admissions
for selected countries from 1980 to 1985.

While critics of U.S. refugee policy have been quick to point out the
obvious ideological bias in this country's refugee admission policy, notwithstanding the provisions of the Refugee Act, they have not been as quick to
answer the government's implicit and simple answer to these assertions—
"so what?" The new refugee standard speaks of admitting refugees who are
of "special humanitarian concern" to the United States.[57] The position of the
Reagan administration has been quite straightforward. Those fleeing authoritarian regimes are generally not refugees, while those fleeing totalitarian
regimes are presumed to be refugees and also presumed to be of "special
humanitarian concern" to this country.[58]

It is interesting to note that although the U.S. government has repeatedly
denied that human rights conditions in other countries have any bearing on
refugee status or admissions, the reliance on such factors is inescapable, but

Table 1
Grants of Asylum and Refugee Admissions for Selected Countries, 1980–1985

	# Asylum Applicants	# Asylum Granted	%	Refugees Admitted
Afghanistan	2,000	1,126	56	15,944
Bulgaria	43	22	51	732
Cambodia	25	8	32	108,472
Czechoslovakia	276	132	47	5,702
E. Germany	25	8	32	1
El Salvador	20,699	561	2	96
Guatemala	1,193	8	1	0
Hungary	651	220	33	2,778
Laos	33	9	27	48,024
Mexico	12	2	16	0
Nicaragua	16,589	2,244	13	6
Philippines	404	100	25	69
Poland	6,950	2,071	29	22,090
Romania	864	446	51	20,548
S. Africa	81	54	66	68
USSR	249	128	51	24,854
Vietnam	267	78	29	199,896
Yugoslavia	348	36	10	67

Figures provided by the Immigration and Naturalization Service. Note that statistics on admissions are based on the fiscal year, while both the Amnesty International Report and the State Department Report are based on the calendar year.

selectively employed. For example, the explanation why those from Eastern bloc countries are of "special humanitarian concern" to the U.S. is given in these terms:

Since the end of World War II, persons from Eastern Europe and the Soviet Union have been considered to be of special humanitarian concern to the United States because of the oppressive policies of the communist governments of those states. . . . The only official justification for emigration acknowledged by Soviet authorities is family reunification with relatives abroad. Those who leave, however, cite abuses resulting from religious and political beliefs as their principal reasons for departure.[59]

The debate on U.S. refugee practices has arrived at a stalemate. What follows is an attempt to provide some common grounding and rationality in an effort to revive this debate. We will explore whether there is a statistical correlation between human rights violations in other countries and U.S.

Table 2
Human Rights Rankings, 1980–1985

	1980 AI	1980 SD	1981 AI	1981 SD	1982 AI	1982 SD	1983 AI	1983 SD	1984 AI	1984 SD	1985 AI	1985 SD
AFGHAN	5	5	5	5	5	5	5	5	4	5	5	5
ALBANIA	3	3	3	3	3	3	3	3	3	3	3	3
ANGOLA	3	3	3	3	3	3	3	5	3	3	3	1
ARGENT	5	4	5	3	3	3	3	3	2	2	2	1
BANGLAD	3	3	3	2	3	3	3	3	4	2	3	2
BRAZIL	3	2	2	2	3	2	4	2	4	2	4	3
BULGAR	3	2	3	3	3	3	2	3	2	3	3	3
BURMA	–	3	–	3	–	3	3	4	3	3	3	4
BURUNDI	2	2	–	2	–	2	2	2	2	2	3	2
CAMBOD	0	3	3	3	3	4	3	4	4	3	3	4
CHILE	4	4	5	3	4	3	4	3	4	3	4	3
CHINA	3	3	2	3	3	2	3	2	2	3	3	3
COLOM	4	3	4	3	5	3	4	3	4	3	4	3
COSTA	–	1	–	1	–	1	2	1	2	1	–	1
CUBA	3	3	3	3	3	3	3	3	3	3	3	3
CZECH	3	3	3	3	3	3	3	2	2	3	2	3
DOMREP	3	2	–	2	–	2	–	1	3	2	–	1
ECUADOR	–	2	–	2	–	2	–	2	–	2	3	2
EGYPT	3	1	3	3	3	3	3	3	3	2	3	2
ELSALV	5	4	5	4	5	4	5	4	5	4	4	4
ETHIOP	4	5	4	4	4	4	4	4	3	4	4	4
FRANCE	2	1	2	1	2	1	2	1	2	1	2	1
E.GERM	2	3	3	3	3	3	3	3	3	3	3	2
GHANA	3	1	–	2	3	3	3	3	3	2	2	2
GREECE	2	1	2	1	2	1	2	1	2	1	2	1
GUATEM	5	4	5	4	5	4	5	4	5	4	5	4
GUINEA	3	3	3	2	3	2	4	1	3	3	3	2
GUYANA	–	3	–	3	–	3	–	3	3	3	2	2
HAITI	4	3	3	3	3	2	3	3	3	3	3	3
HONDUR	4	2	4	3	4	2	4	2	4	3	3	3
HUNGARY	2	2	2	2	2	2	2	2	2	2	2	2
INDIA	4	3	4	3	4	3	3	3	3	3	3	4
INDONES	4	3	5	3	4	3	4	3	5	3	4	4
IRAN	5	–	4	5	5	5	5	5	5	5	5	5
IRAQ	4	4	4	4	4	4	4	5	5	4	5	5
ISRAEL	2	2	2	2	2	2	2	2	3	2	3	2
ITALY	2	1	2	1	2	1	2	3	2	1	2	1
JAPAN	–	1	–	1	1	1	2	1	1	1	1	1
JORDAN	3	2	3	2	3	3	–	2	2	2	3	2
KENYA	–	2	2	2	3	2	3	2	4	3	2	2
S.KOREA	3	3	3	2	3	3	3	3	3	3	3	3
LAOS	3	3	3	3	3	3	3	4	3	4	3	4
LEBAN	–	–	–	–	–	–	–	–	–	–	–	–
LESOTHO	2	2	3	2	3	2	2	2	2	2	3	3
LIBERIA	3	3	3	2	3	2	3	3	2	3	3	3
LIBYA	4	4	3	4	3	3	3	3	3	4	3	3
MALAYS	3	3	3	2	3	3	3	3	2	3	3	2
MEXICO	3	3	3	3	3	3	3	2	3	3	3	3
MOZAMB	3	3	3	2	3	3	3	5	3	3	4	5
NAMIBIA	4	3	3	–	3	–	3	–	4	3	4	4
NICARA	–	4	2	3	3	3	2	4	3	4	3	4
PAKIST	3	3	4	3	5	3	4	3	3	3	3	3
PERU	3	2	3	2	4	2	4	3	4	4	5	4
PHILIPP	4	3	4	4	4	3	4	4	4	3	4	4
POLAND	3	3	3	2	3	3	3	3	3	3	3	3
ROMANIA	3	3	3	3	3	2	3	3	3	3	3	3
SENEGAL	–	1	–	1	–	2	–	1	2	2	3	1
SEYCHEL	–	2	2	2	2	2	–	2	2	2	2	2
SILEONE	–	2	2	1	–	2	3	2	2	2	2	2

Table 2 (*continued*)

	1980		1981		1982		1983		1984		1985	
	AI	SD	AI	SD	AI	SD	AI	SD	AI	SD	AI	SD
SINGAP	3	3	3	2	3	2	2	2	2	2	1	2
SOMALIA	3	3	3	2	3	2	3	3	3	3	3	3
S.AFRI	3	3	3	2	3	3	4	2	3	3	4	4
SUDAN	3	2	3	3	3	2	3	2	3	3	3	3
SYRIA	5	4	5	5	5	5	4	4	4	4	3	4
TAIWAN	3	3	3	3	3	2	3	3	2	2	2	2
THAILA	3	3	3	3	3	3	-	3	2	3	3	2
TURKEY	4	3	4	3	4	3	4	3	3	3	4	3
USSR	3	3	3	3	3	3	3	3	3	3	3	3
UGANDA	4	4	5	4	4	5	5	5	4	4	5	5
VIETNAM	3	3	3	3	3	3	3	3	-	3	3	3
N.YEMEN	-	3	-	3	-	3	-	3	2	3	3	3
S.YEMEN	3	3	3	3	2	3	2	3	2	3	3	3
YUGOSLA	3	2	3	3	3	3	3	2	3	3	3	3
ZAIRE	4	3	4	3	4	3	4	3	3	3	3	4
ZIMBAB	3	2	3	2	3	3	4	5	5	4	4	5

refugee policy. The reasons why one would expect a direct relationship have already been expressed above.

The approach used here was first developed by Stohl et al.[60] and by Carleton and Stohl.[61] Countries have been coded (Table 2) on a scale from 1 to 5 (as listed) according to the level of political violence and terror that country experiences in a particular year based on a "terror scale" originally developed by Freedom House.

Level 1: Countries . . . under a secure rule of law, people are not imprisoned for their views, and torture is rare or exceptional. . . . Political murders are extremely rare. . . .

Level 2: There is a limited amount of imprisonment for nonviolent political activity. However, few persons are affected, torture and beating are exceptional. . . . Political murder is rare. . . .

Level 3: There is extensive political imprisonment, or a recent history of such imprisonment. Execution or other political murders and brutality may be common. Unlimited detention, with or without trial, for political views is accepted. . . .

Level 4: The practices of Level 3 are expanded to larger numbers. Murders, disappearances, and torture are a common part of life. . . . In spite of its generality, on this level terror affects those who interest themselves in politics or ideas.

Level 5: The terrors of Level 4 have been expanded to the whole population. . . . The leaders of these societies place no limits on the means or thoroughness with which they pursue personal or ideological goals.

The data for the coding comes from two sources: The State Department Country Reports (SD), and Amnesty International Reports (AI). In the construction of an index for each year for each report, countries were scaled as if the reports were accurate and complete. Thus, any biases exhibited in the annual reports of the two organizations should be evident in the indices.[62]

The countries that have been coded are those from which nationals have been accepted as refugees/asylees in the United States.

Human Rights and Grants of Asylum

The first analysis we present examines the degree to which successful applicants for asylum reflect the varying levels of human rights violations that exist in the world. Simply stated, are successful asylum applicants more likely to be from countries with the worst human rights records, those in Levels 4 and 5? The data indicate that successful applicants are by and large from countries with the worst human rights records; Table 3 presents our findings. For example, in 1984 the United States granted asylum to 8,191 individuals, of whom 63 percent were from Level 5 countries (using data based on the State Department Report), 21.9 percent from Level 4, and 13.6 percent were from Level 3. In many respects this is prototypical of what we would expect. Two years that go against this general trend are 1980 and 1981. In 1980, 46.9 percent of those granted asylum were from Level 3 countries (using Amnesty International), and only 23 percent of the successful applicants were from Level 5.

HUMAN RIGHTS AND REFUGEE ADMISSIONS

While U.S. asylum practice appears to reflect varying levels of human rights conditions in the world, in contrast, U.S. refugee policy shows little relationship to the level of human rights conditions in other countries. In fact, it is safe to say that refugee admission is the special preserve of individuals from Level 3 countries, rather than Levels 4 or 5 (see Table 4). For example, in 1981 fully 87.7 percent of the refugees admitted to the United States were from Level 3 countries (using data from the State Department Report), and only 7.3 percent were from Levels 4 and 5 *combined*.

What our findings strongly suggest is that to a much larger extent than asylum adjudications, refugee admissions are premised on something other than humanitarian concerns. Individuals from countries with the worst human rights violations are being bypassed in U.S. refugee admissions. One possible explanation, of course, is that refugees from Level 4 or Level 5 countries have found a safe haven elsewhere. However, in light of the teeming refugee populations in some of the world's poorest countries, this offers a weak rationale indeed. We believe that policymakers should completely rethink U.S. refugee policy and make a much more concerted effort to gear refugee admissions to meet the very serious needs that are not being met under present policy.

Table 3
Human Rights and Grants of Asylum

Levels	1980 (1,049 granted)		1981 (1108)		1982 (3752)	
	AI	SD	AI	SD	AI	SD
5	23.0%	34.5%	19.3%	29.0%	75.5%	74.0%
4	25.0	10.3	30.4	23.6	7.8	8.9
3	46.9	47.5	19.3	33.2	15.8	14.1
2	3.9	5.9	29.9	13.4	0.7	2.8
1	0.0	0.1	0.0	0.0	0.0	0.0
NC	1.2	1.7	1.1	0.8	0.3	0.2
	100.0	100.0	100.0	100.0	100.1	100.0

Levels	1983 (4550)		1984 (8191)		1985 (4577)	
	AI	SD	AI	SD	AI	SD
5	76.4%	75.1%	65.8%	63.5%	63.3%	63.5%
4	4.7	10.1	3.6	21.9	6.4	16.3
3	13.5	13.2	29.0	13.6	27.5	18.5
2	4.8	1.5	1.5	0.8	2.0	1.7
1	0.0	0.0	0	0.0	0.0	0.0
NC	0.2	0.1	0.2	0.2	0.2	0.0
	100.1	100.0	100.1	100.0	99.9	100.0

Table reads: In 1980, 1,049 individuals were granted aylum in the U.S. Using Amnesty International as a data base, 23% of those granted asylum were from Level 5 countries, 25% from level 4, and so on.

Asylum Acceptance Rates

Our analysis above showed that as a general rule most successful asylum applicants were from countries with the worst human rights records. Before concluding that U.S. asylum policy solidly reflects the level of human rights violations in other countries, it is necessary to look at asylum acceptance rates at each Level. Here U.S. policy does not fare nearly as well (see Tables

Refugee Admission

Table 4
Human Rights and Refugee Admissions

	1980 (81,752 refugees admitted)		1981 (136,793)		1982 (61,492)	
	AI	SD	AI	SD	AI	SD
Level						
5	1.4%	2.0%	3.5%	3.8%	5.6%	5.6%
4	2.6	1.4	4.0	3.5	9.8	20.0
3	84.2	95.1	90.9	87.7	83.5	68.5
2	0.5	0.3	0.8	4.1	0.7	5.6
1	0.0	0.3	0.0	0.2	0.0	0.0
NC	11.4	0.8	0.8	0.8	0.3	0.3
	100.1	99.9	100.0	100.1	99.9	100.0

	1983 (73,643)		1984 (77,926)		1985 (59,435)	
	AI	SD	AI	SD	AI	SD
Level						
5	5.2%	7.4%	4.1%	6.7%	6.7%	10.1%
4	5.8	41.6	30.5	51.2	3.1	29.5
3	87.8	48.1	63.1	41.2	84.1	59.2
2	1.1	2.7	2.1	0.2	2.6	0.9
1	0.0	0.0	0.0	0.0	0.0	0.1
NC	0.1	0.1	0.2	0.2	0.2	0.2
	100.1	99.9	100.0	100.0	100.1	100.0

Table reads: In 1980, the United States admitted 81,752 refugees. Using Amnesty International as a data base, 1.4% of the refugees admitted were from Level 5 countries, 2.6% from Level 4, and so on.

5 and 6). The asylum acceptance rate for individuals from Level 5 countries can best be described as moderate. Although in our view such rates are low, given the widespread disappearances, murders, and torture that mark those countries, still, to some degree the rates do reflect the human rights situation there.

Of far more serious concern are the extremely low asylum acceptance rates

Table 5
Asylum Acceptance Rates According to
Level of Human Rights Violations by Year, 1980–1985

		1980		1981	
		AI	SD	AI	SD
Levels					
	5	.69 (241/349)	.80 (362/448)	.37 (214/567)	.41 (321/769)
	4	.62 (262/421)	.52 (108/206)	.25 (337/1323)	.24 (262/1094)
	3	.55 (492/890)	.58 (498/859)	.16 (214/1283)	.27 (368/1381)
	2	.71 (41/ 57)	.48 (62/129)	.39 (331/ 851)	.18 (148/ 826)
	1	0 (13/136)	.06 (18/194)	.06 (12/ 213)	.05 (9/ 163)
Total		1049/1853		1108/4237	

		1982		1983	
		AI	SD	AI	SD
Levels					
	5	.49 (2831/5724)	.60 (2778/4642)	.39 (3498/8846)	.65 (3418/5270)
	4	.25 (291/1156)	.16 (335/2043)	.21 (213/989)	.07 (459/5922)
	3	.18 (594/3290)	.16 (528/3146)	.29 (615/2123)	.28 (601/2140)
	2	.18 (25/135)	.24 (104/439)	.13 (217/1612)	.26 (66/255)
	1	0 (0/0)	.03 (0/9)	.03 (0/0)	.03 (0/4)
	NC	.05 (11/209)	.03 (7/205)	.03 (7/242)	.03 (6/221)
Total		3952/10514		4550/13812	

Table 5 (*continued*)

Levels		1984		1985	
		AI	SD	AI	SD
	5	.24 (5386/22694)	.60 (52.3/8688)	.46 (2897/6176)	.47 (2906/6174)
	4	.27 (296/1092)	.07 (1792/24520)	.08 (317/3582)	.08 (746/8488)
	3	.16 (2374/14555)	.22 (1115/5017)	.15 (1260/8574)	.24 (847/3460)
	2	.16 (119/737)	.07 (65/853)	.39 (91/232)	.17 (76/435)
	1	0 (0/0)	0 (0/0)	1.00 (1/1)	.05 (2/39)
	NC	.03 (16/534)	.03 (16/534)	.35 (11/31)	0 (0/0)
Total		8191/34612		Total	4577/18596

Table reads: In 1980, of the 349 applications for asylum from individuals from Level 5 countries (using Amnesty International) 241, or 69%, were successful.

Table 6
Cumulative Asylum Acceptance Rates According to Level
of Human Rights Violations, 1980–1985

AI

Level	# Asylum Applications	Asylum Granted	%
5	44,356	12,170	.274
4	8,563	1,716	.200
3	30,715	5,917	.1926
2	3,624	824	.227
1	–	–	–

SD

Level	# Asylum Applications	Asylum Granted	%
5	25,991	14,988	.576
4	42,273	3,702	.087
3	16,033	3,957	.246
2	2,937	521	.177
1	73	3	.041

for applicants from Level 4 countries. This is particularly true given the State Department Report. For example, in both 1983 and 1984 only 7 percent of the asylum applicants from Level 4 countries were successful, and in 1985 this number was only 8 percent. In fact, the cumulative asylum acceptance rate (Table 6) for individuals from Level 4 countries (using the State Department Reports) was only 8.7 percent, 3,702 successful applicants out of the 42,273 who applied. One explanation for this result is that a large percentage of the applicants from this Level were from El Salvador and Guatemala. However, notwithstanding which countries were involved, the very low percentage rates strongly indicate that in playing the vital role that it does in asylum determinations, the State Department apparently ignores its own data.[63] That is, the harsh depiction that it gives of other countries in

Table 7
Rank Order Correlations Between Human
Rights and U.S. Refugee Admissions and
Grants of Asylum

		AI	SD
1980	Asylum	.2963	.4082
	Refugee	−.0096	.1264
1981	Asylum	.1663	.3349
	Refugee	.0594	.0315
1982	Asylum	.3117	.4009
	Refugee	−.0931	.0975
1983	Asylum	.2454	.3208
	Refugee	−.0211	.1618
1984	Asylum	.2208	.4426
	Refugee	.0468	.2618
1985	Asylum	.1938	.3731
	Refugee	−.0288	.1833

Coded for countries with 15 or more asylee/refugee applicants.

the State Department Country Reports is not necessarily reflected in asylum determinations.

Another oddity of our findings is the fact that individuals from Level 2 countries are much more successful in their asylum applications than we would expect. For example, in 1985 fully 39 percent of the applicants from Level 2 countries (using Amnesty International) were successful. Moreover, this result is occasionally mirrored in other years as well. These are nations without much political terror, and these findings are difficult to explain, particularly in light of the very low acceptance rates for individuals from Level 4 countries.

Correlation Analysis

The last analysis that will be presented involves the correlation between the level of human rights violations and both refugee admissions and asylum acceptances (Table 7). The correlations are generally quite low, particularly with data from the Amnesty International Reports, as evidenced by several negative correlations. However, even employing the State Department Reports as a data source, the Spearman rank-order correlations are not particularly impressive, and certainly not what one would expect given the legal and moral duties in the 1980 Refugee Act.

One reason why one would expect much high correlations, beyond those already explored, is that there is a great deal of self-selection involved in U.S. refugee admissions and asylum applications. In terms of refugee admissions, the location of refugee processing centers, and the refugee priority guidelines themselves, serve to exclude large portions of the world's refugee population. In terms of asylum applications, while the United States cannot refuse to hear a claim for asylum from an alien already in this country, it can seek to prevent those who might apply for asylum from ever arriving in this country, as it has with the interdiction of Haitian boatpeople.

DISCUSSION

Several points need to be made about the results of this study. We are not suggesting that those who have been admitted as refugees are not, in fact, bona fide refugees. The empirical evidence presented here is looking at macro level occurrences, and on one level such data is not relevant to the claims of any single individual. Having said this, however, the data are troublesome in the sense that countries where there is a great deal of persecution in the form of massive killings, torture, disappearances, and the like are not necessarily the countries whose citizens are receiving refuge in the United States.

Excerpts on human rights conditions in El Salvador in 1981 from both the State Department and Amnesty International have already been offered.[64] Contrast this with the State Department's depiction of human rights conditions in Hungary in 1981:

According to Hungarian officials, the number of political prisoners is about fifty. Emigration is possible within limits; visits abroad, including to western countries, are possible within wider limits. Practice of religion is tolerated within the framework of agreements reached between the Hungarian churches and the government. Secret police and prosecutorial discretion, powers, and methods have been somewhat curtailed. . . .

. . . . There are no known recent instances of torture.

There have been no known summary executions in Hungary in recent years. . . . There does not appear to be deliberate and willful or other systematic mistreatment of prisoners.

There have been no reported disappearances in Hungary in the past year.

Citizens generally are free from arbitrary arrest.[65]

Under our coding, the data from the Amnesty International Report had El Salvador as a "5," and using the State Department as a data source we coded it as "4" (which is a good indication of how conservative our coding scheme is). Hungary was coded as a "2," employing data from both the State Department and Amnesty International. In 1981 the United States admitted 441 individuals from Hungary as refugees and granted asylum to an additional 21. As mentioned earlier, in contrast, the United States did not admit a single refugee from El Salvador that year (and only ninety-six since 1981), and only two asylum claims were successful.

Our position is that the persecution in Hungary is qualitatively different from the persecution in El Salvador. It should be clear from the State Department Report that persecution in El Salvador is far more pernicious than that in Hungary. Persecution in El Salvador takes the form of torture, death, and disappearance. Persecution in Hungary does not take these forms. If all else were equal, admitting Hungarians ahead of Salvadorans would not be objectionable. However, the degree of persecution in El Salvador and Hungary is not equal.[66] Far more people in El Salvador than in Hungary face "serious" persecution. Our position is that U.S. refugee/asylum policy ought to reflect these differences.

CONCLUSION

This chapter has attempted to break new ground by presenting an empirical examination of U.S. refugee/asylum policy. Its focus has been on the relationship between the level of human rights violations in other countries and the United States response in terms of refugee admissions and grants of asylum. The results are quite troublesome. As a general rule there is little relationship between the level of political terror in other societies and U.S. refugee/asylum policy with regard to individuals from these countries. More specifically, the beneficiaries of U.S. refugee admissions are almost all from Level 3 countries. What this means is that individuals from countries that have the worst human rights records in the world are systematically ignored by U.S. authorities who decide refugee admissions.

Asylum adjudications are more difficult to categorize. To a certain extent it can be said that there is a closer relationship here between the level of political terror and U.S. asylum adjudications. However, this relationship is weak at best. Our conclusion is that both refugee admissions and asylum practice need serious reexamination by policymakers.

NOTES

We would like to thank Alex Aleinikoff and Guy Goodwin-Gill for their very useful comments on an earlier draft of this chapter. We would also like to thank a group of undergraduate and graduate students at Purdue who carried the brunt of the tedious coding for this project: Gilbert Arroyo, Michael Becker, Luis Lavergne, Frank Owens, Mark Ulanowicz, and Susan Young.

1. Refugee Act of 1980, Pub. L. No. 96–212, 94 Stat. 109 (1980).

2. It should be noted that rather than employing the old seventh preference of the Immigration Act, which ostensibly governed refugee admissions, the attorney general would quite frequently "parole" refugees into the United States. Through use of this power hundreds of thousands of Cubans were admitted to the United States in the early 1960s, the mid–1960s, and even in 1980 *after* passage of the 1980 Refugee Act. Ideology dominated admissions under this avenue as well. Arthur Helton computes that before 1968, the attorney general paroled 925 refugees from non-Communist countries and 232,711 from Communist countries. For the period 1968–1980, there were 7,150 refugees paroled into the U.S. from non-Communist countries, compared with 608,365 from Communist countries. Arthur Helton, "Political Asylum Under the 1980 Refugee Act: An Unfulfilled Promise," *Michigan Journal of Law Reform* 17 (1984): 246, 248.

3. H.R. Rep. No. 608, 96th Cong., 1st Sess. 13 (1979).

4. The terms "refugee" and "asylee" are often used interchangeably here. Refugees seek admission under such status from outside our borders, while asylum applicants apply for refugee status from inside our borders. Although the statutory standard is the same, the Immigration and Naturalization Service (INS) itself has noted that in practice the actual standards of proof have differed. See note 39 and accompanying text.

5. Geneva Convention Relating to the Status of Refugees, Art. 1, done at Geneva, July 28, 1951. In 1968 the United States became a signatory to the 1967 United Nations protocol relating to the Status of Refugees, January 31, 1967, 19 UNTS 6223, T.I.A.S. No. 6557. Among the protocol's provisions are Article 33 (nonrefoulement), which provides that contracting states shall not return a refugee to a country where his or her life would be threatened because of race, religion, or nationality. Article 34 provides that contracting states shall, as far as possible, facilitate the assimilation of refugees.

6. It should be noted that in order to be considered a convention refugee, the applicant must be "outside the country of his nationality and is unable or . . . unwilling to avail himself of the protection of that country." U.S. law has expanded this standard to also include individuals who are still within the country of their nationality. 8 U.S.C. Section 1101(a)(42).

7. U.S. Department of State, *Country Reports on Human Rights Practices for 1981* (Washington, D.C.: Government Printing Office, 1982), 424–425.

8. Ibid., p. 427.

9. *Amnesty International Report 1982: A Survey of Political Imprisonment, Torture and Executions* (London: Amnesty International Publications, 1982), p. 133.

10. U.S. Department of Health and Human Services, *Refugee Resettlement Program*, Tables 7 and 8, A–11 and A–12, January 31, 1986.

11. Ibid.

12. The various positions attributed to the executive branch are taken from the testimony and remarks of Elliot Abrams, formerly assistant secretary of state for human rights and humanitarian affairs, Doris Meissner, executive associate commissioner, Immigration and Naturalization Service, and Alan Nelson, commissioner, Immigration and Naturalization Service. U.S. Cong., House, Hearings on H.R. 4447 before the Subcommittee on Immigration, Refugees, and International Law of the Committee on the Judiciary, *Temporary Suspension of Deportation of Certain Aliens*, 98th Cong., 2nd sess. (1984).

13. U.S. Coordinator for Refugee Affairs, Report to the Congress for Fiscal Year 1987, *Proposed Refugee Admissions and Allocations for Fiscal Year 1987* (Washington, D.C.: Government Printing Office, 1986), p. 13.

14. Patricia Weiss Fagen, "Refugees, Human Rights and Foreign Policy: A Case Study of U.S. Politics" (paper prepared for presentation at the Workshop on Human Rights and Foreign Policy, Freiburg, March 20–25, 1983), p. 21.

15. As of July 31, 1983, there were over 244,000 Salvadoran nationals in the countries of Mexico and Central America. Note, "Salvadoran Illegal Aliens: A Struggle to Obtain Refuge in the United States," *University of Pittsburgh Law Review* 47 (1985): 324.

16. *Proposed Refugee Admissions and Allocations for Fiscal Year 1987*, p. 7.

17. Ibid., p. 5.

18. "Recommend that the UNHCR should continue to express its concern to the U.S. government that its apparent failure to grant asylum to any significant number of Salvadorans, coupled with continuing large-scale forcible and voluntary return to El Salvador, would appear to represent a negation of its responsibilities assumed upon its adherence to the Protocol." *United Nations High Commissioner for Refugees, Mission to Monitor INS Asylum Processing of Salvadoran Illegal Entrants*, September 13–18, 1981, reprinted in the *Congressional Record*, February 11, 1982, S. 827–831.

19. During the congressional hearings on the question of granting temporary refuge, or extended voluntary departure status (EVD), to Salvadorans, Assistant Secretary of State Elliot Abrams referred to a State Department study of 482 returnees to El Salvador. Although Abrams offered this by way of proof of the safety of returnees, only one-third of those listed had been contacted. Hearings on H.R. 4447, 93. During the 1985 hearings on this same piece of legislation, Laura Deitrich, deputy assistant secretary of the Bureau of Human Rights and Humanitarian Affairs, briefly alluded to an ICM (Intergovernmental Committee for Migration) follow-up contact study that seemed to show what the Reagan administration has been saying publicly. U.S. Cong., House, Hearings on H.R. 822, before the Subcommittee on Immigration, Refugees, and International Law of the Committee on the Judiciary, *Temporary Suspension of Deportation for Nationals of Certain Countries*, 99th Cong., 1st. sess (1985). The General Accounting Office has recently concluded that some of the Salvadorans sent home from the United States had experienced "personal security problems." General Accounting Office, "Illegal Aliens: Extent of Problems Experienced by Returned Salvadorans Not Determinable" (May 1987). The most rigorous study in this area has been conducted by William Stanley, "Economic Migrants or Refugees from Violence? A Time Series Analysis of Salvadoran Migration to the United States," reprinted in Hearings on H.R. 822. Stanley's time series analysis

shows strong correlations between the levels of violence in El Salvador and the number of people exiting that country.

20 See, for example, the letter from Alvin Paul Drischler, assistant secretary of state for congressional relations, to Senator Edward Kennedy (reprinted in 128 *Congressional Record*, S. 831, daily ed., February 11, 1982), suggesting that conditions in El Salvador are not as bad as they had been in Nicaragua, Lebanon, or Uganda when nationals from these countries were granted EVD.

21. Raymond Bonner, "Sandinistas Aren't the Worst," *New York Times*, September 14, 1984, p. 29.

22. The Reagan administration not only claims progress in human rights for refugee purposes, but also that El Salvador meets conditions for granting foreign and military aid under Section 728 of the International Security and Development Cooperation Act of 1981, Pub. L. No. 97–1143, 95 Stat. 1519, 1555–1557 (1981) (codified at 22 U.S.C. Section 2370 note [1982].

23. Quoted from Gilburt Loescher and John Scanlan, *Calculated Kindness: Refugees and America's Half-Open Door, 1945–Present* (New York: Free Press, 1986), p. 179.

24. The most notable exception to this judicial deference, at least in terms of Salvadoran claims, is *Orantes-Hernandez v. Smith*, 541 F. Supp. 351 (C.D. Cal. 1982). For a discussion of judicial deference in the area of alien admissions generally and a critique of this policy, see Mark Gibney, "The Role of the Judiciary in Alien Admissions," *Boston College International and Comparative Law Review* 8(1985): 341–376.

25. 692 F. 2d 595 (9th Cir. 1982).

26. The term "asylum" is used here to include asylum as well as claims for the suspension of deportation, although the forms of relief differ. For present purposes, the most significant source of difference involves the burden of proof. In suspension of deportation hearings the claimant must show a "clear probability" of persecution. *Stevic v. INS*, 104 S. Ct. 2489 (1984). In asylum claims the burden of proof is a well-founded fear of persecution, which, the Supreme Court has recently held, is a lower standard of proof, *INS v. Cardoza-Fonseca*, 107 S. Ct. 1207 (1987).

27. It should be noted, however, that the same charge has generally not been made against the 9th circuit. See, Carolyn P. Blum, "The Ninth Circuit and the Protection of Asylum Seekers Since the Passage of the Refugee Act of 1980," *San Diego Law Review* 23(1986): 327–373.

28. *Bolanos-Hernandez v. INS*, 767 F. 2d 1277, 1284 (9th Cir. 1984).

29. The federal circuit courts in the United States have split in terms of the kind of evidence that the petitioner for relief must present. In the *Bolanos* case the court granted the petitioner's claim for relief under both 243(h) (suspension of deportation) and 208(a) (asylum). In this case Bolanos-Hernandez claimed that because of his former ties with the Salvadoran army, his present effort to remain neutral would open himself to persecution from guerrilla rebels. Although Bolanos-Hernandez was not able to offer any corroborating evidence of the death threats that he claims were made against him, the court held that his testimony of such threats was sufficient to grant the relief sought. The court reiterated the position that the human rights violations in El Salvador were not, by themselves, conclusive of the petitioner's claim; however, the conditions were germane to the seriousness or credibility of this claim.

Contrast *Bolanos-Hernandez* with *Dally v. INS*, 744 F. 2d 1191 (6th Cir. 1984), where the court strongly believed one of the petitioners' testimony of past persecution and the likely prospect of its happening again in the future, but refused to grant the relief sought because of the lack of corroborative evidence. It should be noted that the UNHCR has taken the position that because of severe problems asylum applicants will have in collecting evidence to support their claims, they should be given the benefit of the doubt whenever their testimony sounds credible. United Nations High Commissioner for Refugees, *Handbook on Procedures and Criteria for Determining Refugee Status* (Geneva: United Nations, 1979).

30. There is a burgeoning law review literature that is almost universally condemnatory of U.S. refugee/asylum practice with regard to El Salvador. See, for example, Note, "Membership in a Social Group: Salvadoran Refugees and the 1980 Refugee Act," *Hastings International and Comparative Law Review* 8 (1985): 305–338; Note, "The Agony and the Exodus: Deporting Salvadorans in Violation of the Fourth Geneva Convention," *New York University Journal of International Law and Politics* 18 (1986): 703–744; Note, "Ecumenical, Municipal and Legal Challenges to United States Refugee Policy," *Harvard Civil Rights–Civil Liberties Law Review* 21 (1986): 494–601; Comment, "The Expanded Jurisprudence of the Religion Clauses: Will the Sanctuary Movement Benefit?" *Gonzaga Law Review* 21 (1985–1986): 177–197; Note, "Salvadoran Illegal Aliens: A Struggle to Obtain Refuge in the United States," *University of Pittsburgh Law Review* 47 (1985): 295–335.

31. In 1983 the U.S. Congress passed a "sense of Congress" that the secretary of state should recommend EVD status to Salvadorans until they could safely return to El Salvador. Pub. L. No. 98–164, Title X, Section 1012, 97 Stat. 1062 (1983). Because this "sense of Congress" has been ignored by the executive branch as well as the judiciary, there have been continued efforts in this area. On July 28, 1987, the House of Representatives passed H.R. 618, a bill that would grant EVD status to most Salvadorans and Nicaraguans in the United States. The companion legislation in the Senate, S. 332, received a favorable vote in the Senate Judiciary Committee, but floor consideration of the bill was postponed until 1988.

32. Extended Voluntary Departure status has been granted in the following instances: Cuba—1960 to 1966; Dominican Republic—1966 to 1978; Czechoslovakia—1968 to 1977; Chile—1971 to 1977; Cambodia—1975 to 1977; Vietnam—1975 to 1977; Laos—1975 to 1977; Lebanon—1977 to present; Ethiopia—1977 to present; Uganda—1978 to present; Iran—1979; Nicaragua—1979 to 1980; Afghanistan—1980 to present; Poland—1981 to present. See H.R. Rep. No. 142, Part I, 98th Cong., 2d sess. 4 (1984).

33. Hearings on H.R. 4447, p. 17.

34. The original House version of the Simpson/Rodino bill recently passed into law had a provision granting EVD status to Salvadorans and Nicaraguans. The Senate version did not have this provision, and it was removed in the conference committee. *Congressional Quarterly* 44: (October 18, 1986): 2598. The most interesting new development in this area is that in 1987 President José Napoléon Duarte asked the Reagan administration to grant temporary refuge to Salvadorans in the United States. Robert Pear, "Duarte Appeals to Reagan to Let Salvadorans Stay," *New York Times*, April 26, 1987, p. 1. After some consideration, this request was denied. Robert Pear, "Reagan Rejects Salvadoran Plea for Illegal Aliens," *New York Times*, May 15, 1987, p. 1. Several things should be noted about this rather "bizarre twist," to use Senator

Simpson's depiction. One is that President Duarte has based his request on economic considerations, rather than on the safety of Salvadorans. Just as odd has been the fact that Elliott Abrams, assistant secretary of state for inter-American affairs and before this time the staunchest opponent of EVD status for Salvadorans, was in the forefront in supporting Duarte's request.

35. *United Nations High Commissioner for Refugees, Mission to Monitor INS Asylum Processing of Salvadoran Illegal Entrants.*

36. Letter from Kallu Kalumiya, Legal Counsel, UNHCR, Re: *UNHCR Mandate Definition of Refugee and the Situation of Salvadoran Asylum Seekers,* February 1982, p. 10.

37. To date the sanctuary movement comprises over 400 congregations, 22 cities, 3 states, and 12 colleges and universities. For an excellent discussion of the sanctuary movement, see Note, "Ecumenical, Municipal and Legal Challenges to United States Refugee Policy," *Harvard Civil Rights–Civil Liberties Law Review*; see also, Mark Gibney, "The Refugee Act of 1980: A Humanitarian Standard," *Gonzaga Law Review* 21(1985–1986): 585–602.

38. The America's Watch report points out that human rights conditions in El Salvador have become "acceptable" because of the well-publicized view that the violations have, to a degree, abated. Tutela Legal, the human rights office of the Roman Catholic Archdiocese of San Salvador, computed 1,913 civilian deaths in 1985. America's Watch notes a certain irony in these statistics: "There are few places elsewhere where some 1,900 political killings and disappearances in a year—approximately ninety percent of them at the hands of armed forces ostensibly controlled by a civilian democratic government—would be considered routine. In El Salvador, however, where the number of such killings reached a high of some 13,000 in 1981, the comparison to what went before has blunted the impact of the current figures" (*Settling into Routine: Human Rights Abuses in Duarte's Second Year* [New York, 1986], p. 3).

39. *Asylum Adjudications: An Evolving Concept and Responsibility in the Immigration and Naturalization Service* (Washington, D.C., 1982), p. 59.

40. Ibid., p. 80–81.

41. The Organization of African Unity (OAU) has an expanded definition of refugees that covers such situations; it reads: "The term refugee shall mean every person who, owing to external aggression, occupation, foreign domination or events seriously disturbing public order in either part or the whole of his country of origin or nationality, is compelled to leave his place of habitual residence in order to seek refuge" (Organization of African Unity, Convention on Refugee Problems in Africa, art. I, para. 2, September 10, 1969, 1001 UNTS 45).

42. Deborah Perluss and Joan Hartman, "Temporary Refuge: Emergence of a Customary Norm," *Virginia Journal of International Law* 26(1986): 583.

43. Ibid., p. 585.

44. For an excellent argument of why it might be overreaching to conclude that there exists a peremptory customary norm of nonrefoulement, see Kay Hailbronner, "Non-Refoulement and 'Humanitarian' Refugees: Customary International Law or Wishful Thinking?" *Virginia Journal of International Law* 26(1986): 857.

45. Office of the U.N. High Commissioner for Refugees, *Handbook on Procedures and Criteria for Determining Refugee Status.*

46. Guy Goodwill-Gill, *The Refugee in International Law* (Oxford: Clarendon Press, 1983), p. 40.

47. Atle Grahl-Madsen, *The Status of Refugees in International Law*, vol. 1 (London: A. W. Sijthoff, 1966), p. 193.

48. Ibid.

49. Grahl-Madsen seems to be a proponent of the "liberal" school. For example, he is critical of the 1980 Swedish Aliens Act, which limits refugee efforts to persecution that threatens a person's life or freedom or is otherwise of a serious nature. Atle Grahl-Madsen, "Refugees and Refugee Law in Transition," *Transnational Legal Problems of Refugees, 1982 Michigan Yearbook of International Legal Studies* (New York: Clark Boardman Company, Ltd., 1982), p. 69.

50. It has recently been argued that the inability to define "persecution" has made a sham of U.S. refugee policy and, at the same time, has allowed political considerations free reign in this area. Sophie Pirie, "The Need for a Codified Definition of 'Persecution' in United States Refugee Law," *Stanford Law Review* 39(1986): 187.

51. Although Kay Hailbronner takes the position that there is no customary norm of nonrefoulement generally, he also argues that individuals have a right not to be tortured, which creates a peremptory norm of international law to aid those who are the victims of torture. Hailbronner, "Non-Refoulement and 'Humanitarian' Refugees," pp. 887–895.

52. We have purposely refrained from commenting here and elsewhere on whether other countries have helped to cause the refugee population. For an extended discussion of why this matters, and what moral duties arise from harm done to nationals of other countries, see generally Mark Gibney, *Strangers or Friends: Principles for a New Alien Admission Policy* (Westport, Conn.: Greenwood Press, 1986).

53. The State Department's priority guidelines are as follows:

1. Compelling concern/interest: exceptional cases (a) of refugees in immediate danger of loss of life and for whom there appears to be no alternative to resettlement in the United States, or (b) of refugees of compelling concern to the United States, such as former or present political prisoners and dissidents.

2. Former U.S. government employees: refugees employed by the U.S. government for at least one year prior to the claim for refugee status. This category also includes persons who were not official U.S. government employees, but who for at least one year were so integrated into U.S. Government offices as to have been in effect and appearance U.S. government employees.

3. Family Reunification: refugees who are spouses, sons, daughters, parents, grandparents, unmarried siblings or unmarried minor grandchildren of persons in the United States.

4. Other ties to the United States: (a) refugees employed by U.S. foundations, U.S. voluntary agencies or U.S. business firms for at least one year prior to the claim for refugee status; and, (b) refugees trained or educated in the United States or abroad under U.S. auspices.

5. Additional family reunification: refugees who are married siblings, unmarried grandchildren who have reached their majority, or married grandchildren or persons in the United States; also more distantly related individuals who are part of the family group and dependent on the family for support.

6. Otherwise of national interest: other refugees in specified regional groups whose admission is in the national interest.

Source: Refugee Policy Group, Of Special Humanitarian Concern: U.S. Refugee Admissions Since Passage of the Refugee Act (Washington, D.C.: Refugee Policy Group, 1985), p. 45.

This excellent study of U.S. refugee policy is particularly harsh in terms of this priority system. For one thing, it is argued that the priority system drives refugee determinations, not the other way around. Moreover, much like the argument made in this chapter, the Refugee Policy Group criticizes U.S. refugee admissions for ignoring those in the most humanitarian category, the first one.

54. Proposed Refugee Admissions and Allocations for Fiscal Year 1987, Appendix C, p. 39.

55. For a general discussion of how the United States has employed refugee admissions as a foreign policy tool, see Michael Teitelbaum, "Immigration, Refugees, and Foreign Policy," International Organization 38(1984): 428–450.

56. At present there have been strong indications that the Reagan administration is attempting to resurrect officially the ideological barriers found in U.S. law and policy before the Refugee Act of 1980. For example, in 1985, Perry Rivkind, the INS district director for Florida, publicly stated that his office would refuse to return any Nicaraguans back to that country because of the totalitarian characteristics of the Sandinista regime. This was apparently done with the acquiescence of top officials of the Justice Department. Robert Pear, "Key Federal Aide Refuses to Deport Any Nicaraguans," New York Times, April 17, 1986, p. 1. Since then the INS has taken bolder steps to allow Nicaraguans to remain in the United States. "Immigration Rules Are Eased For Nicaraguan Exiles in U.S." New York Times, July 9, 1987, p. 5.

57. For an insightful critique of this nebulous standard see Refugee Policy Group, Of Special Humanitarian Concern.

58. There are a number of quirks about the admission of individuals from totalitarian regimes that need to be explored. To begin, one of the guiding principles of the Reagan administration's foreign policy has been the distinction between "authoritarian" and "totalitarian" regimes. The latter have been a special target of the present regime because they are supposedly worse in that a totalitarian government purportedly dominates all aspects of life in that society, while an authoritarian regime purportedly does not. See Jeane Kirkpatrick, "Dictatorships and Double Standards," Commentary 68(1979): 34–45. Moreover, the argument has been made that some authoritarian, but no totalitarian countries, have eventually become democracies.

In many respects the Reagan administration's refugee admissions can be explained by this authoritarian-totalitarian distinction. What is puzzling is when and why this distinction has been discarded. Given the depiction of totalitarian regimes by the present administration, one is hard pressed to explain how any individuals from those countries are denied asylum in this country. The asylum acceptance rates are certainly much higher for those from totalitarian countries than they are for those from authoritarian countries, but certainly nowhere near 100 percent. Another oddity of U.S. refugee policy concerns the subtle shift currently underway in Southeast Asia. The INS is beginning to characterize some individuals leaving Communist countries in that area as "economic migrants." This shift goes against a decade-old policy regarding Southeast Asian refugees.

Finally, the relatively low number of refugees from Nicaragua bears some examination. Since 1980, the United States has granted asylum to 2,244 individuals, while at the same time admitting only 6 refugees (but see what appears to be a shift in policy, note 56). The Reagan administration has used these figures to claim that ideological biases have been removed from refugee/asylum determinations. We choose to interpret these data in another way, namely, as another indication that there is apparently little connection between human rights violations and U.S. refugee policy. What makes Nicaragua unique, in our view, is that it is purportedly a totalitarian regime.

59. *Proposed Refugee Admissions and Allocations for Fiscal Year 1987*, p. 13.

60. Michael Stohl, David Carleton, and Steven E. Johnson, "Human Rights and U.S. Foreign Assistance: From Nixon to Carter," *Journal of Peace Research* 25(1984): 215–226.

61. David Carleton and Michael Stohl, "The Foreign Policy of Human Rights: Rhetoric and Reality from Jimmy Carter to Ronald Reagan," *Human Rights Quarterly* 7(1985): 205–229.

62. Critics might respond in several ways to the human rights study under review here. One challenge might be to our coding of particular countries. We welcome the opportunity to have scholars reexamine the same data and to code countries accordingly. A second challenge would be to attack the premise that there is any connection between human rights violations and the creation of a refugee population. This issue has been addressed rather thoroughly in the first part of this article. Interestingly enough, in Justice Stevens' majority opinion in *INS v. Cardoza-Fonseca*, 107 S. Ct. 1207 (1987) he likened the well-founded fear of persecution test to that of having a "reasonable probability" that persecution would occur. Stevens explained this notion of reasonable probability by stating that a person with a "10 percent chance of being shot, tortured, or otherwise persecuted" might be eligible for asylum. The analysis presented here is similarly based on probabilities as well.

A final criticism we foresee is the argument that the political terror scale employed here is biased against totalitarian regimes, particularly Eastern bloc countries, because the state machinery is so efficient—and the population thus so cowered—that there will be few instances of actual human rights violations in those countries. We feel that in certain respects this would be a legitimate criticism. It is imperative to point out, however, that we are not taking the position that so-called totalitarian states are "just" under any definition of that term. Some citizens of those countries do in fact suffer inhumane persecution. What we do contend, nonetheless, is that the inhumane treatment meted out by the governments of these countries often affects a smaller portion of the population than in countries with worse human rights records under our coding scheme. Moreover, we also maintain that the massive killings, disappearances, and torture that exist in some countries are examples of more "serious" forms of human rights abuses than the imprisonment of political prisoners, despite our detestation of such state practices. See notes 7–9 and accompanying text.

63. 8 C.F.R. 208.7 (1987).

64. See notes 7–9 and accompanying text.

65. *Country Reports on Human Rights Practices for 1981*, pp. 794–795.

66. Even when things appear to be equal, they really are not. One of the more interesting findings in the General Accounting Office report, "Asylum: Uniform Application of Standards Uncertain—Few Denied Applicants Deported" (January

1987), was how differently asylum applicants with the same kinds of claims were treated. For example, of the asylum applicants who stated that they were "arrested, imprisoned, had their life threatened or were tortured," only 3 percent of the Salvadoran and 7 percent of the Nicaraguan applicants were granted asylum, compared with 55 percent of the Poles and 64 percent of the Iranian applicants who made this same assertion.

BIBLIOGRAPHY

"The Agony and the Exodus: Deporting Salvadorans in Violation of the Fourth Geneva Convention." *New York University Journal of International Law and Politics* 18 (1986): 703–744.

America's Watch, *Settling into Routine: Human Rights Abuses in Duarte's Second Year*. New York: America's Watch, 1986.

Amnesty International Report for 1982: A Survey of Political Imprisonment, Torture and Executions. London: Amnesty International Publications, 1982.

Blum, Carolyn P. "The Ninth Circuit and the Protection of Asylum Seekers Since the Passage of the Refugee Act of 1980." *San Diego Law Review* 23(1986): 327–373.

Bolanos-Hernandez v. INS. 767 F. 2d 1277 (9th Cir. 1984).

Bonner, Raymond. "Sandinistas Aren't the Worst." *New York Times* September 14, 1984.

Carleton, David, and Michael Stohl. "The Foreign Policy of Human Rights: Rhetoric and Reality from Jimmy Carter to Ronald Reagan." *Human Rights Quarterly* 7(1985): 205–229.

Dally v. INS. 744 F. 2d 1191 (6th Cir. 1984).

"Ecumenical, Municipal and Legal Challenges to United States Refugee Policy." *Harvard Civil Rights-Civil Liberties Law Review* 21(1985–1986): 493–601.

Fagen, Patricia Weiss. "Refugees, Human Rights and Foreign Policy: A Case Study of U.S. Politics." (Paper prepared for presentation at the Workshop on Human Rights and Foreign Policy, Freiburg, March 20–25, 1983).

Gibney, Mark. "The Role of the Judiciary in Alien Admissions." *Boston College International and Comparative Law Review* 8(1985): 341–376.

———. "The Refugee Act of 1980: A Humanitarian Standard." *Gonzaga Law Review* 21(1985–1986): 585–602.

———. *Strangers or Friends: Principles for a New Alien Admission Policy*. Westport, Conn.: Greenwood Press, 1986.

Goodwin-Gill, Guy. *The Refugee in International Law*. Oxford: Clarendon Press, 1983.

Grahl-Madsen, Atle. *The Status of Refugees in International Law*. London: A. W. Sijthoff, 1966.

———. "Refugees and Refugee Law in Transition." *Transnational Legal Problems of Refugees, 1982 Michigan Yearbook of International Legal Studies*. New York: Clark Boardman Company, Ltd., 1982.

Hailbronner, Kay. "Non-Refoulement and 'Humanitarian' Refugees: Customary International Law or Wishful Thinking?" *Virginia Journal of International Law* 26(1985): 857–896.

Helton, Arthur. "Political Asylum Under the 1980 Refugee Act: An Unfulfilled Promise." *Michigan Journal of Law Reform* 17 (1984): 243–264.

"Immigration Rules Are Eased For Nicaraguan Exiles in U.S." *New York Times*, July 9, 1987.

INS. v. Cardoza-Fonesca. 107 S. Ct. 1207 (1987).

Kalumiya, Kallu. *Re: UNHCR Mandate Definition of Refugee and the Situation of Salvadoran Asylum Seekers.* Washington, D.C., Office of Legal Counsel, United Nations. February 1982 (copy with author).

Loescher, Gilburt, and John Scanlan. *Calculated Kindness: Refugees and America's Half-Open Door, 1945–Present.* New York: Free Press, 1979.

"Membership in a Social Group: Salvadoran Refugees and the 1980 Refugee Act." *Hastings International and Comparative Law Review* 8 (1985): 305–338.

Orantes-Hernandez v. Smith. 541 F. Supp. 351 (C.D. Cal. 1982).

Organization of African Unity. *Convention on Refugee Problems in Africa.* 1001 UNTS 45.

Pear, Robert. "Key Federal Aide Refuses to Deport Any Nicaraguans." *New York Times*, April 17, 1986.

———. "Duarte Appeals to Reagan to Let Salvadorans Stay." *New York Times*, April 26, 1987.

———. "Reagan Rejects Salvadoran Plea for Illegal Aliens." *New York Times*, May 15, 1987.

Perluss, Deborah, and Joan Hartman. "Temporary Refuge: Emergence of a Customary Norm." *Virginia Journal of International Law* 26(1986): 551–626.

Pirie, Sophie. "The Need for a Codified Definition of 'Persecution' in United States Refugee Law." *Stanford Law Review* 39(1986): 187–234.

Refugee Policy Group. *Of Special Humanitarian Concern: U.S. Refugee Admissions Since Passage of the Refugee Act.* Washington, D.C.: Refugee Policy Group, 1985.

"Salvadoran Illegal Aliens: A Struggle to Obtain Refuge in the United States." *University of Pittsburgh Law Review* 47(1985): 295–335.

Stevic v. INS. 104 S. Ct. 2489 (1984).

Stohl, Michael, David Carleton, and Steven E. Johnson. "Human Rights and U.S. Foreign Assistance: From Nixon to Carter." *Journal of Peace Research* 25(1984): 215–226.

Teitelbaum, Michael. "Immigration, Refugees, and Foreign Policy." *International Organization* 38(1984): 428–450.

United Nations. *United Nations High Commissioner for Refugees, Mission to Monitor INS Asylum Processing of Salvadoran Illegal Entrants.* Printed in *Congressional Record*, S. 827–831, February 11, 1982.

United Nations High Commissioner for Refugees. *Handbook on Procedures and Criteria for Determining Refugee Status.* Geneva: United Nations, 1979.

U.S. Congress, General Accounting Office, "Illegal Aliens: Extent of Problems Experienced by Returned Salvadorans Not Determinable." Washington, D.C.: Government Printing Office, 1987.

———. "Asylum: Uniform Application of Standards Uncertain—Few Denied Applicants Deported." Washington, D.C.: Government Printing Office, 1987.

U.S. Congress House. *Temporary Suspension of Deportation of Certain Aliens.* 98th

Cong., 2nd sess. (H.R. 4447), Washington, D.C.: Government Printing Office, 1984.

U.S. Congress, House. *Temporary Suspension of Deportation for Nationals of Certain Countries.* 99th Cong., 1st sess. Washington, D.C.: Government Printing Office, 1985.

U.S. Coordinator for Refugee Affairs, Report to the Congress for Fiscal Year 1987. *Proposed Refugee Admissions and Allocations for Fiscal Year 1987.* Washington, D.C.: Government Printing Office, 1986.

U.S. Department of Health and Human Services. *Refugee Resettlement Program.* Washington, D.C.: Government Printing Office, 1986.

U.S. Department of Justice, Immigration and Naturalization Service. *Asylum Adjudications: An Evolving Concept and Responsibility in the Immigration and Naturalization Service.* Washington, D.C.: Government Printing Office, 1982.

U.S. Department of State. *Country Reports on Human Rights Practices for 1981.* Washington, D.C.: Government Printing Office, 1982.

Selected Bibliography

Ackerman, Bruce. *Social Justice in the Liberal State.* New Haven, Conn.: Yale University Press, 1980.

"The Agony and the Exodus: Deporting Salvadorans in Violation of the Fourth Geneva Convention." *New York University Journal of International Law and Politics* 18 (1986): 703–744.

Aleinikoff, T. Alexander, and David Martin. *Immigration: Process and Policy.* St. Paul: West Publishing, 1985.

Anker, Deborah. "The Forty Year Crisis: A Legislative History of the Refugee Act of 1980." *San Diego Law Review* 19 (1981): 9–89.

Barry, Brian. "Humanity and Justice in Global Perspective." In *Ethics, Economics, and the Law: Nomos XXIV,* edited by J. R. Pennock and John W. Chapman. New York and London: New York University Press, 1982.

Beitz, Charles. "Bounded Morality: Justice and the State in World Politics." *International Organization* 33:3 (1979).

———. "Cosmopolitan Ideals and National Sentiment." *The Journal of Philosophy* 80(1983): 591–600.

———. *Political Theory and International Relations.* Princeton, N.J.: Princeton University Press, 1979.

Benn, Stanley I., and Gerald F. Gaus. "The Liberal Conception of the Public and the Private." In *Public and Private in Social Life,* ed. Stanley I. Benn and Gerald F. Gaus. London and Canberra: Croom Helm, 1983.

Birrell, Robert, and Douglas Hill. "Population Policy and the Natural Environment." In *Refugees, Resources, Reunion: Australia's Immigration Dilemmas*, ed. Robert Birrell, Leon Glezer, Colin Hay, and Michael Liffman. Melbourne: VCTA Publishing, 1979.

Blum, Carolyn P. "The Ninth Circuit and the Protection of Asylum Seekers Since the Passage of the Refugee Act of 1980." *San Diego Law Review* 23(1986): 327–373.

Briggs, Vernon. *Immigration Policy and the American Labor Force*. Baltimore: Johns Hopkins University Press, 1984.

Brown, Peter G. ". . . in the National Interest." In *Human Rights and U.S. Foreign Policy*, ed. Peter G. Brown and Douglas MacLean, pp. 161–171. Lexington, Mass.: Lexington Books, 1979.

Brownlie, Ian, ed. *Basic Documents on Human Rights*. Oxford: Clarendon Press, 1971.

Carens, Joseph. "Aliens and Citizens: The Case for Open Borders." *The Review of Politics* 49(1987): 251–273.

———. "Migration, Morality, and the Nation-State." Paper presented at the meeting of the American Political Science Association, New Orleans, 1985.

Carleton, David and Michael Stohl. "The Foreign Policy of Human Rights: Rhetoric and Reality from Jimmy Carter to Ronald Reagan." *Human Rights Quarterly* 7(1985): 205–229.

Committee for Economic Development. *The Economic Effects of Immigration in Australia*. Canberra: CEDA, 1985.

Coolidge, Mary Roberts. *Chinese Immigration*. New York: Henry Holt and Co., 1909. Reprint ed., New York: Arno Books and the New York Times Co., 1969.

Doppelt, Gerald. "Walzer's Theory of Morality in International Relations." *Philosophy and Public Affairs* 8(1978): 3–25.

"Ecumenical, Municipal and Legal Challenges to United States Refugee Policy." *Harvard Civil Rights-Civil Liberties Law Review* 21(1985–1986): 493–601.

Fauriol, Georges. "U.S. Immigration Policy and the National Interest." In *The Problem of Immigration*, ed. Steven Anzovin, pp. 96–116. New York: H. W. Wilson Co., 1985.

Feiberg, Joel. *Social Philosophy* (Englewood Cliffs, N.J.: Prentice-Hall, 1973).

Fishkin, James S. "The Boundaries of Justice." *Journal of Conflict Resolution* 27:2 (1983).

———. *The Limits of Obligation*. New Haven, Conn.: Yale University Press, 1982.

Geertz, Clifford. "Ideology as a Cultural System." In *Ideology and Discontent*, ed. David E. Apter, pp. 47–76. New York: Free Press, 1964.

Gibney, Mark. "The Refugee Act of 1980: A Humanitarian Standard." *Gonzaga Law Review* 21 (1985–1986): 585–602.

———. "The Role of the Judiciary in Alien Admissions." *Boston College International and Comparative Law Review* 8(1985): 341–376.

———. *Strangers or Friends: Principles for a New Alien Admission Policy*. Westport, Conn.: Greenwood Press, 1986.

Glover, Jonathan. *Causing Death and Saving Lives*. Harmondsworth, Middlesex, England: Penguin, 1977.

Goodwin-Gill, Guy. *The Refugee in International Law.* Oxford: Clarendon Press, 1983.

Grahl-Madsen, Atle. "Refugees and Refugee Law in Transition." *Transnational Legal Problems of Refugees, 1982 Michigan Yearbook of International Legal Studies.* New York: Clark Boardman Company, Ltd., 1982.

———. *The Status of Refugees in International Law.* London: A. W. Sijthoff, 1966.

Gutmann, Amy. "Communitarian Critics of Liberalism." *Philosophy and Public Affairs* 14:3 (1985).

Hailbronner, Kay. "Non-Refoulement and 'Humanitarian' Refugees: Customary International Law or Wishful Thinking?" *Virginia Journal of International Law* 26(1985): 857–896.

Hare, R. M. "Abortion and the Golden Rule." *Philosophy and Public Affairs* 4(1975): 201–222.

———. *Freedom and Reason.* Oxford: Clarendon Press, 1963.

———. *Moral Thinking.* New York: Oxford University Press, 1981.

Hart, H.L.A. "Are There Any Natural Rights?" *The Philosophical Review* 64(2) (1955): 175–191.

Helton, Arthur. "Political Asylum Under the 1980 Refugee Act: An Unfulfilled Promise." *Michigan Journal of Law Reform* 17 (1984): 243–264.

Henkin, Louis. "The Constitution and United States Sovereignty: A Century of *Chinese Exclusion* and its Progeny." *Harvard Law Review* 100(1987): 853–886.

Higham, John. *Strangers in the Land: Patterns of American Nativism.* New Brunswick, N.J.: Rutgers University Press, 1955.

Hobbes, Thomas. *The Elements of Law.* 2d ed. Edited by Ferdinand Tonnies. New York: Frank Cass and Company, Ltd., 1969.

———. *Leviathan.* (New York: E. P. Dutton, 1950).

Hoffman, Stanley. *Duties Beyond Borders.* Syracuse, N.Y.: Syracuse University Press, 1981.

Hofstetter, Richard R. "Economic Underdevelopment and the Population Explosion: Implications for U.S. Immigration Policy." In *U.S. Immigration Policy*, ed. Richard R. Hofstetter. (Durham, N.C.: Duke University Press, 1984).

Holborn, Louise. "The League of Nations and the Refugee Problem." *The Annals of the American Academy of Political and Social Science* 203 (May 1939): 124–135.

Hutchinson, Edward P. *Legislative History of American Immigration Policy, 1798–1965.* Philadelphia: University of Pennsylvania Press, 1981.

Jefferson, Thomas. *Notes on the State of Virginia.* In *The Portable Thomas Jefferson*, edited by Merrill D. Peterson. Harmondsworth, Middlesex, England: Penguin, 1975.

Jennings, R. Y. "Some International Law Aspects of the Refugee Question," *British Yearbook of International Law* 20: 98 (1939): 112–115.

Kant, Immanuel. *The Metaphysics of Morals*, trans. John Ladd (Indianapolis: Bobbs-Merrill, 1965).

Keohane, Robert O. *After Hegemony: Cooperation and Discord in the World Political Economy.* Princeton, N.J.: Princeton University Press, 1984.

Keohane, Robert O., and Joseph Nye, eds. *Transnational Relations and World Politics*. Cambridge, Mass.: Harvard University Press, 1972.

Kubat, Daniel. "Canada." In *The Politics of Migration Policies*, edited by Daniel Kubat, pp. 19–36. New York: Center for Migration Studies, 1979.

Lichtenberg, Judith. "Mexican Migration and U.S. Policy: A Guide for the Perplexed." In *The Border That Joins: Mexican Migrants and U.S. Responsibility*, ed. Peter Brown and Henry Shue, pp. 13–30. Totowa, N.J.: Rowman and Littlefield, 1983.

Loescher, Gilburt, and John Scanlan. *Calculated Kindness: Refugees and America's Half-Open Door, 1945-Present*. New York: Free Press, 1986.

———. "Human Rights, Power Politics, and the International Refugee Regime: The Case of U.S. Treatment of Caribbean Basin Refugees," World Order Studies Program Occasional Paper No. 14. Princeton, N.J.: Center of International Studies, Princeton University, 1985.

London, H. I., *Non-White Immigration and the "White Australia" Policy*. New York: New York University Press, 1970.

McDougal, Myres, Harold Lasswell, and Lung-chu Chen. *Human Rights and World Public Order* (New Haven, Conn.: Yale University Press, 1980).

Martin, David A. "Due Process and the Treatment of Aliens," *University of Pittsburgh Law Review* 44(1983): 165–235.

Mayo-Smith, Richmond. *Emigration and Immigration*. New York: Charles Scribner's Sons, 1912.

"Membership in a Social Group: Salvadoran Refugees and the 1980 Refugee Act." *Hastings International and Comparative Law Review* 8 (1985): 305–338.

Nardin, Terry. *Law, Morality, and the Relations of States*. Princeton, N.J.: Princeton University Press, 1983.

Nozick, Robert. *Anarchy, State, and Utopia*. New York: Basic Books, 1974.

Organization of African Unity. *Convention on Refugee Problems in Africa*, 1001 UNTS 45.

Perluss, Deborah, and Joan Hartman. "Temporary Refuge: Emergence of a Customary Norm." *Virginia Journal of International Law* 26(1986): 551–626.

Piore, Michael. *Birds of Passage: Migrant Labor and Industrial Society*. Cambridge: Cambridge University Press, 1979.

Pirie, Sophie. "The Need for a Codified Definition of 'Persecution' in United States Refugee Law." *Stanford Law Review* 39(1986): 187–234.

Price, Charles. "Australia." In *The Politics of Migration Policies*, edited by Daniel Kubat, pp. 3–18. New York: Center for Migration Studies, 1979.

Rachels, James. "Active and Passive Euthanasia." *New England Journal of Medicine*. 229(1975): 78–80.

Rawls, John. *A Theory of Justice*. Cambridge, Mass.: Harvard University Press, 1971.

———. "Constitutional Liberty and the Concept of Justice." In *Justice: Nomos VI*, ed. C. J. Friedrich and John W. Chapman. New York: Atherton, 1963.

Refugee Policy Group. *Of Special Humanitarian Concern: U.S. Refugee Admissions Since Passage of the Refugee Act*. Washington, D.C.: Refugee Policy Group, 1985.

Reis, Hans, ed. *Kant's Political Writings*, trans. H. B. Nisbet (Cambridge: Cambridge University Press, 1971).

Rivera, Mario. "Cuban and Haitian Influxes of 1980 and the American Response: Retrospect and Prospect." U.S. Congress, House, *Oversight Hearings: Caribbean Migration*, Appendix 4. Washington, D.C.: Government Printing Office, 1980.

"Salvadoran Illegal Aliens: A Struggle to Obtain Refuge in the United States." *University of Pittsburgh Law Review* 47(1985): 295–335.

Samora, Julian. *Los Mojados: The Wetback Story*. Notre Dame, Ind.: University of Notre Dame Press, 1971.

Saxton, Alexander. *The Indispensable Enemy: Labor and the Anti-Chinese Movement in California*. Berkeley: University of California Press, 1971.

Scanlan, John. "Immigration Law and the Illusion of Numerical Control." *University of Miami Law Review* 36(1982): 819–864.

Scanlon, John, and Gilburt Loescher. "U.S. Foreign Policy, 1959–1980: Impact on Refugee Flow from Cuba." In *The Annals of the American Academy of Political Science*, pp. 116–137. Gilburt Loescher and John Scanlan, special eds. Beverly Hills, Calif.: Sage, 1983.

Schuck, Peter. "The Transformation of Immigration Law." *Columbia Law Review* 84(1984): 1–90.

Schuck, Peter, and Rogers Smith. *Citizenship Without Consent: Illegal Aliens in the American Polity*. New Haven, Conn.: Yale University Press, 1985.

Seddon, George. "Population and the Environment." In *Refugees, Resources, Reunion: Australia's Immigration Dilemmas*, ed. Robert Birrell, Leon Glezer, Colin Hay, and Michael Liffman. Melbourne: VCTA Publishing, 1979.

Shacknove, Andrew E. "Who Is a Refugee?" *Ethics* 95: 2 (January 1985): 274–284.

Shue, Henry. *Basic Rights: Subsistence, Affluence and U.S. Foreign Policy*. Princeton, N.J.: Princeton University Press, 1980.

————. "The Burdens of Justice." *The Journal of Philosophy* 80 (1983): 600–608.

Sidgwick, Henry. *The Elements of Politics*, 2d ed. London: Macmillan and Company, 1897.

Singer, Peter. *Animal Liberation*. New York: Avon, 1977.

————. *The Expanding Circle: Ethics and Sociobiology*. New York: New American Library, 1981.

————. "Famine, Affluence and Morality." *Philosophy and Public Affairs* 1(1972): 229–243.

————. *Practical Ethics*. Cambridge: Cambridge University Press, 1979.

Stohl, Michael, David Carleton, and Steven E. Johnson. "Human Rights and U.S. Foreign Assistance: From Nixon to Carter." *Journal of Peace Research* 25(1984): 215–226.

Teitelbaum, Michael. "Immigration, Refugees, and Foreign Policy." *International Organization* 38(1984): 428–450.

United Nations. *United Nations High Commissioner for Refugees, Mission to Monitor INS Asylum Processing of Salvadoran Illegal Entrants*. Printed in *Congressional Record* S. 827–831, February 11, 1982.

United Nations High Commissioner for Refugees. *Handbook on Procedures and Criteria for Determining Refugee Status*. Geneva: United Nations, 1979.

U.S. Congress, General Accounting Office. "Asylum: Uniform Application of Standards Uncertain—Few Denied Applicants Deported." Washington, D.C.: Government Printing Office, 1987.

————. "Illegal Aliens: Extent of Problems Experienced by Returned Salvadorans Not Determinable." Washington, D.C.: Government Printing Office, 1987.

U.S. Congress, House. *Temporary Suspension of Deportation of Certain Aliens.* 98th Cong., 2nd sess. (H.R. 4447). Washington, D.C.: Government Printing Office, 1984.

U.S. Congress, House. *Temporary Suspension of Deportation for Nationals of Certain Countries.* 99th Cong., 1st sess. Washington, D.C.: Government Printing Office, 1985.

U.S. Department of Justice, Immigration and Naturalization Service. *Asylum Adjudications: An Evolving Concept and Responsibility in the Immigration and Naturalization Service.* Washington, D.C.: Government Printing Office, 1982.

Vlastos, Gregory. "Justice and Equality." In *Social Justice*, edited by Richard B. Brandt. Englewood Cliffs, N.J.: Prentice-Hall, 1962.

Wade, E.C.S., and G. Godfrey Phillips, *Constitutional and Administrative Law*, 9th ed., revised by A. W. Bradley. London: Longman, 1977.

Walzer, Michael. *Just and Unjust Wars.* New York: Basic Books, 1977.

————. "The Moral Standing of States: A Response to Four Critics." In *International Ethics*, ed. Charles R. Beitz, Marshall Cohen, Thomas Scanlon, and A. John Simmons. Princeton, N.J.: Princeton University Press, 1985.

————. *Spheres of Justice: A Defense of Pluralism and Equality.* New York: Basic Books, 1983.

Whelan, Frederick G. "Citizenship and the Right to Leave." *American Political Science Review* 75 (1981): 636–653.

————. "Principles of U.S. Immigration Policy." *University of Pittsburgh Law Review* 44 (1983): 447–484.

————. "Vattel's Doctrine of the State." *History of Political Thought*, Spring, 1988.

Wyman, David. *Paper Walls: America and the Refugee Crisis, 1938–41.* Amherst: University of Massachusetts Press, 1968.

Yergin, Daniel. *Shattered Peace: The Origins of the Cold War and the National Security State.* Boston: Houghton Mifflin Co., 1977.

Index

About the Contributors

JOSEPH H. CARENS is Associate Professor of Political Science at the University of Toronto. He is the author of *Equality, Moral Incentives and the Market* and of several articles in political theory. He is currently working on a book on immigration and political community.

O. T. KENT teaches philosophy at the University of Indianapolis. He received his Ph.D. from the University of Iowa. He was a Rockefeller Fellow at Harvard Divinity School, and has been a visiting philosopher at Michigan Technological University, Rose-Hulman Institute of Technology, and Indiana University, Indianapolis.

JOHN SCANLAN is an Associate Professor of Law at Indiana University Law School, Bloomington, where he teaches Immigration Law and Law and Political Theory. He is the author (with Gil Loescher) of *Calculated Kindness: Refugees and America's Half-Open Door, 1945–Present* and numerous articles on immigration policy and law.

ANDREW E. SHACKNOVE received his Ph.D. in political science from

Yale in 1987. His dissertation topic was "The American Response to Haitian Refugee Migration." He received his law degree from Harvard in 1988.

PETER SINGER is Professor of Philosophy and Director of the Centre for Human Bioethics at Monash University, Melbourne, Australia. He was educated at the University of Melbourne and at Oxford. He has taught at Oxford, New York University, University of Colorado at Boulder, and the University of California at Irvine. His books include *Democracy and Disobedience, Animal Liberation, Practical Ethics, The Expanding Circle, Marx, Hegel, The Reproduction Revolution* (with Deane Wells) and *Should the Baby Live* (with Helga Kuhse). He edits the international journal *Bioethics* with Helga Kuhse.

RENATA SINGER is a principle in the consulting firm of Ellard & Associates. After graduating from the University of Melbourne, she taught in the United Kingdom, the United States, and Australia. From 1985 to 1987 she was coordinator of the Clearing House on Migration Issues (CHOMI) at the Ecumenical Migration Centre in Melbourne, and was editor of the magazine *Migration Action*. Her publications include *The Immigration Debate in the Press 1984, Goodbye and Hello* (with Susie Orzech), *A Rational Approach to Immigration Policy* (with Mark Deasey), and *Skills Development for a Multicultural Society* (with Michael Liffman).

MICHAEL STOHL is professor of Political Science at Purdue University and Associate Director of International Education and Research. He is the author of more than forty articles and book chapters, and author, editor and coeditor of nine books on the subjects of terrorism and violence. His recent books are *The Politics of Terrorism, Current Perspectives on International Terrorism,*(with Robert Slate), and *International Relations: Contemporary Theory and Practice* (with George Lopez).

FREDERICK G. WHELAN is an Associate Professor of Political Science at the University of Pittsburgh. He is the author of *Order and Artifice in Hume's Political Philosophy* and numerous articles in journals such as the *American Political Science Review, Nomos, History of Political Thought*, and *Political Theory*. He is currently working on a manuscript entitled "Membership and Mobility," which treats both the historical and philosophical dimensions of citizenship and the possibility of international movement.

ABOUT THE EDITOR

MARK GIBNEY is an Assistant Professor of Political Science at Purdue University. He is the author of *Strangers or Friends: Principles for a New Alien Admission Policy* (Greenwood Press, 1986). He has also written a number of law journal articles on U.S. immigration and refugee policy, and the judiciary's role in the conduct of foreign affairs.